The Great Atlantic Air Race

The Great
Atlantic
Air Race

PERCY ROWE

McCLELLAND AND STEWART

For Peter, Heather, and Lesley,
who give me pride.

ISBN: 0-7710-7739-4

McClelland and Stewart Limited,
The Canadian Publishers,
25 Hollinger Road,
Toronto, Ontario.
M4B 3G2

Photo Credits: Photos 1, 2 and 44 reproduced by permission of Percy Rowe. Photos 3, 4 and 5 reproduced by permission of W. Pollard. Photos 6, 7, 21 and 24 reproduced by permission of Naval Photographic Centre, Naval Station, Washington, D.C. Photos 8, 9, 10, 11, 13, 14, 15, 16, 17, 18, 19, 20, 22, 23, 25, 26, 27, 28, 30, 31, 32, 33, 34, 36, 39 and 41 reproduced by permission of the Newfoundland Museum. Photo 12 reproduced by permission of Holloway, St. John's, Newfoundland. Photos 29, 35, 37, 38, 40, 42 and 43 reproduced by permission of Captain E. S. J. Alcock. Photo 45 reproduced by permission of the Vintage Aircraft Flying Association. Photo 46 reproduced by permission of Bord Failte Photo.

Printed and bound in Canada by
T. H. Best Printing Company Limited, Don Mills, Ontario

"I am a stranger. I know nothing. I do
not enter into their empires."

> – Antoine de Saint-Exupery,
> Wind, Sand and Stars.

Some of those who people this book are:

Alberto Santos-Dumont, "the first man to fly";
Albert I of Monaco, a scientist-prince;
Alfred, Lord Northcliffe, "the Napoleon of Fleet Street";
His brother, Harold, Lord Rothermere;
Winston Churchill, cabinet minister and later Prime Minister;
Joey Smallwood, reporter, later Premier of Newfoundland;
Orville and Wilbur Wright, whose flights were ignored;
Louis Bleriot, the first to fly the English Channel;
T.O.M. Sopwith, builder of planes;
Fred Raynham, an early distinguished test pilot;
Harry Hawker, "the highest paid flyer in the world";
Jack Alcock, later Sir John, pilot;
Teddy Whitten-Brown, later Sir Arthur, navigator;
Rear Admiral Mark Kerr, sailor-airman-author-poet;
Tryggve Gran, a Norwegian with Captain Scott in Antarctica;
Herbert Brackley, much-decorated pilot;
Glenn Curtiss, American aerial pioneer;
John Towers, commander of the U.S. Navy's first air division;
"Putty" Read, first American to fly the Atlantic;
Robert Lavender, radio specialist, later legal aide in the development of
    the atomic bomb;
Marc Mitscher, pilot, later a famous admiral;
Pat Bellinger, an early U.S. naval flyer;
Kathleen Kennedy, the bubbling fiancee of Teddy Whitten-Brown;
C.W.F. "Fax" Morgan, the most popular flyer in St. John's;
"Mac" Grieve, a phlegmatic Scot;

Muriel Hawker, a woman with faith;
Franklin Delano Roosevelt, Assistant Secretary of the US. Navy, later President;
Charles Lester, cartage contractor;
Geoffrey Taylor, mathematician, later knighted;
Robert Furlong, Boy Scout, later Chief Justice of Newfoundland;
Mrs. Augustus Lester, who danced for Marconi;
Robert Reid, railway tycoon;
The Dooley sisters, who offered coffee flasks and sympathy;
Emory Coil, airship commander;
Mrs. Bride Sutton, who watched the fleet sail into Trepassey;
Captain Adolph Duhn, master of a "tramp" steamer;
Captain E. S. J. Alcock, Sir John's brother.

PART ONE

CHAPTER 1
Le Petit Santos

In February, 1902, the customary collection of royalty and riches was gathered in the small principality of Monaco to enjoy the excitement of the casino, the scent of the flowers and the brilliance of the sunshine. There were entertainers, industrialists, gamblers, hypochondriacs, discreet "other women," masters of cuisine. Amid such a motley group, it was difficult to be different but Alberto Santos-Dumont succeeded.

He was an aeronaut.

Santos-Dumont was already well-known throughout France and he was the idol of Parisians, who had dubbed him *Le Petit Santos* after reading in the press of his astonishing aerial exploits and, in fact, often seeing him for themselves as he soared and swayed above the buildings of Paris, dangling beneath his huge, sausage-shaped balloon. He was the intimate of academicians, particularly the scientifically inclined, and this is how he'd come to Monaco; he'd been invited by His Serene Highness Prince Albert the First, ruler of the principality and a man with a passion for science.

The invitation was particularly important to Santos-Dumont because it would give him an opportunity to fly out over the sea, perhaps for some distance. The visit to Monaco, as it turned out, was also important to the future of trans-Atlantic flight because it brought Santos-Dumont together with an energetic and somewhat eccentric British publisher, Alfred Harmsworth; one of Harmsworth's newspapers later was to initiate a spectacular competition among flyers – and between countries – to be the first to fly across the Atlantic.

Santos-Dumont found the sunshine of Monaco much more to his liking than the mid-winter greyness of Paris. It allowed him to fly his strange machine and, besides, he was used to sunshine; he'd been born in Brazil.

Alberto Santos-Dumont had been a birthday present to his father, a seventh (and last) child, born on July 20, 1873. Henriques, the father, who had conjoined his wife's maiden name to his own with a hyphen in the Portuguese fashion, became forty-one that day. It was a double milestone: the boy was to become one of Brazil's heroes; the father had embarked on the path which was to give him the title of "Coffee King" in that country. Already, by Alberto's birth, his father had planted five million coffee trees. Many millions more were to go in during Alberto's formative years, along with fifty miles of railway track to serve them. It was a highly mechanized operation, for the elder Santos-Dumont was interested in scientific development. The interest rubbed off on the son. Among the boy's first memories was being allowed to drive one of the imported English locomotives on the coffee plantation. But he was a dreamy boy, and his dreams climbed skyward. He recalled later that, at the age of ten, he used to take siestas in the shade of the veranda of the main plantation house and gaze into the sky "where the birds fly so high and soar with such ease on their great outstretched wings. . . So musing on the exploration of the vast aerial ocean, I, too, devised airships and flying machines in my imagination."

The stoker of that imagination had been Jules Verne, and particularly his *Clipper of the Clouds*. Later, Santos-Dumont wrote: "In his (Verne's) audacious conceptions, I used to see, without any shadow of doubt ever crossing my mind, the mechanics and science of the days to come, in which man, solely through his ingenuity, would be transformed into a semi-God."

Even Santos-Dumont's games were aerial. He used to build kites called *passarinho-roa* (little bird flies) in Brazil, and create tiny fire-balloons to light the sky at night on the festival of St. John's Day in late June. From these he moved on to tiny airships, cutting out panels of silk paper, sticking them to bamboo, and sending them skyward with twisted rolls of rubber as their motive force. Then, when he was fifteen, he saw his first balloon ascend with a man in it, at Sao Paulo, and "I wanted to fly in my turn and construct balloons."

Three years later, in 1886, he was in Paris where he hoped to get involved in ballooning. But he was disappointed; Paris was in the aeronautical doldrums and he ran into problems.

The cost of ballooning was not among them. He received a generous allowance from his father, who could well afford it – the older Santos-Dumont had recently sold his estates for more than $5,000,000.

This first Paris visit opened the father's eyes to his son. He recognized the youth's scientific interest, felt he had potential, and gave him every support. On the boy's eighteenth birthday, he took him to a notary in Sao Paulo, acquired deeds which provided Alberto with his majority (so he did not have to wait till he became twenty-one), took him home, opened his safe, and handed the newly created man several tens of thousands of dollars worth of bonds. Then he said, "I have already given you your liberty today. Here also is your capital. I want to see how you conduct yourself. Go to Paris, a most dangerous place for a boy. Find a specialist in physics, chemistry, mechanics and electricity. Study these subjects, and don't forget that the world's future is in mechanics."

Then the father added: "You have no need to worry about earning a living. I will leave you enough to live on," and the young Alberto took it all to heart; to his dying day, Alberto Santos-Dumont never had what is called "regular employment."

But he did work as a serious student in Paris – a considerable accomplishment for a rich youth, alone, in the world's leading city of spectacles, gaiety, and women. He seemed, neither then nor later, to have had much sexual interest in women.

He concentrated on his studies until, when he was twenty-four, he made a trip back to Brazil, and happened to buy the book *To The North Sea By Balloon*, written by two French engineers, Henri Lachambre and Alexis Machuron. Their book described a tragedy. The balloon had set out from Spitzbergen with three men, and was never seen again.

No matter; this did not frighten Santos-Dumont. On his return to France, he hunted out the Paris workshop of Lachambre and Machuron, the balloon constructors.

Would they take him up?

For 250 francs, which included the cost of returning the balloon by rail, they would provide a flight of three or four hours.

On an early morning, Santos-Dumont and the two engineers climbed into a basket, moorings were unfastened, Santos-Dumont's first flight began.

After an hour or so, above the clouds at eight thousand feet, it was time for lunch – eggs in aspic, cold meats, ice cream, fruit, nuts, Champagne, coffee, and chartreuse. It could have been a picnic in the Bois de Boulogne, except that before it was over they had moved into cloud, and then snow. They descended for comfort. Two hours later they landed on the grounds of a chateau owned by a Rothschild.

They had covered sixty miles. Santos-Dumont was brimming: "During the whole flight I observed the pilot . . . . and comprehended perfectly all that he did, it seemed to me that I had really been born for aeronautics."

He was even giddier on the ground. The next morning he was back at the workshop, asking Lachambre and Machuron to build him a balloon; and he spent days with them, supervising details, leaving only to make ascents, many of them solo, several of them dangerous, one through a thunderstorm, at night, to Belgium. Of this he wrote: "On, on I went, tearing through the darkness. I realized I was in great danger, yet the danger was not tangible. With it there was a fierce kind of joy. Up there is the black solitude, amid the lightning flashes and thunderclaps, I was part of the storm."

Santos-Dumont, forever a solitary man, loved the solitude of flying. Within months he had made twenty-five ascents, proved his courage, and was on the threshold of fame. Without deliberately seeking publicity, Santos-Dumont became the darling of the French press. For over a decade, his name increasingly appeared, coupled with his latest forward step in aviation. His most important contribution may have been the inspiration of other men. By the end of the first decade of this century, France had six times as many pilots as Britain, fifteen times as many as the United States. France was the centre of the flying world.

Santos-Dumont revolutionized the way people were thinking about flight. He began talking of using gasoline-engines to power balloons.

Madness, said his friends. Engines would either shake the craft to bits, or sparks from the engine would ignite the hydrogen in the envelope, then – poof!

"If you want to commit suicide," one friend asked, "why not sit on a cask of gunpowder with a lighted cigar in your mouth?"

But Santos-Dumont was an idealist, an innovator, an eccentric.

To test the vibrations caused by a gasoline engine in the air, he and his valet, and two workmen, went one early morning to the Bois de Boulogne. There, his motor tricycle was tied with strong ropes to the branch of a tree. The machine was five feet above the ground. Santos-Dumont opened the throttle. It was a successful experiment; the chassis was not shaken apart by the engine.

This wasn't his only experiment simulating flight. In his house on the Champs Elysées, in which he lived with four servants, Santos-Dumont designed and built a dining room table, suspended by wires from the ceiling. It was six feet above the floor. Beside it, also suspended, was his chair, which he reached by stilts. There he dined, having his food passed up on a tray held high above the head of his valet. Santos-Dumont explained that the idea was to accustom himself to eating high up, as in an airship.

This was the term he used for the cylindrical balloons for which he designed motor, propeller and basket. He also made sketches, bought the right engines, and supervised his assistants' daily work.

All this took months and it wasn't until September, 1898, that No. 1, his first model, was ready to fly.

Santos-Dumont, dressed in a formal suit, shirt with his usual high stiff collar and red silk tie, button boots and cloth cap, bounded into the basket, and took to the air.

At first he manoeuvred gingerly, testing the controls, holding his airship in equilibrium. Then, as it moved easily in response to the rudder, he became more daring, took it up to a thousand feet, headed toward a racecourse. He wasn't up long, but he bubbled with elation: "I have navigated the air."

He went up again for other short trips. They were hardly giant steps forward for mankind – yet. But the small South American immediately captured the imagination of Paris with his courage, effervescence, and optimism. Now they heard of him, saw him floating above their heads, for the first time. For the next few years they were to follow his every aerial move. His native country, Brazil, was in raptures at the far away exploits of the "Coffee King's" son.

Santos-Dumont lapped it all up, dining at Maxim's to be better seen, posing for photographs and sketches. He wore elevators in his shoes to boost his five feet, five inches.

By 1899, Santos-Dumont had begun to wrestle with the problem of providing his latest airship with a backbone. He wanted no more humiliating sights – his No. 2 airship had folded, pillow-fashion, a few minutes after taking off.

His new airship, No. 3, flew successfully toward the Eiffel Tower, over the Champs de Mars, above the suburbs on its first flight. Several more flights were tried. Santos Dumont, a man of emotional ups and downs, was ecstatic. The century had turned and, as if to celebrate it, he announced: "I am going into airship construction as a life work."

France also marked the change. Its Aero Club with a Prince Bonaparte and Gustave Eiffel among its founding members, bought land for aviation, and allowed Santos-Dumont to use it as a base, to put up a hydrogen plant, engine shop, storage buildings and hangar.

There was another marker of the new century. Henri Deutsch de la Meurthe was a very rich man with an inquisitive mind. He was a power in the French oil industry, a patron (like Prince Albert of Monaco) of struggling musicians, and a backer of scientific enterprises. In April, 1900, he put up a prize of 100,000 francs for the first man to fly an airship from the Aero Club's new base at St. Cloud, around the Eiffel Tower and back, in less than half an hour. That was seven miles. Santos-Dumont was determined to win the prize. But to accomplish this feat, he needed an airship which could fly at a speed of at least 14 miles per hour. So he started work on No. 4.

The main difference from his previous airships was that, in No. 4, the aviator, instead of being in a basket, sat on a saddle of a bicycle frame dangling amid rigging.

11

Parisians were to watch Santos-Dumont many times through 1900, breezing above the buildings. What they saw with their eyes or through the viewfinders of their new-fangled cameras was a silken sausage, about 100 feet long and eighteen feet in diameter, lurching through the sky with engine, fuel and water tanks mounted on a pole below it, and the pilot's bicycle frame from which he could reach the controls. If all this seems incongruous by modern standards, what of the pilot? For, although Santos-Dumont was forever innovating with every aspect of his machines, he never changed his dress. Once, while aloft, he beat out a fire with his Panama hat. His high collars, so rigid and expansive, were being copied by Parisians and given the name "Santos-Dumonts."

This most unsuitable aerial garb was finally his undoing. No. 4 had a defect; it couldn't reach 14 miles per hour. Many tests were made to increase the power. Santos-Dumont, to simulate flight, would sit on the bicycle saddle in wet weather on the ground while the revolutions were increased and the tractor propeller in front blew an icy gale around him. He caught pneumonia and had to go to Nice to recuperate. But he did not design warmer clothes for future flights; instead, he changed the position of the propeller so that it was behind him.

By the summer of 1901, Santos-Dumont had tested a new airship, No. 5, and he was prepared to bid for the Deutsch prize. He notified members of the Aero Club of the day and time of his departure from St. Cloud.

On a beautiful still July morning, the members arrived. Santos-Dumont, wearing a silk shirt with the customary enormous collar, a tie with pearl stick pin, and a straw hat, took his position (he was now back to a basket rather than the bicycle saddle). M. Deutsch solemnly shook hands. The airship began to rise at 6.41 a.m. It rose quickly, and, backed by a breeze, reached the Eiffel Tower in ten minutes. Then trouble started. The engine began to falter and airship No. 5 started to drift. The engine conked out and the ship subsided, stern first, into chestnut trees in the grounds of Edmund de Rothschild's villa. What followed was like a scene from comic opera. From the left streamed the de Rothschild servants, from the right came the illustrious members of the Aero Club. Airship No. 5 and its pilot were stuck up a tree. Nobody, however, thought this hilarious. The French press did not mock him. The spectators were serious, only concerned with "Le Petit Santos" and his safety, ready to share his ignominy. The next-door neighbour to de Rothschild was practical. She was the Comtesse d'Eu, former princess regent of Brazil. On learning of her countryman's predicament, she ordered a picnic lunch prepared for him. The hamper was delivered up the tree by a footman on a ladder. It would be ungrateful not to appreciate such solicitousness and Alberto partook of the alfresco meal before descending and visiting her salon to offer his thanks. She told him: "Your evolutions in the air make me think of the flight of our great birds of Brazil. I hope you will do as well with your propeller as they do with their wings, and that you will succeed for the glory of our common country." A few days later a package from Cartier's, the jewelery store, arrived at his house. She had sent him a medal of St. Benedict to wear on his flights.

Two weeks later another attempt was made but, after rounding the Eiffel Tower, the airship was again in difficulties. This time it caught on the roof of the Trocadero Hotel, leaving Santos-Dumont tangled in rigging forty feet above the ground. Huge crowds gathered. They could see him, nonchalant in his basket, still wearing a straw hat and smoking a cigarette. When firemen came to rescue him, he joked with them until they could arrange a looped rope to pull him to safety on the roof.

That night, when he took his place at Maxim's for dinner, everybody stood and cheered him.

The ovation was deserved. Although the mishaps he had gone through now smack of burlesque, they were dangerous. Thomas Edison called him the pioneer of the air and praised his introduction of the gasoline engine. There was the constant danger of fire, explosion, and death with these rudimentary engines so close to hydrogen. Santos-Dumont may have displayed a casual air, but each flight was perilous and later he admitted that he'd frequently been afraid. But he was more than brave; he was tenacious. The setbacks would have grounded lesser men. He learned from them, and went on to build other craft, at his own expense.

In the following weeks, he had No. 6 built. He flew it twenty-five times, then informed the Aero Club he was ready to try again. On October 19, before officials of the club and a large crowd, he took off, quickly made the Eiffel Tower turn, then ran into a strong breeze. After considerable difficulty he manoeuvred No. 6 back to the starting point – but he had taken 30 minutes and 40 seconds.

The honour was not immediately awarded. The next day the French press exploded, knowing it had the might of Parisian public opinion behind it. Their message was clear; "le Petit Santos" had been betrayed.

Santos-Dumont thought so himself. He had set his heart on completing the course – what did a few seconds over the time limit matter?

It was one of the two great pinnacles of his flying career, but having reached the peak there were now only morbid thoughts. They were the beginning of a trend that was to grow into a monster.

For two weeks arguments raged – among the members of the Aero Club, and in editorials – as Parisians took aperitifs indoors during the cooling days of autumn. Finally, it was settled. Santos-Dumont would get the honour and the 100,000 francs. He immediately arranged that the prize should be shared by his mechanics and the poor of the city – so Brazil sent him another prize.

Now Santos-Dumont was lionized. Knick-knacks, postcards, photographs glorified his feat. A fellow inventor, Marconi, sent a congratulatory letter. Invitations poured in to lecture, to be the guest of honour at dinners, to attend plays and concerts.

It was time for a new feat, perhaps to fly over sea. The invitation to go to Monaco came at an appropriate time.

CHAPTER 2
The Prince's Yacht Followed

The chart of Monaco that Santos-Dumont studied a few days before Christmas, 1901, would have shown little but *hachures* marking hills. The Prince's palace, surrounded by the old town, was on one hill. The Casino and the *Hotel de Paris* were on a clifftop facing it. Behind was France and the peaks of the Alpes Maritimes.

There was one spot, a beach called La Condamine, perhaps flat enough to take off and land airship No. 6, after flights over the sea – flights that might go all the way to Corsica.

That of course was an astonishing dream; Corsica was more than 100 miles over sea. If Santos-Dumont could fly that distance, everything accomplished before would be insignificant.

He arrived on the sleeping car express from Paris on January 2, 1902, and was given a suite of rooms. The aerodrome was still being readied so he had time to look around. The king of the Belgians was a visitor that winter. *M'Amour,* a play dealing with adultery, was being presented. Each day, hundreds at the gaming tables tried "to beat the bank at Monte Carlo."

Word that Santos-Dumont was there, and even contemplating the possibility of flying all the way to Corsica, spread along the coast, drawing visitors from Nice and Cannes. As for the Corsican adventure, one journalist, Henri Rochefort, wrote that, if it were accomplished, "there will remain little more for the nations to do than throw down their arms."

Near the end of January, Prince Albert returned to his domain from a state visit abroad. He lost no time in coming down from his palace to meet his Latin namesake, Alberto, and inspect the airship.

It carried a pennant with the letters P.M.N.D.A.N. These were the first letters of the words of a Portuguese epic poem, *Por mares nunca d'antes navegados* (O'er seas hereto unsailed). Was he really thinking of heading for Corsica?

No: a month after his arrival in Monaco, Santos-Dumont made his first flight and he headed out over the entrance of the harbour, but then turned and flew parallel with the coast. Eventually he vanished from the view of those promenading in the clifftop subtropical gardens and the larger crowds lining the harbour wall. After an hour he reappeared, at first a speck, then growing larger as he aimed for the harbour. He came in for a perfect landing.

There were cheers as well as praise, but there were also misgivings. Many felt he ought to have guardian boats. So it was that, on his next flight, a whole flotilla put to sea – the wealthy American publisher Gordon Bennett in his yacht; Gustave Eiffel in his; Prince Albert and the Governor General of the principality, unsuitably dressed in morning coat and top hat, in the royal steam yacht; and numerous others eager to follow what was undoubtedly the sensation of the season. Moreover, just to make sure, a couple of wealthy visitors with powerful cars drove along the coast road to keep a check.

Again, after leaving the harbour Santos-Dumont turned east. In about twenty minutes he was off Cap Roquebrune. The Monagesques waved hats and cheered as he wheeled back toward the harbour.

The captain of the royal yacht was forever giving orders for course changes to keep near the hovering airship; Prince Albert had hopes of seizing the dangling guide rope and leading the airship – like a proud owner would lead a race-winning greyhound – into the paddock. Unfortunately, smoke and sparks from the funnel belched up near the bag of hydrogen and threatened to blow the aviator, the Prince, his crew, and most of the following flotilla to kingdom come. Anyway, just at this moment the trailing rope from airship No. 6 swept across the deck, knocking the Prince down.

Albert was severely cut, Santos-Dumont went on alone to land.

Two days later there was the type of weather that had made Monte Carlo such a favourite winter resort for the rich. The afternoon was still, warm and sunny – ideal for flying. Many must have guessed that Santos-Dumont would make another flight.

The royal yacht took up station in the harbour. The airship lifted off. Immediately, it was obvious to the aeronaut – and within seconds to the watching crowds – that something was wrong. The envelope had not been inflated properly. Bracing wires became entangled in the propeller. The engine was stopped. Drifting, rudderless, the No. 6 started to descend. If it followed its course it would either crash on rooftops or on the mountains behind. Santos-Dumont had no choice. He pulled a gas valve and the airship sank into the harbour. Santos-Dumont was saved by a launch.

It was a great disappointment yet, in total, this visit to Monaco certainly had been a success. Santos-Dumont had flown out over the ocean and, again, he had navigated the air, much like a demi-God.

As it turned out, one of the most important aspects of his flights at Monaco may have been the fact that they were seen by the British publisher, Alfred Harmsworth.

CHAPTER 3

"Napoleon of Fleet St."

Harmsworth wrote that, when he was in Monaco, he "went about a great deal with Santos-Dumont." He watched him fly over the sea and he certainly would have been aroused by the idea of flying to Corsica because it was Napoleon's birth place and Napoleon was something of a model for Harmsworth.

Harmsworth was eight years older than Santos-Dumont and much better known. From a few years after his wedding day in his twenty-second year until now – at age thirty-six – Harmsworth had built up the greatest publishing empire the world had ever seen. It would be another fourteen years before he would be called the most powerful man in Britain, but already he had enormous power – and that was his life's grail.

One of his editors, after Harmsworth's death, said he was left with four compelling impressions of the first Viscount Northcliffe (as Harmsworth was to become). They were his ambition for power, though not necessarily money, through his newspapers; his "Britishness"; his volcanic intolerance of slipshod work; and his uncanny instinct, which he called his sixth sense.

Add to that the physical picture of him in 1902: steely blue eyes, clear cut features, a Napoleonic lock of hair, pudgy hands, square tipped fingers, a thick neck, small feet.

It was a portrait a long way from the good-looking boy he had been. But it was equally far from the fleshy hulk of his last years when he could have modelled as a Chicago mobster.

In 1902, when Santos-Dumont was flying at Monaco, Harmsworth was at a pinnacle of his career. Unlike Santos-Dumont, he had not been born with a silver spoon in his mouth. He was one of thirteen children, common by Victorian standards but insupportable for a father who liked drink, flighty girls, and who never mounted from the lower rungs of the barrister's profession.

Alfred was named after his father but his nickname at home was "Sunny" and his schoolmates called him "The Dodger." He was born in a Dublin suburb and went to a succession of English schools. H. G. Wells was a pupil at one of them and, when he later wrote *The New Machiavelli,* its principal character was a thinly-disguised Alfred Harmsworth.

At sixteen and a half, Harmsworth was no outstanding pupil. He spent a good deal of time dreaming of get-rich-quick schemes, although they did not extend to publishing. In any case, as he passed his seventeenth birthday, any plans had to be held in abeyance. First, Alfred had pneumonia; then he impregnated a servant girl who worked for the Harmsworths. This was no extraordinary occurrence in this age. Alfred was a virile youth, the girl was willing. And if there were no precautions taken before an act of this kind, there were usually arrangements afterwards. The girl was sent away to have her child and the boy was despatched to Europe; in Alfred's case, his Grand Tour was as a secretary-companion to a young clergyman. The youth was given a great sendoff for his first trip abroad. The girl, in Essex, was delivered of a son.

On returning, Alfred Harmsworth started making his living as a free-lance writer and editor.

Then, one day in bed (throughout his life he had many of his better ideas while either in bed or laying flat on the floor), he decided he would ask the Iliffes, who owned the cycling paper he edited to publish a competitor to the enormously popular magazine, Tit-Bits. It would be called Answers to Correspondents. The Iliffes turned down the idea but they agreed to print it for a few weeks on credit if he decided to start it. He did. He was twenty-one.

Answers was launched with a thousand pounds and Alfred's brother, Harold, was brought in to look after the financial side. It was full of articles, written by Alfred Harmsworth, about the terror of wearing top hats and the strange things found in tunnels. Its readers were fed trivia – for instance, that the Prince of Wales (later Edward the Seventh) was known to his intimates as "tum-tum" because of "his graceful rotundity of person."

Such intelligence and a number of bolstering contests couldn't even push circulation above 20,000. The venture was in jeopardy.

Then a financial paragraph in the London *Times* and a walk along the embankment beside the Thames changed Alfred Harmsworth's destiny.

He had noticed one day, in the world's most august newspaper, the value of the gold and silver at a specific time in the Bank of England. A little later he was walking with Harold when they were accosted by a down-and-out. Alfred gave him a little money, but he wanted something in exchange – information. He asked the tramp a question: If he could win a prize what would it be? "A pound a week for life" was the answer. Of course. It meant security. It meant, for millions in those days, the chance to move slightly up the class ladder.

The Harmsworths immediately promoted a contest where the prize was a pound a week for life to the Answers reader who came nearest to guessing the amount of gold in the Bank of England at a certain time on a certain day.

Sandwichmen carried boards through London's West End, reading, A POUND A WEEK FOR LIFE! The magazine proclaimed it The Most Gigantic Competition The World Has Ever Seen. The little Answers office was overwhelmed. Twenty temporary clerks had to be employed. Altogether, over 700,000 entries were received; one mail delivery alone brought more than a quarter million postcards. The winner, Sapper C. D. Austin, guessed within two pounds of the correct figure. He died eight years later of tuberculosis. Harmsworth sent his widow a cheque for £50.

The effect of this single contest was to shoot Answers' circulation up to 200,000. Alfred Harmsworth was on his way.

He started comic papers and employed writers such as Arthur Conan Doyle. Within a couple of years, Answers was selling a million copies a week. Alfred Harmsworth, still only twenty-seven, was the talk of the town.

In the years before he saw Santos-Dumont, he bought his first newspaper, the London *Evening News;* started the *Daily Mail* with which he revolutionized newspaper reader habits; extended his string of periodicals. He ran for parliament but was unsuccessful; acquired a property in Kent near a coastal bluff called North Cliff; lived in London next door to a former Prime Minister, Lord Roseberry; travelled more and more abroad, especially in France; acquired his first car.

Harmsworth was to start the *Daily Mirror* (eventually the biggest selling daily newspaper in the world), buy *The Observer,* and own Britain's most respected journal, *The Times,* but he always regarded the *Daily Mail* as his child. And he gave it the attention of a child. A parlour maid had given birth to his illegitimate son, but he and his wife – despite joint visits to physicians – were unable to have offspring. The paper was the alternative.

Harmsworth surrounded himself with young journalists. He initiated competitions, stunts, crusades, without forgetting the value of news. He would not allow vulgarity (he would not permit it in women either, and once stormed when one of his mistresses wanted to go to the *Folies Bergeres).* He prohibited slang.

From the first, the *Mail* "made" news. The *Manchester Guardian* said of the *Mail* that it made life more pleasant, more exciting, for the average man. It was the excitement and the power that enthralled Alfred Harmsworth.

Harmsworth's house at Broadstairs in England, near the North Cliff, was full of books on Napoleon, a bust of the emperor stood in the drawing room, the plates in the dining room were of Sèvres china with "N" engraved on them. Harmswórth could find other affinities. He was born under the same zodiac sign, both he and the Corsican came from large families – in each of which the mother was the driving force. Harmsworth deliberately began to copy some of Napoleon's characteristics; the lock of hair was smoothed down to ape the Frenchman's. He motored hundreds of miles in France, through country Napoleon had criss-crossed so many times. Often he sought out relics of the Emperor; he was delighted when he tried on his hat and found that it fitted.

The journeys were not always with his wife. The marriage was reasonably compatible but hardly made in heaven. His letters show he always respected her, but there were scores of women prepared to offer Harmsworth a good deal more than respect. Many allusions were made in print to his mistresses; it is difficult to sort fact from fiction because the man was so vulnerable to innuendo. There have been rumours that he had many other illegitimate children.

Travel, and meeting with the great and famous, fitted in with Harmsworth's business and he was in his element: meeting the Astors, Vanderbilts and Mark Twain in the U.S.; sailing to Canada to make massive deals for newsprint; visiting western European countries; sending daily telegraph or phone messages to his secretaries, editors, correspondents; meeting with princes; dining with the young Winston Churchill, Sarah Bernhardt, Cecil Rhodes. And, always, he was looking for ideas, ideas, ideas for the *Mail*. It was inevitable that his newspaper should get involved with the newness and the excitement of flight.

CHAPTER 4
"Britain...
No Longer an Island"

Over in the United States, on December 17, 1903, the Wright Brothers made their flight at Kitty Hawk and the extraordinary thing about it, apart from the feat itself – it was the first flight of a heavier-than-air machine – was the fact that it produced not a rush of enthusiastic head-lines but an incredible amount of apathy.

This stunning lack of interest continued throughout the following year when the Wrights made more than a hundred successful flights, some up to five minutes in duration. When one Ohio editor was asked, forty years later, why this was so, he answered: "Well, I guess we were just plain dumb." Even in 1906, the *Scientific American* magazine still made up-roarious fun of the Wrights' claims to flight, without sending anyone to investigate whether they were true.

It is hardly surprising that the United States was so slow to take to fly-ing. And it is now understandable why Santos-Dumont would have con-tinued following his ambition to be the first man to fly a heavier-than-air machine. At first, France hadn't heard of the Wrights. Then, their early flights were disputed. In Brazil, there could be no question; its native son was the pioneer.

Today there are Brazilians who still believe it. Thirty years ago the government of the day believed it. In October, 1941, it claimed Santos-Dumont as the father of modern flight. The Aero Club of Brazil, with the support of many other South American aeronautical associations, had already protested to the United States the commemoration of Pan-Ameri-can Day on the anniversary of the Wrights' first flight.

After Santos-Dumont left Monaco and returned to Paris, his airships became an everyday part of Paris life. But they were still novel enough to become the basis of much of the personal journalism of the day. Witness Andre Fagel, writing in *L'illustration* on July 4, 1903: "I had just sat down on a terrace of a cafe and was enjoying an iced orangeade. All of a sudden I was shaken with surprise on seeing an airship coming right down in front of me. The guide rope coiled around the legs of my chair. The airship was just above my knees, and Mr. Santos-Dumont got out.

"While crowds of people rushed forward and wildly acclaimed the great Brazilian aviator, Mr. Santos-Dumont asked me to excuse him for having startled me. He then called for a drink, got aboard his airship again and went gliding off into space."

The very next day he landed in the Bois de Boulogne and the police had to hold up the traffic, back to the Arc de Triomphe; he took up a passenger, a Cuban girl, then he took up a child. On Bastille Day of that year, he landed his No. 9, at the invitation of the army, at a military parade inspected by the President of France. Already the generals were beginning to see the value of airships in war.

Now the limits were being extended. Ernest Archdeacon, a lawyer, a rich man, and president of the French Aero Club, had put up a prize for the first man to fly a heavier-than-air machine twenty-five metres. The prize was only three thousand francs but this didn't matter; Santos-Dumont was now employing as many as fifteen workers to adapt his airships. More than ever, money was of secondary importance. But he had to win. He had to be the first man in the world to fly. More and more people were believing that the Wrights had flown. In France, new designs of gliders showed that someone else might gain the honour any day.

There was no time to lose. Santos-Dumont built a new series of airships. By 1906 – this was three years after the Wright Brothers' flight – the string had reached No. 14. This one was adapted and adapted again as Santos-Dumont applied his ingenuity to convert it from a dirigible into a plane. It was called No. 14 Bis. It had a fifty horsepower engine. Originally it was a series of box kites attached to the bag of an airship. Gradually, the kite cells were increased, and eventually the bag taken away. It was called a "monstrous hybrid," but miraculous bastard might have been more apt. Aerodynamically, it could just fly. There was no directional control. It could not turn, and could only glide downward or climb upward with difficulty. It was a freak.

But finally, on October 23, 1906, after ten major mechanical failures it flew ten or twelve feet above the ground for a distance of about sixty metres to win the Archdeacon Prize.

The news went round the world. Man had flown.

Le Petit Journal of Paris said, "Santos-Dumont is the first man who has managed in a heavier-than-air machine to leave the ground exclusively by his own means and accomplish a straight flight."

Le Matin called him, "the first to fly before witnesses in a heavier-than-air dirigible."

Illustrated London News ran a long article entitled "The First Flight Of A Machine Heavier Than Air."

Europe obviously took a different view than that of Dan Kumber, editor-in-chief of the Dayton *Daily News,* who, when asked why he had not reported on the numerous flights of the hometown boys, the Wrights, said, "because it seemed to us to be a vain pastime without any importance and of no consequence."

Harmsworth was not about to allow his own newspapers to make the same mistake when it came to Santos-Dumont's accomplishments. When the Brazilian won the Archdeacon Prize, with a flight of sixty metres and a subsequent flight of eighty metres, it was, at first, almost ignored by Harmsworth's papers.

One of them ran the flight story condensed into four lines, in the *News in Brief* column. Harmsworth was on the phone next day, storming to the Scottish sub-editor responsible, telling him that he was "afflicted with all the caution of his race," that he had misread the story, that the short distance covered didn't matter, but that the event meant that "Britain was no longer an island."

It was an astounding, perhaps lucky, measure of a gauche scientific advance. Man could fly – just – Santos-Dumont's few yards in the air seemed to say. Man has created a new world was Harmsworth's prediction. And he had to be part of it.

"Britain . . . no longer an island." It was the kind of simple, sweeping recruiting call one expected of Pitt, or later of Churchill, but hardly of a still young newspaper publisher whom some considered an upstart.

Actually, Harmsworth had been elevated to the peerage some ten months before Santos-Dumont made his flight. He'd first been offered a knighthood but had turned it down, feeling he deserved better. Then he'd been made a baronet and a baron, in succeeding years. As his title, he chose Northcliffe, a one-word combination of the geographical place-name near his home in Kent.

There is little doubt that Santos-Dumont's first heavier-than-air machine spurred Northcliffe. His newspapers promoted a telephone for every London police station, standard bread, better roads for cars – and, after 1906, they (and especially the *Daily Mail)* hammered home demands for British superiority in the air; they promoted contests, carped at the economies of the Cabinet, deplored the lack of warplanes. They set Britain on the search for aerial superiority.

While Northcliffe concerned himself with supplying his newspapers with ideas, his brother, Harold, worried about their supply of newsprint; there was a danger of relying entirely on a European source and Harold sharpened his pencils and headed for Newfoundland to take a look around and start a little horse-trading.

By 1905, the newsprint problems were solved. Newfoundland signed "The Harmsworth Deal," providing a 198-year lease on 2,300 square miles of forest. The British could not understand such figures – a land area equal to Kent, Surrey and Sussex combined.

The Newfoundlanders merely considered the Harmsworths crazy.

In return for the lease, the Harmsworths offered a development project to harness the Exploits River, build huge pulp and paper mills, and create Grand Falls, the second largest town at that time in Newfoundland. Northcliffe journeyed across to be on hand for the official opening of the Anglo-Newfoundland Development Company's plant in 1909.

The trip was strenuous – it ended by crossing Newfoundland on a swaying, jolting train. The ride made him sick but his health was already something less than perfect; a year earlier, he'd written to a male secretary in Britain and confided: "I have been feeble, slow, cross and lacking interest in the sex, always a bad sign with your devoted Chief."

Possibly he was worried he was syphilitic. Wickham Steed, one of his most famous editors, and Evelyn Wrench, one of the more servile executives, believed he contracted the disease between 1906 and 1908.

Still, his energy was prodigious. He continued to pour out his favourite picture postcards, memos, letters. One went to Dame Ethel King, suggesting that the trees on her estate at an airfield at Brooklands, not far from London, might hamper its use as a landing field for planes. Britain's war minister received a pointed note explaining that both the French and Germans had had military representatives at flying trials by Wilbur Wright over Pau, near the French Pyrenees. Lord Esher, a courtier with influence, was told: "Our national muddle-headedness has rarely been seen to worse advantage than in aviation." The *Times* office got a succinct guideline: "Our national position is truly pathetic."

But all those bowler-hatted clerks, domestics, housewives, spending their pennies for the exciting *Daily Mail,* didn't know about this side of Northcliffe's life. What interested them were his prizes for flying. It was the new sensation. At least vicariously, Northcliffe seemed to suggest: try it. He wasn't offering a drug; it was really a preparation. He wanted Britain ready for anything Germany might try – ten years before war broke out, he was warning of German efficiency, bellicosity and bullheadedness; of German preparations.

He wanted Britain prepared, too, so he became the champion of aviation. He recognized quickly the plane's advantages in war. He ran a series of air contests to foster public interest, get more young men flying, put indirect pressure on the government and its service chiefs.

First was a model airplane contest. Next was a real competition, a race: the *Daily Mail* would present £1,000 to the first man to fly the English Channel.

The sorry fact though, was that in 1909 there were still few flyers with machines capable of covering that small distance across the Channel. In Britain, there were none.

Daily Mail staffmen started a search, but the threads all led back to France. That country had most of, almost all, the world's aviators.

But even there, flying was haphazard.

One Frenchman, Louis Bleriot, decided to enter Northcliffe's contest and, when he was preparing to leave Calais on July 24, 1909, he asked somebody, "Où est Dovre?" An arm was pointed northward. Using this as his only navigational aid, Bleriot took off and landed, twenty-seven minutes later, on a grassy slope beside Dover Castle.

Man had successfully flown across a significant body of water; the first important *Daily Mail* air prize had been won.

CHAPTER 5

A Christian
Band of Brothers

Aviation came to Britain sneakily.

A doctor's son, A. V. Roe, who had already received a Harmsworth prize for model aircraft, had to climb over a back fence every day so he could fly. Roe, who was little more than a boy, built a triplane. He kept it locked behind the door of what once had been a stable just outside Manchester and, as long as it was there, society had no protest. But when he brought the plane into the open, he was charged with creating a public danger.

So he moved to Brooklands, twenty miles southwest of London, and built a shed.

He was the first, but soon other flyers owned sheds at this motor racing track. It set them apart as Britain's aerial pioneers.

The manager of Brooklands had been hired for motor racing and he decided to follow the rule book. He closed the track at sunset and locked it for the night.

Roe went through the farce each night. Ceremoniously, he bade everyone goodnight, left Brooklands by the gate, then climbed over a fence so that he could get back to his shed and its important cargo.

This deception wasn't simply because he needed more time to work on his machine – it enabled him to fly at dawn. This was most important on those summer mornings when the air was still. The early machines certainly required calm air; not one of them had flown even in a 10-mile-per-hour wind.

Flying, then, was a series of small steps. At the airfields, at Brooklands, Hendon, Eastchurch in Britain, at St. Cloud in France, at one or two places in Germany, and another couple in the United States, each step – roll, loop, spin, many more – became a milestone.

Flyers who had come to Brooklands were like squatters. The sheds they put up became the centre of their lives. The individual who owned one was in a special coterie. It was a place to store tools, build a bench, place drums of fuel, cook scrappy meals over a primus stove, sleep in a packing case and, above all, protect the precious machine from the weather. Each shed was a headquarters.

The machines were *alter egos,* tuned, mended, rebuilt, fussed over, discussed, given far more attention than their owners were prepared to distribute over the rest of their lives.

Not many of these pilots were married, so the neglecting of wives was no problem. But some did have fiancées, who could sometimes be a nuisance, for example, when they wanted to be taken out to parties or the West End theatre. Some of these young men seemed quite prepared to sublimate sex, at least temporarily, in a whirr of engine propellers, grease, and new visual dimensions above the Surrey hills. The air historian, Sir Walter Raleigh, has likened these early flyers to an early Christian brotherhood. The more popular concept is that they were a bunch of comics, amateurs who didn't quite know what they were doing but were true to the carry-on, England-always-struggles-through belief, and who managed, of course, to ensure that Britannia ruled the air.

In fact, the gradations have to be finer. There were differences – Roe had his first machines towed down the Brooklands track embankments by cars to get sufficient speed for takeoff, the Honourable Alan Boyle always slept beside his plane in a hammock, and Thomas Octave Murdoch Sopwith later created a leading aircraft factory.

Although there was congress among the three air centres in Britain, Brooklands differed from both Hendon and Eastchurch. All were close to London but Hendon, the closest, rapidly became identified with flying as a sport. Eastchurch was favoured by the wealthy, and was a centre of plane building. Sopwith constructed his first planes there. Soon, he was only interested in building winning planes.

Brooklands always seemed to have a slightly more happy-go-lucky air than the other airfields. It was probably exemplified best by its Bluebird Cafe.

The cafe was one of about 120 buildings erected at Brooklands by the end of 1910. A Mrs. Billings acted as a comforting mother earth figure, and dispensed hot drinks and cool wisdom to all the pilots and mechanics of Brooklands who gathered there.

A place to eat was very necessary. The early morning flights were made before breakfast. The empty feeling in the stomach as an engine skipped a beat, the parched mouth of fear as bearings were lost when weather worsened, not to say outright hunger and thirst, could be assuaged most quickly by a cafe right beside the sheds.

But the Bluebird was more than a cafe. It has been described as a parliament. Until it was burned in 1916, it was certainly one of the more exclusive clubs in Britain. Entrance demanded camaraderie, unselfishness, daring, mechanical knowledge, zest. It also helped to have taste buds that were not too demanding.

The fare was essentially tea, sweet and steamy and by the gallon, bread in thick slices, jam. Bacon and eggs, sausages and mash, chops could be and were cooked, but those were the outer limits of cuisine. The jam, especially in summer and most particularly by afternoon, was a problem. It brought wasps. The airmen had a ready answer. They would use bicycle pumps to spray the jam dishes with petrol. The result was not lethal, but it gave a long remembered taste to strawberry or plum-and-apple preserve.

There were big changes in flying, of course, during that first decade; for one thing, the planes reached the point where they were able to face 10-miles-per-hour breezes. But they still looked like dragonflies with bicycle wheels and flying was still filled with romance.

There was enough of it to lure three young men to Brooklands who would eventually meet again in a hotel in Newfoundland as contenders in the race to be the first to fly the Atlantic. Their names were Frederick Philip Raynham, Harry George Hawker, and Jack Alcock. All of them had unlikely upbringings for pilots.

CHAPTER 6

No. 2 –
But Always Trying

Fred Raynham was the first of the three to fly at Brooklands. He got his pilot's certificate on a May day in 1911 and he was not yet eighteen years old.

Officially, he was granted the eighty-fifth aviator's certificate to be awarded in Britain. He was one of six men who became pilots that day and there was a minor celebration at the Bluebird Cafe. But it wouldn't have lasted long; there were still so few flyers that all were needed to try out planes and teach others to fly.

Fred Raynham was the son of a Suffolk farmer. He was an average student, particularly interested in mechanical subjects. He was about to leave school, as a lad of sixteen, when Bleriot flew the English Channel. He was fascinated and he managed to get to London to see the plane when it was put on display.

He had no doubt what he wanted to do in life; he decided to teach himself to fly. He went down to Brooklands and joined A. V. Roe. There was no pay for any work that he did, but he had an arrangement that gave him the use of one of Roe's planes for two hours a week.

All the pilots of that time seem remarkably baby-faced. Astonishingly, some still looked the same nearly ten years later when they were ready to pit themselves against the Atlantic. Raynham, slight and clean shaven, and with his light hair slicked back, looked the youngest of all, yet he was to become one of the best known test pilots of early aircraft. He took up newly constructed planes and balanced like a Blondin above the Surrey landscape, working for Sopwith, Avro, Martinsyde. It was never dull; often it was dangerous.

On one occasion, he was flying one of these imbalanced contraptions at 700 feet when it began to break up. As Brooklands' watchers admired his skill, Raynham reduced the stresses on the wings while bringing the disintegrating plane safely down to land.

On another occasion, only a few months after he had received his "ticket," he was flying through cloud in a biplane on the way from Brooklands to Hendon when he got into a spin. He was possibly the first man to get out of a spin alive. He never knew how he managed to right the plane and the memory of those few moments, fluttering down to certain death, became part of a storehouse of memories of equally narrow escapes.

The spin had taken place on the way to an air meet. He was a major competitor in these weekend attractions that were the vogue in Britain. (By 1913, as many as 30,000 spectators passed through the ticket booths on summer Saturday afternoons at Hendon to watch races.) Men and youths (especially) took to travelling out after their Saturday morning's work in London.

In 1910, before Raynham had become a pilot, there were seven of these aerial meets in Britain, with an aggregate prize money of eight hundred and five pounds, ten shillings and fivepence. By 1912, Hendon alone had thirty meets and fifty-one the year later.

For a nation used to honouring horseflesh, the air races offered the spur of competition. "Aerial Derbies" quickly became the most important annual contests and odds were set by bookmakers on the various pilots. And there were more than races. There were also the thrills of seeing planes of novel shape suddenly appear; aerobatics, with pilots trying some new antic in their puzzle boxes of strut, mesh, and sometimes erratic spatial dimensions; and, greatest of all, the opportunity to fly as a passenger for a fee (which varied greatly according to the renown of the pilot).

Many of the first pilots were French, but gradually Raynham, Hawker and Alcock became the crowds' favourites.

Raynham flew Avro planes and then the Martinsyde monoplanes, generally considered the most handsome of early aircraft. That was on Saturdays, Sundays, and Monday bank holidays. Through the weeks, he was one of the few pilots earning money from aviation – testing, or giving occasional lessons.

Other competitors would fork out about £500 a year to follow their hobby. This did not include the original price of their plane, nor the cost of tuition. The London *Observer* newspaper reported that in 1911 and 1912 the cost of renting a shed at Brooklands was £100 a year; that the total cost of wages for a good mechanic and a boy to help maintain the amateur's plane was £170 to £180 a year, that the cost of fuel for an hour's flying was about 13 shillings. Planes in those giddy days cost from £400 to £1,200 and the cost of tuition, including insurance, was £75.

There were pressures to make flying more than a popular pastime. The Northcliffe press kept telling the War Office to take more interest in flying. In spite of such public clamours, the flying arms of the services had wobbly beginnings. For instance, the Royal Naval Air Service got its start when an Eastchurch flyer, Frank McLean, offered his plane to the Admiralty for the training of three naval officers and one marine officer while he went on a government expedition to Fiji to observe an eclipse of the sun. A little later, an unusual young cabinet minister at the Admiralty, Winston Churchill, was ignoring official channels and encouraging the new service pilots to experiment, to take off from the sea or from ships' decks – and to drop bombs. This was only one step toward preparedness for war; in 1913, Churchill took another step, buying planes from Avro, Vickers, Sopwith, Bristol – companies which had begun only three or four years earlier.

Of the prize money won in 1911, the year Raynham learned to fly, one hundred pounds went to him for the second aggregate time prize for the year's meets. Some of Raynham's exploits were astonishing to spectators. On a February day in 1914 he took an Avro plane to 15,000 feet over Brooklands, cut the engine, put it into a glide and headed for Hendon twenty miles away, where he landed without restarting the engine. Later that summer, he did the whole thing in reverse.

Raynham's greatest rival was Harry Hawker and it seemed that Hawker always edged him out. Once Raynham finished a 100-mile-course just 37 seconds behind Hawker.

October 24, 1912, was an especially bitter day for Raynham. He had already made attempts to win the British Empire Michelin trophy and its accompanying £500 prize awarded to the British pilot who remained the longest time in the air in an all-British aircraft in one flight between sunrise and one hour after sunset.

Raynham took off from Brooklands in an enclosed Avro biplane, climbed gradually to 400 feet above the airfield and slowly began a day of circuits. He started his long, boring flight, round and round in a broad oval. But in late morning he was joined by Hawker in a Sopwith biplane. It was an uncommon duel, two planes lazily circling at the same altitude. It was as if they were locked together like a child's toy. Occasionally a pilot took a nibble from a sandwich. Hawker had a flask of hot cocoa, probably supplied by the Bluebird Cafe.

Through the afternoon, the planes flew, almost at the same speed, almost the same position in relation to each other. Pilots and mechanics left the sheds at Brooklands to watch. People unacquainted with flying did the same thing in the nearby streets of Byfleet and Weybridge, not knowing what was at stake.

Then Raynham's plane began to run unevenly. The gauge showed he was running out of oil. Far from disheartened at this time in the late afternoon, he landed. He had been in the air for seven and one-half hours, easily establishing a new British endurance record. But Hawker stayed aloft. He had started later and it did not seem likely that he could break Raynham's record. But as the sun began to set, he was still there, circling slowly. At darkness, he was still flying. Only after he had been up eight hours, twenty-three minutes did he land.

Raynham had been robbed of victory again. For one hour and thirty-five minutes, until Hawker's wheels touched the grass, he had been the record holder, but the trophy and money went to Hawker. Raynham was still No. 2.

CHAPTER 7
Harry Hawker

The British public of 1913 and 1914 bought their tickets for the Hendon air meets through London theatre ticket agents and they called their favourite by his first name – he was Harry.

Other pilots, Raynham and Alcock, for instance, were held in regard, but they were known by their surnames, possibly because they were English and were paid, and didn't rate first names. The same distinction was made between paid professional cricketers and the unpaid amateur cricketers; the unpaid amateurs were gentlemen so they received initials rather than first names on the scoresheet and in the newspapers.

Hawker was a professional, paid pilot too. He was also Harry because he was an Aussie, and Australians, to the English, were always carefree, and did not really care a damn for the social graces.

Harry George Hawker fitted the bill.

He was third of four children of an Australian blacksmith, grandson of a Cornishman. When he was eight years old, there was a reason for pride that comes to few boys out among the eucalyptus trees of the Australian countryside; his father, a great shot, went back to the "old country" to compete at Bisley in the world's toughest contest of marksmanship, and won the Queen's Prize.

Harry had already run away from several schools, until finally, when he was twelve, he started working for a car firm, Hall and Warden, at five shillings a week.

What a difference! Here there was no attempt to dodge work. By the age of fifteen, he had gained an extraordinary knowledge of cars; designed and built engines; he became known as one of the best drivers in the state of Victoria.

But praise and increases in pay never held him long and he worked for a number of car firms. An Australian colleague described Harry in those days as being good looking, slightly built, with brown eyes and dark, curly hair. Like Santos-Dumont, he was short, and was so sensitive about it that he wore high-heeled shoes. He was also fussy about his dress and, even when he was working on engines, his overalls didn't appear to pick up as much grease as his mates'.

One day, he ran into a friend, Harry Busteed. Both were interested in planes but flying was almost non-existent in Australia so Busteed was preparing to go to Britain. Harry Hawker didn't need much convincing; he said he could be ready in a week. Another mate, Harry Kauper, decided to join them, and they all arrived in London in May, 1911. After some early difficulties, Hawker found a job with a car firm. But he spent most weekends at Brooklands, becoming increasingly absorbed in flying.

His friend, Kauper, got a job at Brooklands as a mechanic for Sopwith and Hawker was soon there with his tool kit, for an interview with Fred Sigrist, Sopwith's works manager.

Harry started work for Sopwith on June 29, 1912. A close relationship soon developed, based on the common zest of these men. Hawker immediately showed his abilities as a mechanic, working seventy-five hours a week for two pounds. Sopwith worked close beside him. At the Brooklands of 1912 it was difficult to tell which of the overalled, oil-stained, individuals was boss, pilot or mechanic.

Harry would have appealed to Sopwith. He was his kind of man, not too strong on theory but pragmatic, ready to try anything out, not foolishly, but by tests and hard work.

Sopwith once took a plane up for its first test flight, even though he had never flown before. He ran it 300 yards over the turf of Brooklands, then he pulled the joystick back sharply. The biplane shot up to forty feet, stalled, and crashed, breaking one wing and the undercarriage. Sopwith scrambled out unhurt, but decided to progress a little more slowly. He became the thirty-first man in Britain to gain a pilot's certificate.

But Sopwith did not remain a pilot. By 1912, when he was still in his early twenties, he began concentrating on construction. He already had chosen well in Fred Sigrist as a helper in building planes. Now he wanted someone to succeed him in the air as a test pilot.

Harry Hawker was more than willing to be that pilot. He had saved £40 to take him home to Australia in case his fortune didn't change, and he used the money to pay for flying lessons. Every minute he could spare from his mechanic's work, he was in a plane. Sopwith quickly recognized Hawker's skill in the air.

Hawker received his pilot's certificate on September 17, 1912, but he was so good that, before he had actually passed the tests, he was working as an instructor for Sopwith. One of his earliest pupils was Major H. M. Trenchard, later to be known as "father of the Royal Air Force."

Harry celebrated his pilot's ticket by purchasing a sixteen horsepower Panhard car. He used it regularly on Saturday nights, driving some of the Sopwith team to a music hall at Kingston.

Harry was always in a hurry: four days after his first lesson, he was flying alone; with only twenty-nine flying hours behind him, he made his first attempt on the British endurance record.

By 1912, Sopwith had become a full-fledged manufacturer. He started a plant at Kingston-on-Thames, a London suburb. From it, came planes for Harry to test. It was dangerous work. There were no testing devices for metal fatigue, no X-rays to diagnose a mechanical fault. The pilot relied on the good craftsmanship of the workers in the factory. Having been a mechanic so recently, Harry had no qualms. Of all the pilots flying in the early years in Britain, he was the one closest to the work bench in his speech, manner, belief. Always through his flying life, he respected what the aircraft mechanics were doing; talked with them, made suggestions, argued, but listened to their counter-claims.

Everybody who ever met Harry Hawker used the same word, "cheerful." Some of them also noted that his wrists and long fingers were like whipcord. In the last months of his life, a few acquaintances mentioned how those fingers twitched.

The twitch was the result of crashes, which also, almost certainly, caused tuberculosis in Harry's spine.

It was hardly likely that he knew he had health problems, not immediately. A first crash, on takeoff, put him into hospital for a couple of weeks with cuts, bruises, and a pain in the back. But he made light of it and went back to flying.

Through 1913 and the early summer of 1914, he was flying Sopwith's new planes in races, altitude and endurance contests. Some of these were more comical than ingenious – one was a "quick starting race" over a short course. Others had the most complicated rules: for example, Hawker got the £500 prize put up by the American sewing machine magnate, Mortimer Singer, by winning the contest for "the first all-British airplane capable of making six 'out and home' flights between two points on land and at sea, not less than five miles apart, in less than five hours, while carrying both pilot and passenger." This meant the plane had to carry both wheels and floats, and Hawker found, after taking off from the water on floats, that the wheels wouldn't go down to a landing position without being kicked. This was a job for his passenger who, incidentally, was the official starter for the contest.

Harry also won a Whit Monday cross country handicap, in which Jack

Alcock must have wondered whether he wanted to continue the vocation after finding the wind was so strong that it began driving him backwards, forcing him to scratch.

On a Whit Saturday at Hendon, Harry had set a new altitude record of 7,400 feet. Then he lost it, then won it back.

He went back to Australia and was lionized as a hero.

At Melbourne racetrack, 25,000 people turned up to see him perform – many of them came on eighteen special trains.

Sydney, the perpetual rival to Melbourne, wasn't to be outdone; there were 20,000 spectators for Harry's stunts at Randwick racecourse on a summer day.

He arrived back in Britain in June of 1914. It was now home for him because it was a centre of flying and experimentation, something he could never find in the skies above Australia. His welcome proved it; he was aboard ship one day, flying at Brooklands the next. Ten days later, he looped the loop for the first time. As if to prove it was no fluke he went up the following day and did the same manoeuvre twelve times in succession.

Another factor made Britain home for him: flying was now his living and, in Britain, it was beginning to be a very good living. The government was placing ever larger orders for planes with Sopwith, and other companies, as war seemed unavoidable. That meant more planes for Harry to test and rising remuneration.

There was another attraction: popularity. Harry Hawker was the darling of the crowds who went to the summer air meets and read the papers for "aviation results." Nothing proved this so forcefully as the Round Britain race organized by the *Daily Mail*.

This contest meant that Hawker had to turn his attention to amphibians, a type of plane on which he'd had little experience. The rules stated that a contestant must start at Southampton Water and the plane had to carry a pilot and passenger, whose combined weight was not less than 264 pounds, and fly 1,500 miles around the British Isles, in less than seventy-two hours, landing at certain prescribed places. There was considerable doubt among the thousands who lined the shore at Southampton and the esplanades of southcoast seaside resorts that anyone could fly such a distance in three days and nights.

Harry was going to try. He chose as his passenger, his Australian mate, Harry Kauper, and off they went – wearing ordinary boots and trousers, but waterproof caps in recognition that their entire route was over the sea. They didn't take any food because they "couldn't be bothered."

At first all went well. Huge crowds looked up from their sand pails or trays of tea, and other pier and beach delights at Brighton, Hastings,

Ramsgate, and saw the plane, up about 1,000 feet, moving at 60 miles per hour. But, after landing at Yarmouth, Hawker suddenly collapsed. At first it was said the collapse was due to exhaust gases from the engine. Then the sun was blamed. In any case, Hawker could not fly on, and Sydney Pickles, another well-known Australian flyer, took his place. In the end, a storm forced the plane out of the contest at Scarborough.

Harry recovered by the following week and he decided to make another attempt with Kauper. This time, he wore flying helmet and goggles – presumably to avoid sunstroke. And everything went like clockwork for three quarters of the route. He landed at Scarborough, Aberdeen, Oban, strictly according to the rules, with plenty of time in hand. Then, near Dublin, engine trouble developed and the plane suddenly sideslipped into the water. Harry was unhurt but Kauper's arm was broken, and the plane wrecked. They had covered 1,043 miles in a flying time of twenty-one hours, forty-four minutes.

The *Daily Mail,* which had gained plenty of ink from the adventure, decided to give Hawker a thousand pounds as consolation. It brought to a total of £24,570 – a very considerable sum – that the *Mail* had given to keep flying before the public. Winston Churchill, the young First Lord of the Admiralty, was aboard a yacht off the Kentish coast near Deal when Hawker flew overhead and a letter from Churchill duly appeared in the *Mail:* "Mr. Hawker has achieved a wonderful result . . . the accident in no way detracts from the merit of a feat at once memorable and serviceable."

By then, the accident was one of many and they all helped make Hawker that much better known – so well-known, in fact, that as early as 1913, he had impersonators. One man got free drinks in a Lincoln hotel after identifying himself as "Harry Hawker," and promising to take everybody up for a free flip.

But Harry had more serious flying accidents.

A crash into the banks of the River Wey in Surrey put him into hospital with a nagging pain in the back.

And there was a serious crash into wooded St. George's Hill, close to the Brooklands field.

This one had happened because Harry had been taunted in the Bluebird Cafe. Other pilots had suggested that the closed-in, streamlined effect of a new Sopwith plane meant that it would be difficult to control; they'd said that, if it went into a spin, no pilot could bring it out. Hawker had gone over to the Sopwith line of aircraft and taken the offender up. He'd climbed, put it into a loop, and come out of it successfully. Then he'd done it again, but at a lower altitude. This time, when the power had fallen, the plane had gone down, too – in a spin. It had crashed, from 500 feet, into trees. Again Hawker had gone to hospital.

Again he made a quick recovery. Four days later he took a plane of the same type up to eight thousand feet, put it into a spin, and successfully brought it out. Once more he proved to himself what could be done with a plane.

CHAPTER 8
Two Manchester Boys

On a cool April morning in 1910, while it was still dark, Jack Alcock, who was then a stocky, red-cheeked youth, was moving around his simple, terrace home in the Manchester suburb of Fallowfield.

He and his father were up early for an air race: Lord Northcliffe's *Daily Mail* had offered £10,000 to the first man to fly from London to Manchester. Both Alcocks were interested in flying, the father, who was essentially a horse dealer, and the youth, seventeen years old, a mechanic who worked on cars.

They were not alone. There was considerable early movement that morning around Fallowfield, West Didsbury, Salford, in Manchester proper, as crowds started moving out before 5.00 a.m. to Fogg Lane where towels had been laid out on a field to mark a white path for the winning pilot.

The two Alcocks moved around quietly, getting their early tea and snack, because there were others in the household, asleep – Mrs. Alcock and four other children.

The newspapers, and the more knowledgeable of young Jack's benchmates at work, figured it was a race between the Frenchman, Louis Paulhan, and the Englishman, Claude Grahame White. But it was almost no contest. Paulhan's Farman biplane touched down first, leaving the Englishman far behind, near Birmingham.

Young Jack Alcock was hardly a great scholar but he had a bent for machines and, in a city which had made many men's fortunes out of cotton machinery, that was considered more important. When he attended local schools, he had made hot air balloons as much as twelve feet in diameter, of tissue paper, paste and strips of wood, and sent them up by means of a heating system which relied on wads of cotton wool soaked in methylated spirits. And, like Santos-Dumont in his childhood a quarter century before, Alcock had made box kites.

Jack Alcock left school at sixteen to enter the Empress Motor Works as an apprentice. He had a good nature and he was remembered there as being happy-go-lucky and game for anything. He once drove one of the firm's trucks into a brick wall on a dare. The manager surveyed the damage and forbade him to touch an Empress vehicle again. But this didn't include aircraft; it was at the Empress works that Jack tinkered with a plane for the first time.

By 1910, when Louis Paulhan won the *Daily Mail's* £10,000, Jack Alcock had met Norman Crossland, a founder/member of the Manchester Aero Club who had his own motor engineering business. One day Crossland asked Jack whether he would like to join him as a mechanic at his Salford works. But Alcock must have entered into a loose working arrangement with Crossland because, when the French pilot, Maurice Ducrocq, sent an engine for repair to the Empress Motor Works, Alcock was recalled by Empress to help work on it. After the repairs were made, Alcock was sent south to Brooklands to install the engine in Ducrocq's plane. The Frenchman was impressed. He offered Alcock a job as his mechanic. Soon Alcock was learning to fly. Ducrocq gave him his lessons, sitting in front of him in the cockpit. Alcock, behind, leaned over him to handle the controls. Two hours of this instruction and Alcock was ready to go up alone. He made many solos before becoming Britain's 368th official pilot in November, 1912 by taking off properly, performing the requisite number of figure-eights, and landing a plane precisely on the inspector's mark.

Two days later, he made two cross-country trips. A week later, he entered his first race and won, on handicap, beating, among others, Tom Sopwith.

Many beside Sopwith recognized Alcock as more than an enthusiastic amateur; here, as in the case of Hawker, was that rare combination – a great pilot and mechanic. The Sunbeam Motor Company recognized this too, and asked Alcock to become its racing pilot.

Through 1913, Alcock's life was not unlike that of Harry Hawker. There were air meets, planes to be tested, and pupils to be instructed.

His sister, Elsie, moved to Brooklands to keep a small house for him, but one day Jack Alcock was flying low over the Thames when he spotted her below in a punt with two young men whom he considered bad company. That night, he packed her off home to their mother.

When Alcock was twenty-one, and at Brooklands, Teddy Whitten-Brown, six years and a bit older, was in Manchester, working for Westinghouse, where his father was an executive.

Teddy's grandfather fought at Gettysburg and both his parents were American. His father trained as an engineer in Pittsburgh and brought his young bride, Emma Whitten, to Glasgow where the son was born. A few months later his father was sent to Manchester to help establish the British Westinghouse plant there.

The young family (Teddy was an only child) moved into a home on Oswald Road in Chorlton-cum-Hardy. It was very different from the home of the Alcocks, in Fallowfield, for the Whitten-Browns were of the middle class, edging into the upper middle class. Arthur Whitten-Brown was a professional man and their three-storey house was not in a row but had small stone gateposts and a name – Ellerslie. Young Teddy had a range of hobbies which could easily be indulged by his fairly wealthy parents. There were the novels of H. de Vere Stacpoole and other romantics, a lot of poetry, a dark room to experiment with colour photography; then a motorcycle for bird-watching trips in Wales and to the Island of Anglesey.

Teddy went to Manchester schools. He had blue eyes, wavy brown hair, was of medium height, with a finely drawn face. He was shy and did not make friends readily.

When he was sixteen he had been taken on as an electrical apprentice by the British Westinghouse Company. A condition of his employment with Westinghouse was that he attend evening classes, so he went to Manchester's Municipal School of Technology (now part of that city's university) for four years.

By day, he worked in a number of departments of Westinghouse. After four years, it was noted that he was "a reliable apprentice who made the most of the opportunities offered." So he was offered a job. He accepted.

It was hardly exciting work, but at least he travelled.

He kept a diary, a small, red book in which entries were made in his minute writing. What it revealed, more than anything else, was his dullness. The first entry was a timetable, Manchester to Bolton; after it, were some addresses. A couple of weeks later, the diary records: "Picture frame from Boots" (the chain of English chemist stores) and there are some drawings of women wearing hats. Nothing about Teddy himself.

The most interesting comment of all was inserted several months after he began the diary: "Told to leave for U.S. on Wed. per St. Louis from Southampton to investigate car lighting and starting sets. To sign a 2 yr. agreement at 25 pounds a month."

What did he think of the Atlantic crossing? We shall never know.

Generally, he went to industrial cities of the English North and Midlands to supervise the installation of electrical equipment, but in 1910-11 he was in South Africa to install or check machinery in mines. Then, at the end of 1913 he was off to America. But his stay there didn't last long; war was threatening and he returned to Britain.

It was in 1913 that Northcliffe announced his most dramatic aviation contest: Ten thousand pounds would be awarded to the first man to fly the Atlantic non-stop.

This venture was quite different than anything that had brought aviators prize money before. The English Channel was something Britons could understand; on a clear day, from Dover, it was possible to see across the Channel to France. London to Manchester was even more understandable. Trains made the journey every day. There were flat farmers' fields to land on should something go wrong. Even a flight "Round Britain" wasn't too much of a mystery; the flyers would not be out of sight of land.

But the Atlantic! It was incomprehensible.

To cross it by liner was still an odyssey. By tiny plane with one engine, (or, at the most, two) was simply a madman's dream.

Brown, quite naturally, ignored the challenge; he'd never even been in a plane.

Alcock was just too busy. He was already known as the Brookland's pilot who would go up when all others feared the weather, the man with the highest number of flying hours in his logbook. (By the time he was ready to fly the Atlantic in 1919, he had 4,500 hours in the air.) Most of those hours were made up on short flights but he gained five or six hours flying from London to Manchester, and back, in the last major race before the war broke out. He flew through a storm, wearing an ordinary cloth cap back to front as a helmet, and he came in third.

There was one other meet in 1914; it was at Hendon on the August Bank Holiday. But there were few spectators. A much denser crowd stood outside Buckingham Palace where Britons tend to gather at eventful moments in their history. And Britain was at war.

CHAPTER 9
The Admiral,
A Norwegian, and "Brackles"

Raynham, Hawker, and Alcock were to pilot three of the four British planes in the attempt, in 1919, to be the first to fly the Atlantic and, before World War One, they were among the best pilots in Britain; their names were known. Kerr, Gran, and Brackley, were names most Britons had never heard of, yet these three were to be the principal crew members of Britain's largest plane in that 1919 Atlantic race.

Kerr, christened Mark, was old enough to be the father of the other pilots. By 1914 he was already an admiral, acting as commander in chief of the Royal Hellenic Navy.

Tryggve Gran, born in Norway, had been the ski expert for Captain Scott on his last attempt to reach the South Pole.

Herbert George Brackley – nicknamed "Brackles" – had only just started working for a news agency.

Before the war, they didn't know each other.

Only Gran's name had been in the newspapers.

Jens Tryggve Harman Gran was born in 1889, the son of a shipbuilder. He was a rambunctious youth who gave his mother "many hours and days of worry." He was one of those boys who, on seeing a stone, must throw it. The burghers of Bergen, where he grew up, had to withstand a barrage of pebbles rained on their windows. One day an elderly widow was a special target of a major window breaking spree for a whole gang, led by Tryggve. But when the others fled, he stayed, rang the doorbell, introduced himself, and told the widow to send the glazier's bill to his mother.

He was determined to become a Norwegian naval officer and, when he was still in his 'teens, he managed to get himself hired on a ship and, for the next two years, he learned of ports in South America and Africa.

Back home, he became a naval cadet; he must have realized the importance of some formal education.

He was one of his country's outstanding skiers, a good sailor, near fluent in English. He failed to graduate from secondary school but later he went back to school in Oslo and managed, barely, to get a diploma. Three days after winning it, he set out, as a young man of twenty, with Captain Robert Falcon Scott for the Antarctic.

Scott hadn't chosen him because he had matriculated, but because of his skiing experience. Gran sailed for New Zealand in June, 1910 to participate in the race to be the first to reach the South Pole (eventually won by the fellow-Norwegian, Amundsen).

Gran was on the expedition on which five men, including Scott, reached the Pole (after Amundsen) then died so tragically on the return journey.

Gran experienced all the agonies of the Antarctic, the blizzards of the Polar Barrier, frostbite, hunger, exhaustion, and pure frustration.

There were ponies, as well as sled dogs, to haul supplies, and each member of the expedition had a pony to care for. Gran's was "Weary Willie" and, as only one example of the horrors of the expedition, Gran later recalled how it fell behind and was attacked by a hungry dog team; Gran drove off the dogs, but "Weary Willie" arrived at that night's camp without its sled and covered with blood.

Gran spent three years in the Antarctic and his mother said later: "Down there, he lived like a savage," then she added, "a life to his taste."

As soon as Tryggve was back in Europe, he shaved off his beard and affected long woollen scarfs in the fashion of the English blade. He decided to become an aviator.

He went to France, joined Bleriot's flying school, and was soon looping-the-loop – the tenth in the world to perform the manoeuvre – for which he received a thousand francs.

It wasn't enough. He had only a skittish acquaintanceship with aerial navigation, but now wanted to be the first to fly the North Sea. A few days after officially becoming a pilot, he bought a Bleriot plane and found a girl, Grete Somme, to christen it.

The plane, named Nordsjben (North Sea), was shipped to a field near the Cruden Bay Hotel, north of Aberdeen, in Scotland. Lloyd's of London was approached for insurance and demanded a premium of 75 per cent.

There was reason for haste: on July 27, 1914, it was announced that, because of the threat of hostilities, no civil aircraft would be allowed to leave Britain after July 30. At nine minutes past one in the afternoon of that final day, Gran took the monoplane off toward the sea. His own notes tell what he faced in the subsequent flight of four hours and ten minutes, before landing in Norway. It was the longest flight out of the sight of land to that date:

"2.15, one hour has passed. I have no choice, it must break or land now. It is difficult to write. The machine is heaving. The compass is steady and working well. Have passed through thick fog. Seen the sun a moment. Strong seabreeze. Steering 4 east. Time 3.15. Thought all was over. Threw the machine up against the wind. 3.45. The engine runs well. 1,200 rotations. Have eaten a little bit. The rubber tube connection between the bottle and mouth functions excellently – comes in drops. Time 4.15. Lovely to be on right course. The machine heaving very much, difficult to steer. Working with hands, feet – boiling hot. Time 4.25. Worse than ever. Black fog. The wind is southwest. Impossible to stay on course. Tank 2 lost the pressure, must pump. Seasick. Trying to steer straight east. 5 o'clock. Just through the fog. 6,000 feet. Lovely sunshine. Like sailing over a snowcountry. Tank 2 empty. Don't have to pump. Barely 1 hour gas left. Believe it will do. 5.10. Hurrah – Believe I see mountain – want to loop. Descending to the sea."

Then, he noted, as he came down, he saw animals and people and a few of them rushed away to hide from the strange apparition from the sky. He landed his plane on a hard beach beside a lake, scrambled out and ran past astonished villagers and over knolls and walls to a farm with a phone so that he could send messages to his mother, Norway's king, his team at Cruden Bay, and the *Daily Mail*. He received a letter of congratulations from Northcliffe; an adulatory poem from Amundsen, great receptions in Stavanger, Bergen, and Oslo. Three days after he landed he was appointed a lieutenant in the Norwegian air force.

Before the war, Kerr was over in Greece, being nice to its king. He was always nice to kings – and kaisers. Some would say he was the born courtier; others that he was simply an apple-polisher. But ordinary people, ordinary seamen, liked Kerr the British admiral.

He was the son of an admiral. So his biographic basics fit a military style: Admiral Mark Edward Frederic Kerr, b. Sept. 26, 1864, s. of Adml Lord Frederic Kerr; m. 1906, Rose, d. of late William Gough of Royal Dragoons.

Everything Mark Kerr did was proper. He entered the Royal Navy when he was thirteen years old and spent two years on the three-decker training ship, *Britannia*. He shared wardrooms with young royals. He climbed the ladder, rank by rank.

Kerr showed prowess on almost every kind of sports field. He played polo, rode to hounds, had a whack at cricket, was a keen shot. He was also a poet, though a bad one. From *Flying* we get:

"Quietly stealing across the blue sky,
Out-pacing the Eagle the Air-craft will fly;
Caring for nothing in Heaven and Earth,
For this is a new life come into birth."

Kerr flew as a passenger in 1911, and he became fascinated by flying. He fought press attempts to sensationalize aerial accidents, mingled with many famed pilots of the times, and tried to lobby His Majesty's Lords of the Admiralty to accept planes for the Navy. (One myopic Lord thought two planes would be enough in the event of war.)

Then Kerr was sent to the Mediterranean to head a British Naval Mission helping to plan development of the Greek navy. He thought it should have an air arm and reasoned, logically, that, if he set an example by becoming a pilot, young Greeks would follow.

Equally logical in his eyes, was his claim that he would be a good pilot because of the good hands he had developed at polo, as a jockey (he had twice been invited to ride in the English Derby, but was never able to get his weight low enough) – and at the tiller of a sailing boat.

Kerr chose as his flying base Phalerun on Eleusis Bay in Greece and a British pilot named Collyns Pizey as his instructor. Pizey gave Kerr three dual flights in a Sopwith, then three solo flights. They totalled just eighty-two minutes in the air. Then Kerr was ready for his test. On July 14, less than three weeks before war started, he was granted Royal Aero Club aviator's licence No. 842 as well as the first flying certificate ever given by the Greeks. He was the first flag officer of the Royal Navy to fly.

Herbert Brackley was a few months short of twenty in 1915. "Brackles" was the second child of seven born to a London tailor. His full name was Herbert George, the father was George Herbert; British parents did not wander far in naming their young.

When he was in his early teens, young Herbert was considering the priesthood. He cycled fifteen miles each way each Sunday to act as a server for eucharist in a high Anglican order. This was only part of a very full life. He also used to ride fourteen miles a day to school. He was good at cricket. He learned to swim after other boys had thrown him in a pond, then regularly won school medals for swimming and diving. He played the violin in small orchestras. Photography was a hobby. He was meticulous in his dress.

Instead of going into the priesthood, "Brackles" left school at sixteen to become an office boy at Reuter's news agency for ten shillings a week. Two years later, he was playing in a large orchestra, serving as a cadet officer in the Church Lad's Brigade, and beginning to work his way up through journalism.

Then the posters with the picture of Lord Kitchener and the pointing finger went up all over Britain. In April, 1915, Herbert Brackley joined the Royal Naval Air Service. He still hadn't smoked or drank because he was six months short of twenty-one; he had promised his mother he wouldn't until he reached that age.

During those six months, he became a pilot.

CHAPTER 10

Slow Start
in the U.S.A.

When Northcliffe offered the prize for flying the Atlantic, the United States trailed Britian in aviation by a fair distance. Yet there was one major challenger in America, an aircraft builder named Glenn Curtiss.

Curtiss designed a huge flying boat which was ready shortly before the outbreak of the First World War. But it was obvious, immediately, that the plane would never be able to take off with a load of fuel sufficient to carry it across the Atlantic. So Curtiss began redesigning it.

Then the war intervened. When it appeared that the U.S. would be involved, Curtiss began building aircraft for the American armed forces.

The Curtiss plane did cross the ocean but in the cargo hold of a liner; it was used as the pattern for a large type of flying boat produced for the Royal Naval Air Service.

Four years later, when the war came to an end the Americans revived their efforts to fly the Atlantic. This time, they planned to use not one but four Curtiss flying boats (though only three took off). And they planned to back their challenge with the support of dozens of ships of the U.S. Navy, which would be strung out across the Atlantic to guide the aircraft and to provide whatever help might be needed.

The men who made the attempt became the U.S. Navy's NC Seaplane Division No. 1. The NC stood for Navy-Curtiss and the planes soon became "Nancies."

The man who commanded them was John Towers, a smooth and charming civil engineer from Rome, Georgia, who first met Curtiss in 1911.

There were five men in one flying boat, six in each of the others. Many were greenhorns, which wasn't surprising; when war broke out in 1914 the U.S. Navy had one air base and thirty-seven pilots.

Towers was twenty-nine when he first met Curtiss. He had graduated from the Georgia School of Technology, been round the world in a U.S. battleship, and specialized in gunnery. He reported to Curtiss for pilot training in 1911, at a time when many in the navy looked down on flying. The U.S. Navy had no qualifications for flyers, and Towers graduated under the regulations of the Federation Aeronautique Internationale. It was considerably later that he was granted, retroactively, Naval Aviator's Certificate N. 3. He flew for the Navy and he did some experimental flying at the Curtiss plant in San Diego Bay.

And he had a spectacular accident that took him as near death as any flyer had been and still survived to talk about it. He was flying with Ensign William Billingsley, 1,500 feet over Chesapeake Bay, when their bamboo frame machine was suddenly struck by a strong downward gust which threw Billingsley out of the cockpit to his death. Towers was also thrown out, but he managed to hang on to a strut and he survived.

He was badly injured and was in hospital for several weeks and Curtiss came to interview him there; it was rare to find a survivor of a plane mishap who could describe what had gone wrong.

As the result of that bedside chat, Curtiss designed a basic seat strap to hold the flyer into his open cockpit. It became standard equipment for planes of the future.

Towers had less painful claims to early fame. He set a world's record of six hours, eleven minutes for sustained flight before both Raynham and Hawker beat it over England. And he commanded the navy's first aviation unit – it was aboard a collier, which showed what the Navy brass thought of these new upstarts of the air.

Though Towers commanded the NC division, he also commanded one of the flying boats. Another was commanded by Albert Read, a couple of years younger than Towers and as quiet and shy as Towers was friendly. Read's nickname said all. It was "Putty," and there are two stories of how he got it. One is that he returned to school from a vacation in the sun with a face as untanned as when he left. The other story is that he got the name because of his always immobile expression. There are very few photos of a smiling "Putty" even in his moments of glory.

He always was a very gung-ho officer. He stood fourth in his Annapolis graduating class of more than 200 students in 1907, and he ended up a Rear Admiral.

There was never doubt about his professionalism; everybody said Read always did a thorough job even if they sometimes indicated this made him a bit of a bore.

The third Nancy flying boat was commanded by Patrick Bellinger.

Bellinger was born in South Carolina the same year Towers was born in neighbouring Georgia. He went through naval academy and became interested in the science of flight. He was among the first ten pilots of the U.S. Navy and, for a short time, he held a flight endurance record.

And he gained another distinction: at Vera Cruz, in the short U.S. war against Mexico, Bellinger's plane was the first to return with holes through its fabric. They were made by rifle bullets.

The crews of the Nancies came from many parts of the United States.

Elmer Stone was from Norfolk, Virginia, a navy town. The appeal to join it was strong but, instead, he went into the Revenue Cutter Service, predecessor of the Coastguard. He passed his exams to become a cadet when he was twenty-three.

He was in command of a small boat that rescued seven men from a shipwrecked schooner (he was commended by the Assistant Secretary of the Navy) and it became apparent, during the search for the floundering ship, that planes might be valuable in rescue work. So he applied for naval air training and became the thirty-eighth navy pilot to obtain his certificate – and the first pilot in the U.S. Coastguard.

Marc Andrew Mitscher was also a pilot. He was the same Mitscher who was to become an American admiral and, later, hero of World War Two, with his photo in the newspapers always showing him wearing his trademark, a baseball cap. The papers were fond of repeating his dictum as he swept through the Pacific: "The recipe for victory is to kill so many of them (the pronoun was sometimes replaced by dashes) that they fail to exist as a nation."

Mitscher was born in the little Wisconsin town of Hillsboro. Marc was a poor student and fared so badly at the naval academy that he failed to qualify as a midshipman. Then, as soon as he went to sea, he proved more than adequate.

He was soon convinced of the importance of planes to the navy of the future, and pounded Washington with requests to go to the Florida naval air base of Pensacola for pilot training. In 1916 they were granted.

Lieutenant Harry Sadenwater, a radio man, was born in Brooklyn. Clarence Kesler, chief machinist's mate, was from Ohio. He worked on the NCs alongside Machinist Rasmus Christensen, who had been born in Germany.

Walter Hinton was also an Ohioan. He differed from the other pilots; he came through the ranks. Rather than swab decks, he decided he would be one of the first enlisted men to apply for flight training. He did so well that he not only received a commission but was made chief instructor on twin-engined planes.

A few crew members, like Lieutenant Commander Robert Lavender, were not trained to fly. Others, like Commander Holden Richardson, were among the nation's authorities on aeronautics.

Lavender always knew he would enter the Navy. When he was in high school, he had a telegraph set and it was an interest that spurred him to become a radio officer. He went through Annapolis and, by the time the U.S. entered World War One, he had taken special scientific courses, served as chief radio officer for sixty-five destroyers at Guantanamo, and had his first taste of flying.

On one early flight, the plane in which he was a passenger spun into a Cuban bay. Lavender's arms were broken and his nose was crumbled. But when the NC seaplane division was created, he became its chief radio officer, the man who would fly with Towers in the flagship plane.

Holden Chester Richardson was a pioneer of naval aviation, the thirteenth officer to win his wings. Richardson was a tall, broadbacked, clear-eyed individual, who claimed his start in aviation came with the box-kites he built and flew from the decks of the battleship *North Carolina*.

In 1910 he had built a glider and had a car tow it across the parade ground at Philadelphia Naval Yard. On the sixth attempt it became briefly airborne, then stalled. Richardson was bruised – as he was in many other crashes after that.

By wartime, Richardson had become one of the two or three leading U.S. authorities on seaplane design.

He was an obvious choice to help in the American push to be first across the Atlantic.

CHAPTER 11
The Interruption of War

Many of the men who would later compete to become the first to fly the Atlantic spent the 1914-18 years trying to win the war, putting in much of the duration in their countries' infant flying services.

Arthur Whitten-Brown was one of those who compressed a lifetime of experience into months. He'd been twenty-eight years old when the war had started and, though he'd lived most of his life in Britain, he was still an American citizen. So he could have avoided the services for a long time. But there was never any hesitation. He became a British subject, and enlisted in the Universities and Public Schools Battalion when it was formed only one month after the declaration of war. Four months later he was a subaltern.

In one year, 1915, he served through the gas attacks of the Second Battle of Ypres, survived trench action on the Somme, transferred to the Royal Flying Corps, trained as an air observer, was posted to No. 2 Squadron, took part in artillery spotting missions and bombing raids on enemy lines, was shot down, injured, and taken prisoner.

He had a bullet wound in the left foot, his leg broken, thigh dislocated, his lower shin terribly smashed, a bowel wrenched, several teeth knocked out and a lip cut. But he still managed to destroy all maps before German soldiers pulled him from the wreckage.

He was a prisoner for nearly two years. During the first part he was in hospital receiving treatment for his leg. It allowed him to walk – but he had a limp for the rest of his life and, sometimes, he had a certain degree of pain.

The injury restricted his exercise when he was placed in a prisoner-of-war camp so Whitten-Brown looked for something to occupy his time. Through the Red Cross, he obtained books on aerial navigation. The books were skimpy because such navigation was a new, very undeveloped art (most flyers in 1916 simply used their eyes, a map, and the seat of their pants to get from any point A to any point B). But from the books, from conversations with other downed flyers, and from articles sent to him by his parents, he acquired a very substantial theoretical knowledge.

By the time he had been moved to Switzerland, where he was to be interned nine months, he was offering devices for aviation to the American legation in Berne. It was possible that he knew he would be a cripple for life.

Whitten-Brown was repatriated in 1917. After a leave with his parents in Manchester, he reported to the Air Ministry in London, looking for something to do. What he wanted was to be an air observer again and practise the navigation he had taught himself. But his records showed he was unfit for active service. As far as the Air Ministry was concerned, he could go back to "civvy street." Instead, by some cajoling, he managed to get seconded to the Ministry of Munitions, and joined the aircraft production department to help design aero-engines.

Brown went to work with a Major David H. Kennedy, who had two daughters. One, Kathleen, was nineteen. She kept pestering her father about going to work to help the war effort. Possibly because he was afraid she might go and work in a factory, Kennedy found his daughter a job in the ministry too. There she met Teddy Brown.

His home was in Manchester, too far to visit very often. Kathleen had a home at Penn, in the pleasant county of Buckinghamshire, and she took Teddy home.

Most people who knew Kathleen's mother considered her a snob but a lieutenant with a hyphenated name must have been sufficient for Kathleen. On October 10, 1918, the engagement of Teddy and Kathleen was announced. No immediate date was set for the wedding.

Harry Hawker was married during the war.

The young Australian was turned down by the forces because of his back injury, but he continued for Sopwith work that was at least as valuable as that of any pilot over the western front. Indeed, most people who knew him, claimed this was the most important part of his career. Every day he tested planes that were sent into battle. If the flyers of the Royal Flying Corps and Royal Naval Air Service faced risks, at least these had been cushioned by the daily work of men like Harry.

Of all the family of planes made by Sopwith's and tested by Hawker the most famous was the Camel, a biplane with the wing span of a large living room, urged on by an engine of 110 horsepower. The plane could move at 115 m.p.h. and climb to 19,000 feet, nearly four miles above the earth. Pilots swore by the Camel. In one four-month period, more enemy planes were shot down by Camels than by any other aircraft produced in the war.

It was Hawker's job to ensure that Sopwith planes could provide this superiority. He had to take them up, put them through every manoeuvre, recommend changes, take them up again. It was not a job to be taken lightly. The risks were enormous. So were the rewards; he was the highest paid pilot in Britain.

From July 13, 1914 to October 20, 1916, he flew 295 different machines on 199 different days. All but a dozen of these aircraft were being taken into the air for the first time.

In the middle of it all, he met Muriel.

It was like a rehearsal scene from a musical. Muriel was in a little car, driving with a girl friend, through Richmond Park, just outside London, an enchanting place for a trifling Sunday morning flirtation in April. Also driving in the park that day was Harry Hawker, in his Gregoire. He had a pal with him, Basil.

The girls were stopped, and had what they called "the bonnet" up.

Pretty girls and a machine that needed fixing – the combination was too much for Harry. He stopped.

The girls of course weren't very mussed because somewhere, sometime, there was going to be some young gallant who would stop and actually do the work. Nevertheless, there was the mating ritual to be followed.

Harry's first offer of help was refused.

Off he went round the park.

But he came back to find Muriel (half an eye cast down the road) playing the amateur mechanic. At least she had found out what was wrong. Harry had already guessed.

"Was it petrol, after all?" he asked when he had stopped again.

How did he know?

"Because if a girl breaks down, she will invariably take down everything detachable before looking in the tank," he replied.

This sounded as if Harry knew a lot about women, and it added to the spice. But Muriel didn't want to be too forward. Harry was obviously older than she was – she was, well, she hadn't had her twenty-first birthday party yet, and he was, maybe twenty-five or twenty-six.

But after Harry had transferred some of the gasoline from the tank of his car to hers, she did agree to give him a phone number.

The following Sunday Muriel was sitting at home when she was called to the phone to take a message from the police. It was Harry, who said he had just bought a Daimler, and would she like to come out and try it. The girl friend and Basil went along, as they did for several succeeding Sundays. Muriel's parents weren't told about these first drives in a Surrey park with a young Australian.

Eventually, though, Harry was asked home for dinner, and afterwards, though he loathed playing cards, he made up a four at whist. Muriel suspected such self-sacrifice indicated that Harry might soon ask her to marry him. They were married two years after they'd met.

They moved into a house called Ennadale at Hook in Surrey. It had extra space next to the garage where Harry fitted up a workshop. He had bought two 225 horsepower Sunbeam aero engines (one to be used as a spare) and the chassis of a 35 horsepower Mercedes. With these principal components, Harry intended to build himself a powerful car. He already had a Talbot, a Gregoire, and a Ford.

Muriel realized that if she weren't going to be alone in the drawing room while Harry was outside in his workshop during that last winter of the war, she should learn to become a craftsman. It is to her honour that she learned to operate a rivetting gun.

She didn't always hold a rivet gun. When she was pregnant, she read to Harry while he worked on the car, articles from such motoring and aeronautic magazines as the "Automobile Engineer" and "Flying"; and the entire Bram Stoker novel, *Dracula*. This suited Harry well; he'd always found reading an ordeal.

Occasionally, he had to deliver a plane to France and, on one trip, he made a forced landing in a snowy field. He tried to pull the machine out of a drift, and strained his back. It put him in bed for two weeks.

The back was to give him more and more trouble. Damage to his spine had prevented him getting into the forces. Other accidents compounded the problem. One such accident was in a car, driving into Brooklands. This time the car had to be lifted off him because his arm was pinned by the steering wheel. His shoulder was put out, his arm was in a sling for a few days, but that didn't stop him from test flying three planes.

While Hawker built himself a car during the war, Jack Alcock built a plane. He had gone to Eastchurch at the outbreak of war, and become a warrant officer instructor for the Royal Naval Air Service. One of his pupils was Herbert George Brackley.

For a year, Alcock was an instructor. He found it chafing. Most of the time he had to be on the ground while his pupils practised solo flying. It was better after December, 1915. Alcock was promoted to Flight Sub-Lieutenant, and made head of the school of aerobatics.

Still, he was not content, and he pestered the Admiralty for active service. Finally, a year later, he was sent to No. 2 Wing of the Royal Naval Air Service at Mudros on an island in the Aegean Sea. It was an important base, an airfield for long-distance bombers, fighters, reconnaissance planes and anti-submarine patrols.

Active service suited Jack Alcock. He had a natural genius for flying, a good knowledge of navigation, absolute self-reliance. The small Greek islanders at Mudros considered him the typical Englishman. He was over six feet tall, had a strong frame, powerful forearms. He was ruddy and had almost flaxen hair. His eyes were blue. He was a warm, generous man and he would have liked the sunny, relatively simple life of a Greek island. When he wasn't flying, he enjoyed life on the ground, in the tavernas, drinking retsina and mixing with the local girls.

Alcock flew both as a bomber and fighter pilot in any plane that was available. His flying hours mounted. He piloted a Handley Page bomber, the biggest plane of its time, for eight hours, on the 600-mile return journey, the longest raid of its time, to drop explosives on the major city of Adrianople. There was a lot of night work like that, blowing up munitions dumps, factories, ships.

There was day work too. Once, Alcock was in a bath when a German reconnaissance plane appeared over Mudros with two fighter escorts. Alcock pulled on pyjamas, tore across to a Sopwith Camel, and took off. In the dogfight that followed, Alcock shot down both fighters (part of a total of seven he is credited with during his posting at Mudros). For this exploit he received the Distinguished Service Cross. The citation mentioned his "great skill, judgement and dash."

One of the pilots Alcock shot down between bath and breakfast that day was a German named Muller. His plane landed in the sea and remained afloat long enough for Muller to scrawl out a message of *Ich bin tot* and the address of a girl in Varna, Bulgaria, on the propeller of the plane. He then tried to cut his wrists with the penknife with which he had written his last message; he was rescued but he died later of his wounds.

The propeller was picked up by a launch and the message duly sent to the address in Bulgaria.

Two years later, when Alcock's name was known through Europe, he received this letter:

Dear Sir:

I apologize for taking the liberty to write to you without being known by you – the liberty to write to you and have your attention just for a moment to follow these lines.

Therefore I must introduce myself to you. I am the young lady to whom the German pilot Muller, that you brought down two years ago, had written in his last greetings on the propeller of the wrecked seaplane. Sometime ago I received the number of the Daily Mirror

57

which contains a picture of the propeller and your photo. I was very curious to know something about you . . .

My friend Muller was a very good pilot, he was one of the best, and I see that he has had a worthy ending, more than that, you must have excelled him to have beaten him down . . .

I began by introducing myself, and I must say something more to let you have a complete picture, I am a Bulgarian and am a graduate of an American college; I lived several years among English and American people, and learned to love your language and literature . . . I shall be immensely please if you send me a good photograph of yourself, and if you add some snapshots of your seaplane too. I shall enjoy them none the less, and with the picture in the Daily Mirror I shall highly treasure. I shall not say how I would wish to possess the famous propeller, but rightly it belongs to you; it is your trophy, for it you have risked your life.

Believing you will answer my small request,

I am, with very best wishes,

Yours sincerely
STRAOKA ILIEVNA

It is not known whether Alcock ever replied to the young lady and the whereabouts of the propeller itself became a mystery. For some time, Alcock's parents had it. For a while, it leaned against a tool shed in the small back garden of their Manchester home. Then it disappeared.

While he was at Mudros, Alcock decided to design and build a scout plane.

When it was finished, it travelled at 20 miles per hour faster than any other plane on Mudros. Unfortunately, all Alcock's work was wasted. Soon after testing, while it was standing empty, it was wrecked when another pilot landed a fighter right on top of it.

On the night of September 30, 1917, Alcock was sent to bomb railway marshalling yards on the Asiatic shore of the Bosporus. His plane was hit by anti-aircraft fire and crashed in the sea half a mile from Anzac Beach. Alcock and his crew were not hurt – and the Handley Page bomber floated.

They scrambled ashore through sniper fire and eluded capture for sixteen hours.

The German air force, not for the first time, sent a plane to Mudros and dropped a message from Alcock and his companions, giving the news of their capture and requesting that a British plane fly them a parcel of clothes and other supplies. This was done.

Later, Alcock and his crew were taken by their Turkish captors to Constantinople, a city Alcock had bombed. As if in retribution they were placed in a stinking prison cell for a month. About the only consolation was a letter Alcock received from his commanding officer at Mudros, which read: "Your baby has just been given a new suit of clothes and is learning to walk. It is the best infant in the school." Interpreted, this meant that the plane he had built had been repaired. There was nothing to do in the prison and a fellow prisoner recalled later that Alcock talked a great deal about the requirements of making a flight across the Atlantic; Alcock obviously remembered Northcliffe's prize offer.

Then Alcock was moved nearly 300 miles to a prison camp at Kedos where he stayed until he was sent back to England after the armistice.

He was uninjured, in good health, able to spend this "peace Christmas" at home. But he itched to be flying again. He started looking for a job.

Freddie Raynham already had a job. Like Harry Hawker, he was a test pilot throughout the war and Flight magazine once remarked on his insatiable appetite for this kind of work: "We no sooner hear of him delivering an Avro somewhere than he is testing a Martinsyde at Brooklands. Next he is at Hendon putting a B.E.2C through its paces." It wasn't quite as smooth as the magazine suggested. The centre of gravity of one plane was too far aft, and Raynham had to crash-land. The tail of another broke while he was looping over Brooklands. But he got through the war relatively unscathed.

The man who was to serve as Raynham's navigator in the attempt to cross the Atlantic did have war scars. His official name and rank was Captain C. W. F. Morgan of the Royal Navy, but the "F." stood for Fairfax, and he was best known as "Fax."

Morgan had joined the Navy as a cadet in 1904 and served mainly as a navigation officer at sea. At the outbreak of the war, he transferred to the Royal Naval Flying Service.

Morgan liked to claim he was a direct descendant of the buccaneer, Sir Henry Morgan, that each of his male ancestors had been a nautical man, and that he was the first in the family to take to the air. He did it meritoriously; he received the Distinguished Service Order and Croix de Guerre for the German planes he brought down. It wasn't done without cost. Like Arthur Whitten-Brown, he was left a cripple, a leg devastated by bullets.

When the war ended, the pilots of the great Atlantic race had yet to meet their navigators: Alcock had not met Brown, Raynham had not met Morgan and Hawker had yet to meet Lieutenant-Commander Kenneth Mackenzie-Grieve.

Grieve was a navigating officer during the war. He served much of it aboard the *Campania,* a former Cunard liner, converted into a mother ship for a seaplane squadron attached to the Grand Fleet.

Like Morgan, Mackenzie-Grieve was a descendant of naval men. He was the youngest son of a Royal Navy captain, the brother of another. He had joined the Navy at fourteen and a half years of age. By the time most young people today are coming out of high school, he had seen China and Australia, and served with the Mediterranean fleet.

Mackenzie-Grieve was thirty-nine and considerably older than Harry Hawker. The men were very different. Harry was bouncy, well-known. Nobody had heard of "Mac," and he didn't look like a hero. He was tall but he was thin, with sunken cheeks and a large nose. He was the epitome of the phlegmatic Scot. This didn't matter to Hawker. They got along well because "old Mac" was a good navigator, a cool customer, not given to fancy airs. Those were the things that counted for Harry. After Grieve was chosen Harry's navigator, he took six days' flying training and he graduated. But he never advanced any claim that he was an aviator and this was the kind of honesty Harry Hawker appreciated.

Rear Admiral Mark Kerr arrived back in Britain on August 31, 1917 after being commander in chief of a Royal Navy squadron in the Adriatic.

Twenty-one years before, he had come home from Italy, an invalid with "Mediterranean Fever." Three doctors in London had told him he would die soon but the bounding bantam (he was only five feet, four inches tall) ignored them, lived through two world wars, and eventually died at the age of seventy-nine. Kerr was always much more than the Edwardian caricature of the shootin' and huntin' Englishman. Once, without asking permission, he threaded his destroyer flotilla through the merchant ships in the Pool of London because he thought it would be a good idea for Londoners to see their Navy.

He was recalled from the Adriatic, in that summer of 1917, because the Admiralty had a more important task for him in Britain. The Royal Air Force was going to be formed as a single air arm and Kerr was given the job of helping to create it. Seven months later, when the Royal Air Force was born, Kerr was made the first deputy chief of air staff.

But he differed with others so much on strategy that he asked for a switch. He was then given the rank of Major-General, and put in command of the southwest air force area in Britain. From his headquarters at Salisbury he controlled sixty stations.

When the first of Britain's aircraft companies, Handley Page, was looking for a commander to fly its entrant in the Atlantic air race, Kerr was an obvious choice. He was still an active man despite his years, one of the "fathers" of the RAF, a man who would lend prestige to their undertaking. They already had the plane, a four-engine monster designed to bomb Berlin, a warplane so ahead of its time that its wing span was not exceeded until the Lancaster bomber was built in World War Two. So Handley Page had the plane and a commander. Who would be the pilot and navigator?

Kerr considered young Herbert Brackley as the best big plane pilot in the world.

In that hectic year of 1915, "Brackles" had flown many types of plane, crossed enemy lines, had his first crash, and his first injuries (he received a concussion and was unconscious for two weeks).

The following year he became a noted bomber pilot. "The conspicuously good work as a pilot of a bombing machine" brought him the Distinguished Flying Cross and promotion to flight commander. It was followed by a D. S. O. for his "persistence and determination" on one raid. His old employer, Reuter's news agency, sent along an inscribed cigarette case to mark the event, and the London Diocesan Church Lads' Brigade added a letter of congratulations.

During one stretch, Brackley led bombing raids on sixteen consecutive nights; on several occasions, he made three raids in the same night. He was, in the words of one squadron commander, "a night-flying pilot of exceptional ability." Brackley was waiting to lead a bombing raid on Berlin, in the huge new Handley Page four-engine aircraft, when the armistice was signed.

Tryggve Gran, who became another member of Kerr's crew, had been commissioned a first lieutenant in the Norwegian Air Force as part of his reward for his flight over the North Sea. But Gran found the commission somewhat of a hindrance. In 1915 he was in both Britain and France, studying means of countering air attack. He tried to join the Royal Flying Corps, but this was difficult for an officer of a neutral country so he got himself discharged from the Norwegian forces (although he never gave up his citizenship). Then he joined the R.A.F.

He was wounded in an air battle, served on the western front, and, for a brief spell, was with the Archangel expedition to the Arctic to support the White Russians against the new revolutionary regime.

By the end of 1916, only twenty-six Americans were wearing the gold wings on the left breast of a forest green tunic which, with peaked cap of the same colour surmounted by the eagle, made up the new uniform of a U.S. Navy aviator officer. In addition, there were thirty students in training, and three technical specialists including Holden Richardson and Dr. Jerome Hunsacker, a brilliant pioneer who established an early course in aviation science at Massachusetts Institute of Technology.

There were also ninety-three enlisted men with the rating of airman,

125 enlisted men taking aviation courses, and another 233 mechanics and others who had undergone some study related to aviation.

It wasn't much to go into war with, as the United States did a few months later.

However, quality was certainly a considerable counter-check for lack of quantity. So was vision.

There were few naval air bases. Rockaway (originally shared with the Army) and Montauk, both on Long Island, were among the first. A full lieutenant – Marc Mitscher – was commanding officer of Rockaway. A full lieutenant commander – John Towers – controlled the aviation desk of the Office of Naval Operations in Washington.

In 1917, when the U.S. entered the war, the Germans, with their U-boat packs, were winning at sea. Some new measure to fight them had to be considered. By August, 1917, Rear Admiral David Taylor thought he had one.

Taylor was sure the solution lay in creation of big flying boats which could survey any part of the Atlantic in any kind of weather. One of their major duties would be to spot German submarines in European waters before they slipped out into the sealanes.

But these flying boats would have to fly over to their bases in Europe, Taylor reasoned. If they had to be transported by merchant ship, many would be lost.

The idea was discussed with Glenn Curtiss, whose last plane built to fly the ocean had eventually crossed it by ship, and Curtiss submitted two designs of giant flying boats. The hull design for both was revolutionary. It has been described as looking like a Dutch wooden shoe, and – by Towers – as "rather queer." Washington decided on the smaller, three-engine model.

Work began at the Curtiss plant at Buffalo, but such was the urgency that Curtiss, his engineers, blueprints, models, some components, were all boarded onto special rail coaches one Friday night, hooked up to the New York train, and taken to Garden City on the eastern seaboard, where a special factory was established to create the new planes. Work started there the following Monday morning on Navy-Curtiss No. 1 – the first Nancy.

Among items brought to Garden City for assembly were sixty-eight panels, some measuring twelve feet by forty feet, which made up the tail and wing frames of the aircraft. They were built by a firm in downtown Manhattan, and had to be transported gingerly nearly twenty-five miles. This was done at night, when the streets were clear, in special horse-drawn wagons used originally for moving theatrical sets. The wagons were preceded and followed by two cars carrying Navy officers who swung red lanterns. The whole operation was like a race to bring in a much revised show for a Broadway opening by a certain date.

By September, 1918 NC-1 was at Rockaway; on October 4 it made a few taxiing tests and then took off. But the plane would never hunt submarines. Two months later the war had ended.

Northcliffe hadn't waited for war's end. Four months before, on July 17, 1918, his *Daily Mail* renewed the offer of a prize of £10,000 for the first to fly the Atlantic.

The timing of the announcement didn't surprise anyone. Northcliffe, now one of the best known men in the world, was recognized for his eccentricity. The offer was considered premature, and both the Air Council and the Royal Aero Club of Great Britain, which would regulate flights in connection with the prize, indicated no attempts could be made until there was peace. But already various British manufacturers were discussing their prospects, making individual plans.

Whichever one should have the first aircraft across the Atlantic would have a tremendous commercial advantage in selling planes around the world. The "war to end all war" was ending and these plane designers and builders could see nothing but boom times in the everlasting peace that lay after it. Under such conditions, commercial aviation was bound to flourish, and especially for the manufacturer of a plane which had flown the Atlantic non-stop.

For this was a condition of the *Daily Mail* contest. Anybody, except enemy flyers, could enter. The flight had to be completed within seventy-two hours. It could be from any point in North America to any point in Europe. If a seaplane were used, it could alight on the sea and still be eligible if it took off and completed the flight without outside aid.

The latter condition, in the eyes of most British manufacturers, did not matter. Planes with much greater range had been developed in the five years since the prize was first offered in 1913. Now, said Tom Sopwith, 1,880 miles was no problem. The head of Vickers Aviation confirmed this, referring to the Vickers Vimy's ability to fly the 1,880 miles in about twenty hours. Handley Page chimed in by pointing out that a year before one of its bombers had flown 2,000 miles; it was quite capable of flying the Atlantic in one stage.

The 1,880 miles the aircraft makers mentioned was from Newfoundland to Ireland. It was the natural course – the shortest distance, with prevailing, backing winds.

In the U.S., the *Daily Mail* prize aroused nearly as much interest as in Britain. At one air base forty pilots petitioned their commanding officer for permission to fly their bombers across the Atlantic for delivery to the Western Front, immediately. They were turned down.

By December, the whole American air effort had returned to its leisurely pace, which was just as well because the early tests of the NC-1 indicated major modifications would be necessary.

In early 1919 a committee report went to the U.S. Secretary of the Navy, Josephus Daniels. Part of it read: "In view of the fact that the first successful airplane was produced in this country and that the United States developed the first seaplane, it would seem most fitting that the first trans-Atlantic flight should be carried out upon the initiative of the United States Navy."

Daniels, a newspaper publisher from North Carolina and one of the greatest civilian backers the Navy had ever had, couldn't agree more. And he received complete endorsement from his young Assistant Secretary of the Navy, a man still in his thirties and an ardent supporter of naval aviation – Franklin Delano Roosevelt. With support at this level, the Americans were in; the race was on. And it had changed its complexion. It was no longer a contest between individuals. It had become a duel between nations.

There were a couple of points that seemed, at first, to take the edge off the rivalry.

The Americans agreed that, since their final jumpoff point would be Newfoundland, a British colony, the British would be offered, in exchange, the services provided by U.S. surface ships. And the American naval flyers would not be able to accept the *Daily Mail* prize. The man who, as a later president, was to be known simply by his initials of FDR, announced: "We cannot see how the American Navy could be a contestant for a prize given by private enterprise."

But Josephus Daniels, the U.S. Secretary of the Navy, made a statement that brought all the rivalry to the surface. He was asked whether the U.S. Navy hoped to beat the British in making the first flight and he trumpeted:

"We hope to beat the world!"

PART TWO

CHAPTER 12

Starters
and Non-Starters

Three days after peace was signed, the Royal Aero Club in Britain announced the lifting of a wartime ban on the Atlantic race and, on the very next day, November 15, 1918, it received an entry. By the following spring, it had ten more. Scores of pilots dreamed they might be the first to fly the Atlantic. There was the excitement and the honour and, of course, there was all that prize money; the £10,000 offered by the *Daily Mail* was later boosted by additional offers – £1,000 from a businessman, Lawrence Phillips, and £2,000 from the Ardath Tobacco Company.

Some of the entries in the race popped up for a day or so in the press, then vanished. Many efforts were more serious but many of these ran into trouble.

The Boulton and Paul company in Britain set out to adapt a Bourge bomber, but it crashed while being flown over England by its chief test pilot. There was no time to prepare a second entry.

The Alliance Aeroplane Company, also British, built a single-engine biplane, the Seabird. The cabin was big enough to move around in and, the London *Times* reported, one of the two men could lie down to rest. "We will be able to send radio messages 300 miles and receive them from 2,500 miles away," said J. A. Peters, the pilot. But the plane was the product of a firm controlled by the big London store of Waring and Gillow which decided that the aircraft should first fly to Madrid and other store branches before going to Newfoundland to try the Atlantic. By the time other aircraft were being readied in Newfoundland, the Seabird was still sitting on its field at Acton, just outside London.

Fairey Aircraft Company, another British firm, entered a seaplane and chose the Australian, Sidney Pickles, as its pilot. But time ran out and neither Pickles nor the plane reached Newfoundland.

Nor did Captain Hugo Sundstedt, a well-known, Swedish-born pilot in the U.S., who had been the first to fly across the Baltic. He made several test flights over the New Jersey coast, in a giant seaplane, the Sunrise, always endeavouring, beforehand, to arrange that there should be plenty of reporters and photographers to observe him. So there were many witnesses when he made the error of handing over the plane to a happy-go-lucky Russian, Commander Czenzski. Before a large audience, Czenzski went into a spin only 400 feet above Bayonne Bay. He was rescued, but the Sunrise gurgled down below the water.

A plane called the Shamrock, built by the large British firm of Short Brothers, also ended up in the sea. This attempt was a mixture of sound preparations and naivete. The plane was painted white, hardly a suitable colour if it were forced down in pack ice, though it was decorated with a large Union Jack. The main fuel tank was shaped like a torpedo and fitted with a quick-emptying device so that, if the aircraft had to make a forced landing, the tank could be converted to a lifeboat.

Major J. C. P. Wood was the pilot and Captain C. C. Wylie was the navigator. What they were trying to do was to fly the Atlantic, east to west, against the prevailing winds, heading for North America with no exact knowledge of where its landing fields might be. Wood and Wylie, like so many British flyers, spoke as though they had just finished reading one of Northcliffe's early weeklies for boys. Whenever the newspapers reported the flyers' comments, they were filled with understatement or self-deprecation, or a bit of chuckle when the first personal pronoun was used; patriotism was implicit; "the team" was all; everything had to be offhand, sporting, unsentimental. There was something odd about those interviews: certain skeins of the human condition – sexual drive, fear, ambition, hardship – were never mentioned.

Instead (as one example), *Daily Mail* readers were treated to a discussion, by Wood and Wylie, of their vague notions for picking their way over the Atlantic: "We shall look to the sun, the pole star and a clear horizon to fix our position, and then with a new machine, something like a sextant, we can tell where we are, within 20 miles, night or day." It didn't occur to them that Atlantic clouds, not to mention Newfoundland fog, often hid the horizon, or that, when mountains and cliffs endanger the end of a journey, something more than the rough-and-ready 'within 20 miles' is called for.

Not to worry. "By means of a ready reckoner, we shall be able to steer a fairly accurate course," said Wylie. "Not the least instrument is a chronometer watch." One hopes so.

The pair was obviously confident that the weather would be ideal for the flight and visibility unlimited. Wylie also said: "passing ships will be asked to provide their positions. Ships on main shipping routes will also

66

be asked to make smoke from funnels at the end of every watch. This is a simple matter for the stokehold crews, and oil-burning vessels will leave a patch in the sky which we can see for 60 or 70 miles."

This came from an officer who had gained most of his navigational experience at sea level. Wylie's faults were common ones: he assumed that maritime navigation could be applied directly to the air; he thought that, from above, a broad view could always be had to help in the fixing of the plane's position.

Wood and Wylie started from Eastchurch on April 18, 1919, planning to land, first, at the Curragh racetrack outside Dublin, and again near Limerick. They flew northbound over England and then North Wales. Next, they crossed the large Island of Anglesey, which is separated from the mainland by a bridge. At Holyhead they finally reached the open sea. It was only a short crossing to Dublin. But they had gone just twenty-two miles over water when an air-lock caused their engine to die. It was a calm day and they ditched easily. Much of the gasoline had been jettisoned so the empty fuel tank held them up. The Shamrock proved seaworthy. A trawler came alongside, took off the two men, and started to tow the plane into Holyhead.

Twenty hours later, the first serious east-to-west crossing ended when it was found that salt water had damaged many of the plane's controls beyond repair.

There were other entrants that turned out to be of only passing interest. One aircraft outfit, with the unwieldy name of Prodger-Isaac Aviation Company, said a plane was being prepared "and an entry can be expected in a few days." That made as much sense as the much later (and more mysterious) statements by Lieutenant Leth Jenson, late of the French Navy, who arrived in St. John's, Newfoundland, in the midst of the elaborate and advanced preparations of a number of other pilots and let it be known that a French, single-engine plane would arrive soon, but "more I cannot say at present."

It became apparent, as announcement followed announcement in the papers of that spring, that talk was cheap but that it would cost a lot of money and time for a serious attempt. That could come only from a government or a large company.

A serious attempt entailed the construction or modification of a plane, the assembling of a large ground crew as well as a pilot and navigator, the purchase or rental of land for takeoff in Newfoundland, and an organization to accommodate and feed men there. There was also the shipment of plane, spare parts and fuel. Whims were not enough.

But certainly there were serious entrants, planes and teams of men who did reach the starting point in Newfoundland. They were, from Britain:

– Hawker and Mackenzie-Grieve in the Sopwith, single-engine plane, Atlantic.

– Raynham and Morgan in the Martinsyde single-engine plane, Raymor.

– Kerr, Brackley, Gran and Wyatt in the converted Handley Page four-engine bomber, also called Atlantic.

– Alcock and Brown in a two-engine Vickers Vimy.

There were also American entrants: three U.S. Navy flying boats under the overall command of John Towers. These were the NC-1, commanded by Lieutenant Commander Patrick Bellinger; the NC-3, commanded by Towers; the NC-4, commanded by Lieutenant Commander Albert Read.

In addition to the planes, there was a U.S. Navy airship, the C-5.

The flyers were optimistic, naturally. Harry Hawker, for instance, expected it would be simply a matter of assembling his plane, having one or two quick test flights, then he'd be off. It would be all over in a couple of weeks.

But Newfoundland is ruled by weather; it is part of the language. Weather sayings were taught to the children as fact: "Winter thunder means summer hunger," and "A red sun has water in its eye."

And everyone knew that, for all the hardness of winter, spring could be even more fickle. Spring in Newfoundland lasts a long time – running from the muddy lanes which greeted Hawker through to the last iceberg of late June. There are, on average, several hundred of these massive bergs moving down the eastern side of Newfoundland each year, and some springs they can total 1,600. They're called "growlers" because they're so big they scrape along the bottom of bays. Breaking away from the polar icefields in the warmer waters off Greenland, they move south, are a hazard to shipping and, with the larger fields of pack ice, can exert a major influence on daily weather.

This ice is directed by wind and, if it is from the wrong direction, fields of ice, hundreds of miles long, twenty or thirty miles across, lock the coast in a scabbard. Harbours such as St. John's can be so sealed that men are able to walk across them on ice. A change of wind and the ice will float out into the ocean within hours.

There is also the mixing of warm and cold airs, which produces swaddling fogs, so often that one amateur pilot in St. John's claims that it is possible to enjoy his hobby on only eighty clear days per year.

And there is rain. Newfoundland gets so much of it that the steep streets are often brooks. The wearing of a sou'wester is protection against this, and it is usually part of a uniform that is completed with a sweater. For Newfoundland can be cold, even when the calendar says it is spring.

That particular spring, of 1919, offered a mixture of heavy snowfalls, gales, some fog, and freezing nights.

On April 15 and 16 a heavy storm raged, there was considerable snow and 50 m.p.h. winds in St. John's – all trains were suspended because of drifts.

The rest of the month wasn't much better. A meteorological history of that April makes dismal reading – seventeen days with some rain, five with some snow, two with fog, sixteen with ten-tenths cloud, a mean temperature for the thirty days of 36° Fahrenheit. Near the end of April, bookies in England were offering seven-to-two odds that nobody would fly the Atlantic before the end of May.

The frustrations were worse in May. The flyers learned that England had one of its best springs ever. Warm, sunny weather brightened London nearly every day. The English couldn't understand, given these unusually pleasant conditions, why Harry hadn't started on his flight. And where was Fred Raynham's old fighting spirit?

In Newfoundland, May offered nineteen days with some rain, three with fog. And it was cold; the temperature reached 62° on only one day.

Even June wasn't much better. Just before the middle of the month, icebergs were spotted off Cape Race. The month of white flannels on English cricket greens, and of vendors selling thirst-quenching drinks to sports crowds sweating in Baltimore and Boston was something different in Newfoundland. That month, St. John's had seven days with a clear sky, seventeen days with some rain, four that were foggy, and eleven overcast. In addition, there were other days when the wind was too strong for a safe takeoff.

That was only one of the problems facing the weathermen – Lieutenant Lawrence Clements in St. John's, Geoffrey Taylor at Harbour Grace, Newfoundland, and a whole team aboard the American ship, *Aroostook* at Trepassey Bay in Newfoundland. They also had to know what the weather was like over the Atlantic, in Ireland, and the Azores.

Arrangements had been made for all Royal Navy vessels and many merchantmen operating in the Atlantic to radio regular reports. Similarly, the Americans had reports sent to Trepassey from its destroyers strung across to the Azores. There was considerable sharing of information between British and Americans. But out of all the facts, one message was clear, day after day: conditions were too bad for trans-Atlantic flight.

In those days, it must be remembered, aircraft had limited abilities to surmount the weather by climbing; they had few instruments so "blind flying" was dangerous; some planes were light enough to be damaged by gale force winds. In addition, the American Nancies were flying boats so they would have to land on the ocean, and the strength and state of the sea, as much as the turbulence of the air, was an important factor.

This side of weather lore, what it was like away out over the Atlantic, was something the people of St. John's couldn't understand. When there was the rare fine day, they wondered why the planes were still there. Some of the flyers wondered too.

CHAPTER 13
Newfoundland

Even if it were possible to overlook the incredibly rotten weather, it would be difficult to imagine a more unlikely focus for world attention and excitement than Newfoundland at the end of World War One. For the Newfoundlanders themselves, the air race was a surprise. The village of Trepassey, for instance, had five or six hundred residents; suddenly it was host to eight thousand U.S. sailors who were helping to launch the American flying boats.

It was still winter, in 1919, when the people of Newfoundland got their first real news of the race. Fairfax "Fax" Morgan arrived in St. John's aboard the *Digby*. He was a "front-runner" from Freddie Raynham's team and his mission was to find a suitable air strip for the tests and the takeoff.

The *Digby* was a Furness Withy ship, a major link between Newfoundland and both Britain and mainland Canada. The one-way fare to England was eighty-five dollars; it was thirty-five dollars to Canada. Letters, at the time, could be mailed to England at two cents an ounce, or one penny. The mail, of course, travelled by sea.

There would have been mail on the *Digby* when she arrived in St. John's. But what was much more important was that she brought Sergeant Thomas Ricketts home from the recent war. He was Newfoundland's first Victoria Cross winner and he was already such a folk hero that there was a song called "Ricketts' V.C.," a common part of the self-entertaining repertoire in many Newfoundland homes. Ricketts received all the attention when the ship passed through The Narrows to tie up in St. John's harbour.

Naturally, he would be interviewed by newsmen but he was too important for the new reporter on the St. John's *Evening Telegram*. This reporter, Joey Smallwood, had been hired right out of school and he made up in ambition what he lacked in size; he was determined to make a name for himself as a journalist. While his colleagues concentrated on Ricketts the hero, Joey went after "Fax" Morgan, who was rumoured to be associated with an attempt to fly the Atlantic. Anyway, for Joey, Ricketts represented the past; Fairfax Morgan was the future. Besides, Morgan was a captain and Joey, then as ever after, was impressed by rank.

When Morgan arrived in St. John's, he was suffering from the Spanish Flu, so he was transferred to the town's General Hospital. There, Joey, the eager-beaver reporter, went to see him, and learn about his mission.

Well, of course, Joey knew all about Newfoundland, and especially this part of the island, better than any Royal Navy officer was going to discover in a month of Sundays, and, if somebody were looking for a piece of flat land, he couldn't do better than choose a piece beside Quidi Vidi Lake, running toward Cuckold's Bay. The land was almost outside the hospital window. Besides, flat land was scarce in Newfoundland.

So right there, a bargain was practically signed, sealed, and delivered: Freddie Raynham and "Fax" Morgan would use the flat land on the north side of the lake as the base for their plane, which was to bear a name that was a compound of their first syllables – Raymor.

Joey wrote his story and it was exciting news in St. John's. By tradition, the newspapers' front pages were taken up with advertisements, shipping movements, official proclamations from Newfoundland's governor, "sealing messages" (in season), train arrivals. The second page, apart from a few ads, contained the serial, which was interminable.

The serials were always victories of virtue over vice, especially where young ladies were concerned, with titles such as "The Girl of the Cloisters," "The Heir of Rosedene," and "The Gamekeeper's Hut." The start of Chapter 29 in the issues of March 22 will tell you all you need to know about the style: " 'Ah, yes, that horrible, horrible money!' murmured Edna, drooping on his loved bosom."

The Newfoundland that Hawker and the others came to, in that spring of 1919, had much poverty. One sixth of the people were illiterate.

Newfoundland, when it was suddenly thrust into the world's eye as a major airbase for Atlantic flight, had a population of about a quarter million. This was spread through the bays and inlets of a 6,000-mile coastline that was frightening even to the map-maker. It looked like a dinosaur's knuckle.

St. John's, the capital, at the eastern end of what is one of the world's largest islands (considerably bigger than some European nations) had only about 30,000 people. The rest of the islanders were scattered in villages, isolated one from the other. They were the outporters, or "baymen." St. Johnsmen were "townies."

Their highway was the sea, a sea which was both their livelihood and their enemy. It had to be their living; the interior of Newfoundland was mainly rocks, lakes, gigantic forests, and bog. Since there was little arable land, fresh milk and beef were luxuries.

So were roads. Six years after these pioneer flyers were there, the whole of Newfoundland had only 130½ miles of "good motor road." In the year of the air race, the second largest city, Cornerbrook, had one car.

For most, education was also a scarcity. Geoffrey Taylor, later knighted for his work in mathematics and physics, a professor at Cambridge University, and used to what the English usually associate with "the finer things of life," was in Newfoundland in 1919, acting as weatherman and teacher of celestial navigation for the crew of the Handley Page aircraft. He recalls that nowhere else in his travels had he come across such a gulf between the very rich and the other ninety-five percent of the population, who were very poor.

Newfoundland was controlled by a handful of merchants and the occasional tycoon such as Robert Reid, who built a railway that was named after him. He was typical of the powerful people of the colony. In 1898, he agreed to build and operate a railway for fifty years for certain considerations, among which were: a subsidy of 5,000 acres of Newfoundland for each one of the 648 miles of track he laid; an annual mail subsidy of $100,000 to help make a substantial profit with the steamers he operated around the coast; the sole right to operate Newfoundland's telegraph system for half a century; and the streetcar, electric light, and power franchises for the city of St. John's.

With such concessions, one might assume that the railway would be an example for all the world, with luxurious rolling stock and split second timing. Instead, between 1904 and 1921, it lost nearly six million dollars and became a joke for the people of Newfoundland. "The railway," said a member of Newfoundland's House of Assembly, "isn't a railway. It is two streaks of rust running across the island."

Finally, in 1923, four years after the air race, the railway didn't operate at all for a week and it had to be taken over by the government.

Newfoundland's "merchant princes" operated along Water Street, and their wharves pushed out behind their stores, into the harbour. Water Street was the oldest thoroughfare in North America and some of the merchant dynasties had been established for centuries.

The baymen, the people who lived in the little specks of villages dotting the scraggly coast, were constantly in debt. The merchants had agents all over Newfoundland who would advance the outporters nets, oars, fuel, sacks of flour, seed potatoes, and much else, against their future catches. Some families barely saw cash throughout their lives.

73

For eleven months of the year, the typical bayman lived as precariously as one could imagine. His subsistence came from the cod he caught in the inlets, fishing from his small dory. Usually, he also had a patch of rocky land behind his village home; he'd have a goat or two, sometimes a pig, and a crop of potatoes. The one advantage these villagers had was that their land and home had cost them next-to-nothing. Apart from fish, the island's wealth was timber. The trees were there for the felling.

Families were large, confirming the euphonious definition of Newfoundland as fog, cod, and fornication. But families were large for reasons other than lack of birth control. Large families were needed. Boys could be helpful in crewing the boats and the mortality rate was one of the highest in North America. Smallpox and tuberculosis, among other diseases, ravaged the island.

The sea coloured a bayman's language: "As busy as a one-armed nailer in a gale of wind"; a "tickle," which was a passage between islands; and, "fish in the punt, pork in the pot."

Newfoundland expressions, in general, were among the most colourful in the English language. "The heel of the day" was sunset. "A hat of woods" was a low-growing copse on the brow of a hill. "To go dog for. . ." was to accompany someone as a helper.

The sea was dangerous but never more so than during the annual seal-hunt, when fatalists turned suicidal. There was an imbecilic exhilaration to this annual trek north. The hunters had a toast: "Bloody decks, and many of them!" Rich scions of North American families, who had heard of the adventure, would bribe the captains to get berths. Young, poor Newfoundland boys, in the thinnest of clothes, would go off to the ice-packs, partly drawn by the unbelievable riches – twelve dollars for a pelt in 1919.

When the little boats were jammed solidly in pack ice, the men, in small parties, would jump out on the ice, carrying bats or gaffs, and strike the slithering seals fatal blows on their skulls. The animals would be split open, with knives, their pelts taken, and the fat removed for rendering. The ice would be splayed with blood, intestines and spilled fat from the pots. The ice would sometimes split, and men would fall into the freezing water and drown. Sometimes floes would break off, with a man or two on them. The current would sweep them away from their comrades and the haven of their little boats. The gap of water would widen. Gradually, they would be lost to sight, to die of cold and starvation, alone.

The successful hunters took their pelts to St. John's and, with a little money in their pockets, it was an exciting place. There was the Star Theatre, showing, at various times, D. W. Griffith's "supreme triumph," a thirteen-reeler called "Hearts of the World"; Theda Bara in "A Fool

There Was" (a six-part film serial inspired by Rudyard Kipling's poem, The Vampire); and Charlie Chaplin in "The Count."

Newfoundland had been the first part of North America to introduce Prohibition but there were ways of bypassing the law. One dodge was to get liquor for medicinal purposes. That meant going to a doctor, who would issue a prescription to the value of one, two, or three dollars, according to the "sickness" of the patient. This "scrip" was taken to places such as Peddigrew's drug store, suppliers of curative liquor. For years after Prohibition ended, there was a home, of a Doctor Harvey, on Duckworth Street, that was known as "The House Built of Scrips." (When "Fax" Morgan arrived in Newfoundland, he was taking no chances. One of his crates, labelled "spares," was filled with liquor.)

If one of the seal hunters went looking for a girl, he probably found there were girls looking for men. Losses at sea and on the ice floes meant that normally there were more women than men in Newfoundland and the imbalance had been worsened by war.

Newfoundland was ignored for centuries by Britain, which did not contribute to social services, but the island replied to Britain with a blind fealty. Newfoundland, when World War One broke out, was a place proud to call itself a colony, fly the Union Jack, stop for tea, and rush off to help in the mother country's wars. Six thousand, two hundred and forty-one Newfoundlanders were overseas in World War One. The troop ships hadn't brought all of them back in the spring of 1919; one fifth would never return. A great number had been killed on July 1, 1916, at Beaumont Hamel on the Western Front. The Newfoundland Regiment had gone "over the top," eight hundred strong. An hour after the attack, only sixty answered the roll call.

Generally, the spring of that year was a time of hope for Newfoundland. The war was over, the boys were coming home. The economy, for once, was good. And now there was talk of a great new role for Newfoundland. People began thinking of it as the air cross-roads of the world. Reporters like Joey Smallwood wrote speculative pieces about the Newfoundland of tomorrow's air age and, eventually, the advertisers joined in. Bishop Sons & Co. Ltd., of Water Street ran the following in one of the papers:

> Newfoundland is on the lips of the whole world. Apart from the Peace Conference, Newfoundland holds the attention of the world at the present time. Our boys of the army and navy, by their daring, have made the whole world sit up and take notice. Hawker, Grieve, Morgan, Raynham, the world's most daring flyers, have selected our island for one of the world's greatest historical events. And now the Patrician shoe for ladies has taken up its permanent abode

among us, and is now to be had at Bishop's, the leading store in Newfoundland.

The flyers themselves were treated hospitably, especially by the top families of St. John's. In fact, the city's elite had more than altruistic reasons for their hospitality. Some had marriageable daughters, and some of the flyers were dashing bachelors. Nearly all held commissions and, in the limited social activities of the Newfoundland capital, any newcomer of the right class infused new interest. Finally, there was the undoubted aura that reflected on the hosts by being associated with those adventurers.

Hawker and Grieve stayed at the Cochrane Hotel which, although Hawker jokingly referred to it as "The Cockroach," was estimable by the lights of Newfoundland society. There was cut glass on the tables and chiffoniers off the main dining room, which also had potted palms. There was a billiard room to which the men could retire after dinner. The bedrooms were spotlessly clean, despite Hawker's crack. They were looked after by maids who were always impeccably uniformed. There were Persian rugs and, beneath them, highly-polished floors.

The hotel was home to three spinster sisters, the Dooleys, who could have stepped out of one of those newspaper serials. A fourth Dooley sister, Lizzie, was married to the owner of the Cochrane, William Drayton, a St. John's merchant. Lizzie, too, was as unworldly and fragile as any heroine of the serials; she was the chatelaine and she never did any work of consequence. The three other sisters, Kitty, Minnie and Agnes, helped run the hotel. Agnes used to have flasks and sandwiches ready for the airmen each morning after breakfast, to carry with them in case they took off.

Hawker and Grieve and their plane, in crates, had to make the journey across Newfoundland on Reid's miserable railroad because their ship couldn't get into St. John's harbour; it was throttled by ice.

The great race actually began with slovens, platforms made of timbers, ten inches by ten inches thick, and pulled by as many as five pairs of horses. In summer, the slovens had wheels and in winter they were pulled on sled runners. But in spring, when Hawker and his crew needed them to move his plane, neither wheels nor runners were effective.

Hawker and Grieve were the first to reach St. John's. They arrived March 30, 1919. Freddy Raynham and most of his party reached St. John's eleven days later, on April 10. It was more than a month later before Alcock and Brown arrived. And the fourth crew – Kerr, Brackley, Gran and Wyatt, with their big Handley Page – arrived in the Newfoundland capital about the same time as Alcock and Brown.

The first three British teams all required those cumbersome slovens to get to their sites. Hawker and Grieve set up on an open field, forty acres, at Mount Pearl, six miles from the St. John's railway station. Raynham and his crew settled onto the site that "Fax" Morgan, their advance man, had found through Joey Smallwood, the helpful reporter. Alcock and Brown started off using Raynham's air strip, on the east side of the city, then moved to a potato patch northwest of St. John's.

Kerr and Brackley and their crew did not need a sloven. They moved the Handley Page by train, to a site at Harbour Grace on Conception Bay, eighty miles northwest of St. John's.

None of the air strips came even close to being ideal. Joey Smallwood described the one at Harbour Grace: "It wasn't one field, but a series of gardens and farms, with rock walls between them. These all had to be removed, as did three houses and a farm building. There was another considerable obstruction, a barracks, which had to be destroyed. Gangs of men carried out this work and then, when all was cleared, a heavy roller, drawn by three horses and weighed down with several hundred pounds of iron bars, eliminated the hummocks. The result, after a month, was a bumpy aerodrome."

CHAPTER 14
Four British Teams

Harry Hawker's first sight of his "airfield" outside St. John's was a jolt. He said later: "We knew from maps before starting that Newfoundland was the last place to look for spacious landing grounds but, if anything, the maps seemed to flatter the country." The airstrip was L-shaped, about 400 yards on one limb, 200 yards on the other. High trees were close to the uphill end of the short leg and there were low trees making an avenue on either side of the long one. And the elevation made it a windy spot.

In the Newfoundland lexicon, a "skimmer" is a spectator, a voyeur. The arrival of Hawker's plane soon had the "skimmers" trekking out from St. John's to look on idly as the aircraft was assembled. Some found the odd paid job. A gang of sixty men was employed to fill in the soft spots of the airstrip.

Joey Smallwood was filling the *Evening Telegram* with articles about the flyers. (He claimed he'd guided Hawker from the railway station to the Cochrane Hotel and thus stolen a march on all other reporters.) There were also pieces, taken from English and American newspapers, about flying the Atlantic and about those who intended to try it. One article suggested that Hawker was the highest paid pilot in the world, making $100,000 a year.

Such reporting was enough to turn the head of many a boy, and it was boys who eagerly made up additional, volunteer labour at Hawker's field. One was Robert Furlong, later Chief Justice of Newfoundland. In 1919, he was a Boy Scout – one of the first in Newfoundland. His job at the airfield was to help lay stones over soft ground at the entrance to the hangar so Hawker's plane, the "Atlantic," could be wheeled out to the patched airstrip.

It took a week to assemble the plane – the kind of delay that would normally annoy Harry. Despite the delay, and terrible weather, he was still confident that he and Grieve would get away by mid-April. The plane had been thoroughly tested in England. He had taken it up once for more than nine hours; another time, he covered 1,800 miles. While he and Grieve waited for the plane to be ready, they paddled about in a pond to test the fuselage-boat of the plane, and they checked their flying suits.

They made their first flight April 10. One newspaper said the Sopwith plane "appeared to get into a vacuum at takeoff, and those assembled thought she would crash, but the plane got off by skilful management." It was also the first flight in Newfoundland but there were few on hand to watch because the airfield at Mount Pearl was too far from the centre of St. John's. But thousands in the city saw the plane – and not all were enthusiastic. A day or so after the test, one man wrote a letter to a newspaper, saying the noise of the flight had had a bad effect on his laying hens.

*   *   *

Freddie Raynham and his team began preparations the moment Raynham arrived in St. John's on April 11, the day after Hawker's flight.

"Fax" Morgan was as busy as any of the Raynham team but he heard of Hawker's lifesaving gear and how it was built into Hawker's plane, and he found time to get a crack off to a reporter: "I'm afraid those lifesaving gadgets are of little use," Morgan said. "For myself, I have decided that I may as well take one deep breath if we strike the sea. We will be a very small speck in a big ocean out there."

The loss of a leg and a breezy personality combined to make Morgan one of the most popular flyers. He always had a greeting for the lowliest St. John's urchin, and a smile for the little girls, yet he would mingle with the upper echelons of Newfoundland society. One wealthy gentleman, Gerald Harvey, loaned Morgan and Raynham his Sheffield Simplex car, which was splendid in looks and performance – on the flat. Unfortunately, not much of St. John's is flat. Consequently, the flyers found the only way they could bring the car back up the slope to the Harvey house was to put it in reverse.

This sort of stunt helped make Morgan, particularly, known as a "good 'un" to the St. Johnsmen. People learned quickly that he would joke about his cork leg, play practical jokes on anyone else, and not be the least perturbed if they backfired on him.

When their plane, the Raymor, began to take shape, Morgan would hold schoolboy audiences spellbound. He would answer questions but he pulled the boys' legs, too – telling them, for instance, that the Verey pistols were for pilots to shoot one another "to end their miseries" in case they crashed.

Seven days after the slovens took the packing cases out to the air strip beside Quidi Vidi Lake the Raynham-Morgan plane took off on a test flight.

The Raymor was wheeled across a road from its tent hangar to the long strip of land. On hand were reporters – and Hawker and Grieve.

Raynham and Morgan decided to play up to them. For their first test, they wore the usual Burberry flying suits and fleece-lined boots, but they topped them off with dashing leopard-skin hats.

They roared away easily, flew over the town, out through The Narrows, up the coast to the village of Torbay, and returned to make a perfect landing. It was simple when there was no heavy fuel load.

*   *   *

In the meantime – it was around the middle of April – Alcock and Brown were still in England, making the first test of their Vickers Vimy, a plane originally planned to bomb Berlin.

They'd met almost casually and gelled immediately as a team. When the war ended and Jack Alcock returned from the Turkish prisoner-of-war camp, he was determined to do great things in flying. In early 1919, he made several visits to the Vickers plant at Brooklands to discuss an Atlantic flight. Vickers wasn't officially entered in the Atlantic race but, since the beginning of the year, the company's leading designer, Reginald (Rex) Pierson, had been working to modify one of the company's aircraft for the race.

Alcock was a "very rare bird" – he knew as much about the abilities of aircraft engines and the stresses on an airframe as he did about piloting. When he returned to Vickers, he was with former friends: Maxwell Muller, the works manager, who, despite his German-sounding name, was a Scot who had received his pilot's licence at Brooklands; and Archie Knight, the company superintendent. Both knew Alcock's record well. They now worked as a triumvirate. So it was that Alcock chose the plane which he would take on a ship, westward, across the Atlantic. It was the thirteenth Vimy off the production line.

Arthur Whitten-Brown, the engineer-turned-flyer, waffled at first after the war. As a prisoner-of-war, he had studied aerial navigation but, on his return to England, he worked in an office. Then he showed up at Vickers one day in 1919, looking for a job. He was interviewed by Muller, the works manager, who realized, during the conversation, that the applicant knew more about aerial navigation than the straight map-reading which was the experience of most who had flown over the Western Front. Muller blurted out: "Would you like to fly the Atlantic?"

Brown didn't waver.

In that instant, he changed gears. He made up his mind to defy his future mother-in-law, the dragonish Mrs. Kennedy, and put off his wedding.

"Then come and meet the pilot," said Muller.

They met: Brown, shorter, slighter, quieter than Alcock, a formal man, not usually given to snap decisions; Alcock, younger, but a leader, a bachelor and enjoying it, ambitious. Both from Manchester, both wartime flyers, but neither like the other.

Alcock warmed to Brown from their first meeting. "I liked him because he was so quiet," Alcock said later. There was a lot of give and take between the two. Brown sensed that Alcock was a superb pilot and natural leader. Alcock, in turn, was always careful to stress Brown's qualities as the navigator.

So, in mid-April, the Vimy made her first flight over Surrey, a month after Alcock had chosen her. Other tests were staged quickly and all were successful, even though, with a fuel load of 865 gallons, the plane weighed half a ton more than the maximum specifications of its design.

Alcock made light of the Atlantic flight. "It's a piece of cake," he said. "All we have to do is to keep the engines going and we'll be home for tea."

Not one of the Alcock-Brown team members (there were thirteen of them) had been in Newfoundland before. So it was something of a shock when they reached that ancient island of rock buffed by glaciers. Alcock and Brown, this tweedledum and tweedledee, received little attention when they docked in Halifax. And when they arrived in Newfoundland, they had to take a depressing two-day train journey across the island, arriving in St. John's at night. There was still patchy snow and cold wind, though it was May 13. And they had trouble getting into the Cochrane Hotel. But they did manage to get rooms, so the hotel wound up with three British crews – Hawker and Grieve, Raynham and Morgan, and Alcock and Brown.

It was agreed that Alcock's plane, the Vimy, would use Raynham's airstrip. At least, that's where it would be assembled and make one flight – meanwhile Alcock would search for a field where the plane could take off with a full load of fuel.

* * *

The fourth British team in Newfoundland was led by Rear Admiral Mark Kerr. He was a pilot, along with Herbert Brackley; Tryggve Gran was to navigate and Frederick Wyatt was the radio man. Colonel E. W. Stedman was in charge of all ground operations for the Handley Page aircraft and Geoffrey Taylor was to help with meteorology and to teach navigation to Gran.

They arrived in St. John's aboard the *Digby,* accompanied by several ironbound cases and 105 smaller boxes. These contained the Handley Page, the largest plane flying in 1919.

They ate and drank at the Crosbie Hotel, the Cochrane's only rival in St. John's, and the cases were moved onto a special train for shipment to Harbour Grace. The airstrip there had been found for Kerr's crew by Robin Reid, son of the railway Reid. Kerr had met the father when his warships visited Newfoundland and he'd met young Reid when the son was in England during the war.

When the *Digby* docked, both Reids were there to greet the flyers. A small crowd gathered, if for no other reason than that the Reids drove Rolls Royces, and these were practically unknown in Newfoundland. One Rolls was turned over for the use of the pilots.

St. John's was getting busy. There was a feeling of excitement. Men were arriving all the time to help, in one way or another, with this great air race, and equipment, cases and cases of it, was arriving, too. At Harbour Grace, mechanics and riggers were boarded in the houses of the little town. There was even a cameraman on hand. Walter Pritchard of the Gaumont Picture Company had come out from England to make a record of the daily life of the air team, the creation of an airfield, the first test flight.

The preparations at Harbour Grace began quickly. A scaffold, fifty feet high, was built over the plane's fuselage, and blocks and tackles were mounted on the scaffold to raise the wings into position. All this work proceeded in the open, with cold winds blowing off the bay's ice floes. It had been planned to assemble the plane in a giant tent hangar but it hadn't arrived.

*　　*　　*

The weather was a hindrance to preparations but it was an irksome frustration for the flyers who were hoping to get started.

Grieve got a letter one day from a couple of women in the cable office of the still existent British War Mission in New York. It read: "Sir, Do buck up and start. We cannot stand the suspense much longer. Best of luck from two Cablettes." Grieve gruffly told Hawker that their suspense was nothing to his own. The flyers got quite a lot of mail from women, including a good deal of bad verse. One lady, again in New York, wrote a particularly smarmy piece that she called "The Vikings of the Air." Some women offered to serve as nurse-waitress-helpmates.

There were also letters from people who wanted autographs, from dubious inventors, from people providing false weather lore, from those who merely sent along good wishes.

The most remarkable offer was received by Hawker, from a former Irish soldier who was living in Manitoba. He had had fourteen years' experience as a bugler in the army, he wrote, and he wondered if they would like him to play his cornet, free, during their flight. He could provide entertainment during the trip itself, and he would be able to signal their arrival over Ireland by playing "Garryowen." If they chose to proceed to England, he could play, "We're Bound For London Town."

If the mail was sometimes funny, the newspapers were often disconcerting; they seemed to indicate that aerial accomplishments were taking place everywhere but in Newfoundland. There was a record non-stop flight between New York and Chicago, of six hours and fifty minutes; post-war civilian flying had started officially in Britain with eleven passengers on a London-Manchester flight; and the government of Australia had put up a £10,000 prize for the first flight from Britain to Australia.

It was worrying to the Britons; around the world, flyers were setting records, and right there in Newfoundland, over at Trepassey, the Americans were getting ready to try and be first across the Atlantic.

Nobody had ever seen anything like the way the Americans were going at it.

CHAPTER 15
Deadman's Bay

The Americans who scouted the jumping-off point for the big navy flying boats ran into Newfoundland's atrocious weather right from the start. It was near the end of March, just as Hawker and Grieve were settling into the Cochrane Hotel in St. John's, when two American officers, Pat Bellinger and Elmer Stone, set out from Boston on the U.S. destroyer, *Barney*. The spring ice floes blocked their efforts to get into Trepassey Bay at the eastern end of Newfoundland so they had to land at Placentia, then go overland to Trepassey.

Trepassey and its neighbour, Mutton Bay, were merely the best choices from a bad selection. Bellinger and Stone said, in their official report: "Newfoundland and its surrounding waters represent the most unfavourable weather conditions for operators of seaplanes of any on the Atlantic coast, and the harbours with their surrounding hills are very unsatisfactory for making a getaway, except when the wind conditions are suitable. Poor holding ground for anchorage is to be expected, due to the rocky bottoms of most harbours."

Trepassey was a village of five or six hundred inhabitants in 1919. It was less than fifty miles in a direct line south of St. John's, more than double that by the tortuous branch railway line (and even now, half a century later, approachable only by a bumpy, twisting, coastal road).

If Newfoundland generally, and St. John's in particular, was still in a state of shock at the limelight thrust upon it during those months, just think of little Trepassey on its rocky, isolated inlet, originally called *Baie des Trepasses* – Deadman's Bay.

Trepassey was like a rare, tiny rock plant that had waited dormant for this single season. For a few days it bloomed bewilderingly, ecstatically, drunkenly, in full knowledge of every one of its few people that such excitement would never come so intensely, so strangely, into their lives again, unless they seeded themselves somewhere else to seek it.

One who had a close view was a newly married, young Trepassey woman. Mrs. Bride Sutton had been brought by her groom to a home on Point Daniels overlooking the bay. Fifty-four years later, she was still looking out on those waters from the home she had never left, upon that bay where the first of the American ships had entered and dropped anchor on the afternoon of Friday, May 2, 1919.

The ship was the *Aroostook* and her arrival had special meaning for Bride Sutton. A first cousin, Lieutenant Richard James, was on board. He had left Trepassey, as so many young men did. He had gone to America and joined the navy.

The *Aroostook's* commander invited Mrs. Sutton and her husband aboard to meet her cousin, and to tour the ship.

The *Aroostook* was there only thirty-six hours when two auxiliary cruisers, the *Hisko* and *Prairie,* arrived. Five destroyers came the next day, and then it was as if the stream would never cease. Many of the baymen, always ready to take a poke at the townies, said even St. John's had never seen such a fleet. As one group of ships arrived on the tide to be fueled, another group would be off on the next.

From her kitchen, Mrs. Sutton kept track of them all. She knew that a field beside the Northwest Arm had been rented from two other Suttons, so crew members could slug a baseball around. It cost the Treasury in Washington seventy-five dollars.

The sailors erected a few prefabricated buildings, on other rented land, but most of the servicing of the ships bound for mid-Atlantic stations and the servicing of the Nancies, when they arrived, was done on or alongside the *Aroostook* and her auxiliaries.

There was plenty of traffic of liberty boats, senior officers' launches, and special tenders between ships and shore.

Trepassey was invaded. But it was far from a confrontation; the meeting was so unusual that it resulted in an immediate alliance. The sailors were from every quarter of the United States and beyond. Many were Filipinos and they found the Trepassey weather bitterly cold.

Mrs. Bride Sutton, for her part, has summed up the sailors in a style of formal address lost to the rest of the world, but still lingering in the outports of Newfoundland. They were, she remembers, "very respectful, moral and orderly. There was nothing done by them in word or deed constituting a breach of the peace."

The morning after the *Aroostook* arrived, one of her small seaplanes was lowered into the water. It went off on a flight over the harbour and the village. For most of the people of what the Americans were already calling Trap-Assy, this was their first sight of a plane flying. And, to compound the interest, within hours everybody in Trepassey knew that one of the pilots aboard the *Aroostook* was young Richard James, who had gone away to America.

That night many of the young Americans came ashore for the first time. It wasn't exactly the kind of Saturday night port they might have wished for. Or, as one had his verdict written in Joey's account, "even to the most optimistically minded, it is not a very modern city."

But, though Trepassey lacked size, its Irish stock were big on talk and warmheartedness.

The one village store was quickly denuded of its goods. Its contents weren't exactly souvenirs, but the American sailors were flush with pay and prepared to buy practically anything. In an upright Catholic village, there was no chance of buying a woman. Prohibition ruled out drink. So they had to resort to cigarettes, candies, foodstuffs, items of men's wear. (This great need for souvenirs was partially satisfied later by an enterprising villager who took the train to St. John's, picked up 200 sealskins, and sold them to the sailors.)

Hospitality abounded. Mrs. Sutton had many of the American sailors up to her house for a meal and she was not alone in her generosity. Every house did what it could to help the men occupy their shore hours. Fishermen would take the Americans for local tours, then home for supper. Balcon Bone, the chief radio officer of the *USS Prairie*, noted that many would charge only 50 cents, despite their poverty, for a meal that would cost $2.50 in New York.

When a meal went with a fisherman's chat, the talk was largely about Newfoundland's weather – for some of the sailors had never seen snow – or about local fishing.

In return for such hospitality, two doctors and Lieutenant Strong, the dental officer from the *Prairie*, came ashore and gave treatment to 150 villagers. For most, it was the first time in their lives they had ever had a tooth pulled or filled by a professional.

On that Sunday of the *Prairie's* arrival, the village's only church (Roman Catholic) was filled by sailors for several masses. Father O'Flaherty was a very busy man. He not only looked after men's souls, he knew where to take them fishing. So on the following weekdays he took various officers and ratings out to neighbouring streams and ponds. Captains Cranshaw and Tombs, of the *Aroostook*, lunched with the priest, and were directed to one of his favourite hideaways where they caught seventy-six trout between them.

Navy and Newfoundlanders tried to outdo each other in warmth of spirit, although it was a one-sided contest as far as numbers were concerned. Entertainment was arranged on the *Prairie* (a little bit too classical, some thought). In return, on May 9, a "Grand Concert" was given by the young folk of Trepassey for those Americans who could squeeze into the Total Abstinence Hall. The program started with the Star Spangled Banner sung by a group of young ladies. Other songs included Sir Cavendish Boyle's "Newfoundland," "Comin' Through The Rye," "When Irish Eyes are Smiling," and "Fling Out The Flag."

The next day Lieutenant James made the first flight of a native-born Newfoundlander over his own soil when he flew a seaplane off the bay, and dipped low in salute over his cousin Bride Sutton's home.

The naval might in the bay and the purses of the sailors on land were stunning revelations to the men and women of Trepassey. It was said that the Americans were prepared to spend a million dollars to get the Nancies across the Atlantic first; the people of Trepassey thought the million was being spent right in their village.

The destroyer patrol, one estimate had it, would cost $300,000. The planes cost $30,000 each. One hundred thousand dollars was going for research. It was too much figuring to add up such sums.

And right here, in Trepassey, there were newspapermen spending as much money to cable a single story to New York as some of the fishermen made in a month from their nets.

More reporters arrived and there were four cameramen working for that newest development in movies, the newsreel.

No wonder attention was straying from the Brits up at St. John's. All the American reporters there had come down to Trepassey. There were no hotels so they lived in a railway car and called it Nancy Five.

Benedict, the U.S. consul in St. John's, and his wife, were other visitors to Trepassey. His Excellency Sir Charles Harris, the Governor of the colony, was invited down to see the departure of the flying boats for the Azores. A Lieutenant C. A. Tinker arrived aboard the destroyer *McKeen* as special representative of Franklin Delano Roosevelt; he was to keep FDR informed of any special requirement, of each new development. Theodore Hedland of the Boston *Post*, an aviator himself, hoped to be the first man to fly his story back to his newspaper, but he never did take off from Trepassey.

But the Nancies still hadn't arrived. The major event still had to be written.

CHAPTER 16
Take off from Rockaway

Not all observers looked on the U.S. effort admiringly. When it was discovered that nearly 100 ships would be involved, including battleships and destroyers, all to get the flying boats across the Atlantic in what was considered fairly easy hops, the less favoured world (notably the competing British) collectively put fingers to its nose. The whole operation became "bizarre" and "unsporting" and "typical of American over-organization."

Even "Fax" Morgan took a swipe at the Americans. He wrote an article in the *St. John's Star* in which he suggested the Americans "might as well fly the English Channel fifty times."

The most important ship of the gigantic fleet would be the *Aroostook* in Trepassey Bay. She had been a minelayer, converted at Norfolk Navy Yard so she could store two single-engine seaplanes, hold 5,000 gallons of aviation gasoline, and mess and sleep a couple of dozen flyers.

The cruisers *Baltimore* and *Columbia* and the destroyer tenders *Melville* and *Shawmut* would serve as base ships too for Halifax in Canada, for Horta and Ponta Delgada in the Azores, and for Lisbon in Portugal.

That wasn't all: every destroyer of the backup force had a special aircraft radio receiver installed; fifteen of them were fitted with weather reporting equipment; a number of officers were given a five day "cram" course in meteorology.

American planning called for a naval ship every fifty miles of the way, as beacons across the Atlantic. With such togetherness, the critics said, there would be hardly need to navigate.

Towers was taking no chances. Before he'd sent Bellinger off to reconnoitre in Newfoundland, he'd given him another job. From the Hampton Roads naval air station, Bellinger flew over the sea to try spotting smoke made by the destroyers *Trippe* and *Wilkes,* under varying weather conditions. He did the same thing at night, checking how far away starshells and searchlights could be seen.

The first of the Nancies had come to public attention almost as soon as it had made its early tests. Sixteen days after the war ended, the NC-1 set a record and a precedent. It flew with fifty-one men aboard, which was a record for a flying boat. One of them was Machinist's Mate Harry D. Moulton; he was the world's first aerial stowaway.

This first Nancy had shown it could ride ten-foot waves – even if it did make crew members sick – and it could carry a good load. It had also flown down to Washington to demonstrate this for the Congressmen who had to answer to the taxpayers.

Then the Nancies faded from the newspapers for a time. They were pushed aside by news of the peace meeting at the Palace of Versailles, and of a rising fighter, Jack Dempsey. People had an almost paranoid fear of a new, strange word, "bolshevik." Then, near the end of March, the Nancies were in the news again. On March 27, a gale hit the Nancies' base at Rockaway on Long Island while the Nancy One was anchored in the waters of Jamaica Bay, which today's incoming jet passenger crosses to land at John F. Kennedy airport. Nancy One rode the waters well. But she dragged her anchor, floated beside a ramp, and her wing was battered to pieces.

There wasn't another lower port wing to spare. So the NC-2 was "cannibalized" to keep the "One" flying.

A few days later, FDR, the Assistant Secretary of the Navy and the man who had cut a lot of red tape, came out to Rockaway to see his friend, Towers. He insisted on going for a flip. Towers was a bit reluctant. It wasn't the best of days, a strong wind was blowing. But FDR went up for nine minutes and he was delighted. He assured Towers everything the Navy could provide would be made available to ensure the success of the Atlantic attempt.

The Nancies were almost all wood, fabric, and wire. Holden Richardson was to say that the Nancy, which Roosevelt flew in, had less metal in it than there was in a symphony orchestra brass horn, and not enough aluminium to make a kitchen saucepan. The planking floors were separated by bulkheads, each with a watertight door. They were so small that the average-sized man had to squirm through them, and Holden Richardson was huge.

The Nancies, among the biggest planes built in the world to that date, could taxi at 60 miles per hour through relatively rough seas. But they could only fly at about 90 miles per hour in smooth air.

The hull of each plane was forty-five feet long, ten feet in the beam. It was divided into six compartments. The forward one had a cockpit for the navigator and an extra man. In the next compartment, the two pilots sat side by side. Then there was a rest compartment for those off duty. Next came two compartments for storage of fuel and for the mechanic's post. The rear of the plane was occupied by the radio man and his sets.

Above the hulls were the wings, linked to each other by wires and struts. The tail assembly looked like a box kite. A Nancy weighed fourteen tons when loaded, a lot for one man to handle.

While Bellinger and Stone were shivering in the rasping wind of Newfoundland inlets, looking for a suitable jump-off spot, "Putty" Read, the main organization man, was in Washington, worrying about the outfitting of the Nancy expedition – everything from 1,200 fathoms of half-inch chain for the mooring of the flying boats, to leather flying suits with helmets and goggles for all crew members, and 120 sets of naval emergency rations, each holding thirteen ounces of bread and meat compound, four ounces of chocolate, plus other foods, all enclosed in watertight cans.

Read had to order thousands of items from naval stores, naval suppliers, and ordinary retail stores. For airframe maintenance, as an example, there had to be one shellac brush, one quart of marine glue, two spools of thread, one package of needles, two yards of plane cloth – a reminder that flying was still done largely "by the seat of the pants."

On April 21, Towers, Read, and others who had been working in Washington, moved to the Rockaway Base, where everything was confusion.

There was only one proven plane, yet Towers announced the starting date for the expedition would be May 5, less than two weeks away.

Rockaway went on a round-the-clock schedule. The Curtiss men were placed on two shifts. On May Day, the last of the three available planes, the NC-4, took off for a first short flight. The following day, it flew twenty miles out to sea in fog and drizzle.

Towers officially announced, on May 2, that the route would be from Trepassey to Lisbon via the Azores.

It was hoped that the three planes, Nancy One, Nancy Three and Nancy Four, would cross from Newfoundland in fifty-four and a half hours in the air and a total elapsed time of sixty-two and a half hours.

On this same day of foul weather, the *Aroostook* slipped into Trepassey Bay as base ship.

The next day, May 4, work was suspended at Rockaway for an hour while the NC's 1, 3, and 4 were rolled out of their hangars, and the crews assembled. Towers stood before men and planes while Captain Power Symington of the Third Naval District read orders from Assistant Secretary of the Navy Roosevelt, commissioning the first seaplane division of the U.S. Navy. A bugler sounded "to the colours." Stars and Stripes were hoisted in the sterns of the aircraft. Towers read aloud orders placing him in command, and then announced the names of the men who would command each of the planes, and the men who would make up the crews.

Towers named himself commander and navigator of the NC-3. This flagship had Holden Richardson and David McCulloch as its pilots.

Pat Bellinger was commander of NC-1 with Marc Mitscher and Lieutenant Louis Barin as pilots.

"Putty" Read was commander and navigator of NC-4 with Elmer Stone and Walter Hinton as his pilots.

On the same day, the base ship *Baltimore* put moorings in Halifax harbour, to await the three flying boats. At Rockaway, the betting started on the outcome of the flight. The odds were two-to-one against all three planes reaching Newfoundland, one-to-five against all three reaching Lisbon.

Some of the crew members learned only a few days earlier that they might be flying the Atlantic. All had been given a choice. Mrs. Read was pregnant, and Towers knew this, so he asked "Putty" whether he wanted a command. Towers received a quick yes.

As his chief radio officer, Towers chose Robert Lavender, probably the most knowledgeable aerial radio man in the U.S. Navy. Lavender hesitated because his wife also was pregnant; he didn't even tell her he'd been picked. In the end, in the close, gossipy naval base, she found out and she told her husband: "It's a wonderful opportunity. You're going."

When Lavender was selected to fly with Towers in the NC-3, he chose two other excellent operators, Harry Sadenwater and Rodd, for the NC's 1 and 4. They helped fit equipment into the planes.

On that May 4, the day of the commissioning ceremony (also the day Alcock and Brown sailed from England for North America) all seemed as near ready as it ever would be at Rockaway.

Then, suddenly, it looked as though the whole venture might be cancelled. In the early hours of the following morning, Towers was asleep, Stone and several other men were still working on the Nancy Four and the Nancy One. Some of them were fueling the planes' 200 gallon tanks with electric pumps.

At 2.15 a.m., a spark from one of the pumps ran down a stream of gasoline from a fuelling hose. In seconds there was a conflagration and twenty men jumped to extinguishers. Flames were kippering the Nancy Four's tail section and eating into the Nancy One's wing.

Eight minutes from its start, the fire was out, but, from the first glance at the damage, it looked as though the operation would have to be cancelled. Nancy Four, on closer inspection, wasn't in such bad shape but Nancy One, missing one wing, was unflyable.

Towers didn't think he could continue with just two planes. Then he changed his mind and decided to proceed without Nancy One. Bellinger wouldn't accept this. He remembered the Nancy Two, already partly cannibalized, but still with one good wing.

In the next few hectic hours, Curtiss workers were brought back to Rockaway. Bellinger and Richardson and others of the Nancy One crew went without sleep supervising repairs.

The weather was on their side because it held up the departure of the other Nancies. It was rainy with poor visibility on the eastern seaboard and Towers and Read weren't going anywhere. There were more bad days, more delays, and, on May 7, there was a shocking accident.

In one forgetful split second, Machinist's Mate Edward Howard, swung his arm round into the arc of a propeller. It chopped his hand off at the wrist. Somehow, he managed to walk to a first aid post, get his stump bandaged, and return to plead with Towers to allow him, still, to go on the Atlantic flight. But the commander couldn't take a one-handed mechanic.

Towers had an announcement on that May 7. He told the press that, because of the continued bad weather, the operation's start was indefinitely postponed.

Then, during the night, the weather changed. Two hours before dawn, the Nancy crews were awakened. Between mugs of coffee they made their last minute checks of engines, charts, navigational equipment, radio sets, emergency signals.

By dawn on May 8, the New York press had word that the American entrants in the first Atlantic air race would start that day. They rushed to Long Island.

Each of the commanders had a farewell word for them, and for America.

Towers said simply, "Guesses aren't worth much but if you want mine, we'll get there."

Read was lengthier: "Whether we get there or not, we are going to get some fun out of it, especially the commanding officers who are also the navigators."

Bellinger spoke the most memorable words. He said, "With the help of God and in spite of the devil – we'll get there."

A few minutes later, to the cheers of about 500 people, honks from cars, whistles of ships, the three Nancies took off in showers of spray, bound for Halifax and their jump-off base, at Trepassey, in Newfoundland.

The Nancy Four at that moment had only five hours in the air. It wasn't much experience on which to fly across the unknown.

CHAPTER 17
The First Legs

The three Nancies flew in formation over Montauk dirigible field at the tip of Long Island on the first leg of their trans-Atlantic flight and the entire personnel of this naval air base cheered them. It was May 8 and the Nancies were headed, at last, for Newfoundland.

Within minutes of their takeoff from Rockaway, the radio operators aboard the plane – Lavender, Sadenwater and Rodd – were receiving and transmitting messages. Montauk sent its greetings. FDR wished them luck. Chatham air base on Cape Cod kept contact.

Visibility was good. From 3,500 feet, the crews could see Block Island, Martha's Vineyard, the elbow of Cape Cod. As they passed over Martha's Vineyard, Read's plane galloped ahead, and it was forced to make a wide circle to come back in formation behind Towers' lead plane.

Towers was in his cockpit with Richard Byrd, amid wires, charts, instruments everywhere "so that we kept getting mixed up like puppies on leashes," and he saw the first of the destroyers ahead, the *McDermut*.

The *McDermut* followed the drill laid down for the whole Atlantic operation. On hearing the plane's engines, the destroyer emitted black and white smoke alternately and headed toward Cape Sable, thus giving the plane's navigators wind direction and an indication of the course they should follow.

But shortly after the Nancy Four spotted the *McDermut*, the plane developed engine trouble and "Putty" Read had to order his plane to land in the Atlantic.

The Nancy One and Nancy Three flew on towards Halifax, as naval ships below went through the same procedure as the *McDermut*, pointing the way to Nova Scotia. A combination of weather problems, and the troubles of the Nancy Four, ended the earlier festive air in the two remaining Nancies.

Cloud ceiling lowered. Each crew member peered ahead for the tell-tale destroyer smoke. Radio contact became more important. The stream of coffee up to Towers and the pilots ended. The flight became bumpy – all the way to Halifax.

In fact, for the One and Three the flight became a good test of men, equipment, navigation, radio and the support ships.

When they reached land, the two planes flew up the Nova Scotia coast. Towers landed the Three first at Halifax harbour. Bellinger brought in the One, ten minutes later. Ships' sirens, factory whistles and the bells of the town greeted the two Nancies when they landed about 6.00 p.m.

The crews boarded the U.S. Navy's *Baltimore* where a weather expert was predicting a fine following morning. But the Nancy Four was down and Captain W. T. Cleverins of the *Baltimore* told Towers, as he stepped aboard, that nobody knew the Four's exact location. The Nancy Four had been sighted by the *McDermut,* but not by the next destroyer on the route, the *Kimberley.* When this had been reported, Captain Cleverins explained, a search was started.

The Nancy Four began to lose speed off Cape Cod and fell behind the other two planes. Read was having difficulty with his intercom and he started to climb from his cockpit, back toward the pilots to find why they were dragging their feet. He was met by Lieutenant Jim Breese, who told him the cause – dropping oil pressure of an engine. It would have to be cut.

It was – and there was no problem; the Nancies were capable of flying on three engines. But not on two. About 2.45 that afternoon, steam erupted from the forward centre engine. A connecting rod sailed out into space. So the Nancy Four was left with only its two wing propellers revolving.

Read had no choice. He crawled again, along the planking floor of the fuselage to the pilots' cockpit, and told them to land. Rodd was already sending out a distress signal. Towers heard it and so did the destroyers *McDermut* and *Kimberley.* But once the plane was down on a calm sea, Rodd couldn't get through to anyone because the destroyers were just too busy talking to each other. It was the first, but not the last, time this operation would be plagued with chatter.

The Nancy Four was down about eighty miles from Cape Cod. Elmer Stone had made a good landing. Read knew his position. It was not possible to make repairs on the sea, so the NC-4 taxied on the two remaining engines, on a smooth sea, toward the Chatham air base on Cape Cod.

Crew members spelled each other at the controls. During the night, everyone, including Read, got a little sleep. There was a full moon and they could see for miles. Around midnight they saw the lights of a ship and chased it, but they weren't fast enough. (One of the last two remaining engines failed at this stage but it was restarted.)

Shortly after dawn on May 9, as they turned into the channel leading to the Chatham base, two seaplanes were roaring away to start the day's search for them. The hunt was called off, word was flashed to the world, newsmen had a new name for the Nancy Four – Lame Duck.

That morning in Halifax, things seemed bright for Towers and Bellinger. The weather was good and word was received that the Nancy Four had reached safety at the Chatham air base.

But it would be another three days before the Nancy One and the Nancy Three left Halifax. Checking the engines of the Nancy Three that morning, Lieutenant Braxton Rhodes and Lloyd Moore discovered serious cracks in the propeller. So Towers ordered a similar check of the props of the Nancy One. There were cracks in two of them. So all had to be changed.

There were spare Olmstead-type propellers aboard the *Baltimore* but no hubs to hold them on. Fortunately, Richard Byrd, who was aboard the Nancy Three, had been commanding officer of the U.S. Navy's air detachment at Halifax only seven months before. He remembered some hubs had been turned over to the Canadians on his departure. So he dashed off in a launch to find them. Next day they were installed.

Then the weather turned worse and added to the delay. Eventually, on May 10, as the *Mauretania* steamed into Halifax harbour with returning troops and Alcock and Brown, the Nancies One and Three took off to continue their journey to their real starting point, the bay at Trepassey.

The One was airborne before 9.00 a.m. and reached Trepassey in under seven hours. The Three had problems with its starter; a new one had to be fitted and it was late in taking off. Then, after only thirty minutes' flight, oil pressure started dropping in its pusher engine. The engine had to be stopped and the plane landed on the sea. A check showed that one of the new propellers was already cracked and, because they had gone only thirty-five miles from Halifax, Towers decided to return.

Lavender radioed the *Baltimore,* in Halifax harbour, to prepare a propeller. The exchange was made in two hours. At one minute before 1.00 p.m. the white plumes of water indicated to watching Haligonians that the Nancy Three was taking off again. She took only five and a half hours to reach Trepassey because of a 35 knot tailwind. This bounced the aircraft around the sky so much that the pilots, Holden Richardson and David McCulloch, had difficulty controlling it. Richardson, who was over forty, found the bumpy ride, from Rockaway to Halifax, tiring; he had held the controls so tightly that his arms became cramped. On the run from Halifax to Trepassey it was worse. It was also much colder, with the temperature in the cockpit around zero.

Down below, as they approached Newfoundland, there were hundreds of ice blocks floating. Lavender, when he first spotted them through cloud wisps, thought they were sheep on grey hills.

After passing over Placentia Bay, the Nancy Three followed the coast of the Avalon Peninsula until the five mile-deep gut of Trepassey Bay was spotted. It wouldn't be an easy landing. The wind was forty knots, the bay at one point was only half a mile wide, and it was getting dark.

Richardson decided to bring the Nancy Three down in a stretch of sea less than a mile in length. In manoeuvring for the approach, the plane nearly went into a spiral dive when gusts pushed up the port wing. He finally brought the plane in for a bumpy landing on the whitecaps.

It was a hazardous arrival on a day when the skies, sea, and land were that pewter colour which is so common to Newfoundland, and one of the Nancy Three's crew called Trepassey, "the most forlorn place on earth."

Towers, the commander, immediately set about getting new parts. He was fed up with the cracking propellers and wanted them replaced by sets of standard Navy oak propellers. These would have to come from the factory at Baltimore.

His request was relayed to the American Propeller Company from Washington on a Saturday morning, shortly before workers were due to end their week. But the newspapers were full of the trans-Atlantic epic, and the workers probably didn't need much persuading to work through Saturday afternoon and Sunday making a dozen ten-foot props.

The work was finished on the Sunday evening. The following morning the propellers, in their packing cases, were placed in a special railway coach and attached to an express train bound for Boston. On the Monday evening they were transferred to a truck, driven to Boston Navy Yard, and put aboard the destroyer *Edwards*. The *Edwards* sailed, full steam, for Trepassey.

Back at Chatham airbase on Cape Cod, the Nancy Four – the Lame Duck – required a forward centre engine, and a considerable overhaul to the aft engine. It meant several days' work and a frustrating delay for Read. Although the One and Three had been stalled in Halifax, they were now at Trepassey, the jump-off point, and Read feared they might try the major Atlantic flight without him. If that happened, he knew there was little chance that the Navy would permit him to fly the main mid-ocean leg alone.

The crew of the Nancy Four worked long days at Chatham to install the engine. Then, the flying boat was delayed by a gale. After that, the starter on one of the engines broke. It was almost too much for the crew. There was no replacement for it at Chatham, so a call had to go to Rockaway to find a replacement. Within an hour, it was aboard a seaplane, flying to Montauk where a plane from Chatham was to pick it up. But this plane ran aground on a sand bar. Next, it was decided to send a blimp from Chatham to pick up the part at Montauk. But there was confusion over this plan and, eventually, the seaplane from Rockaway flew on to the Chatham base on Cape Cod with the part. On Read's instruction it flew through the night, landing at Chatham so that the starter could be installed for a dawn takeoff.

The starter was installed on May 14 and Read ordered the Nancy Four into the air for a six-minute test flight. There was still a wobbling of the forward propeller but "Putty" Read decided if he didn't press on he would lose his last chance at a trans-Atlantic flight. A few minutes past 9.00 a.m. the "Lame Duck" took off. It had been at the Chatham base for five days.

The flight to Halifax took four hours and it showed that the Nancy Four was running far from efficiently. The newly installed centre engine vibrated. The others had dirt in their carburettors. A check at Halifax showed one of the propellers was cracked.

Although he trailed the other planes, which had made it to Trepassey, Read was still being cheered on by Washington. On the flight from Cape Cod, Rodd had passed along a radio message: "What is your position? All keenly interested in your progress. Good Luck, Roosevelt."

Read had dictated the reply: "Roosevelt, Washington. Thank you for good wishes. NC-Four is 20 miles southwest of Seal Island making 85 m.p.h. Read."

Aboard the *Baltimore,* in Halifax harbour, Read learned that the foul weather had been replaced by a general clearing trend which would benefit him on the way to Newfoundland. Moreover, fair weather was general across the Atlantic.

Read knew this meant that Towers and Bellinger could take off without waiting for him.

But the propeller on the Nancy Four would have to be replaced and Read couldn't take off until the next morning, May 15. That meant he wouldn't reach Trepassey until the late afternoon of May 15. And there, at least one engine would have to be changed before the Four tried to fly to the Azores.

Now the Nancy Four was the furthest from the goal. There were two other Nancies and three British crews already in Newfoundland.

CHAPTER 18
May 16, 1919

The network of U.S. ships, stretching from Newfoundland to the Azores, kept a stream of weather news pouring back to the destroyer *Aroostook* in Trepassey Bay. Most of it was bad "it's no go" – but on May 15 the weather pattern began to change.

Nancy Four had yet to reach Trepassey from Halifax but the Nancies One and Three were at Trepassey, ready and eager, and Towers, who was in charge of them, decided they should take off.

On the afternoon of May 15, emergency rations, hot drinks and other last minute supplies had been stored in the crevices of the planes. Twelve men, bulky with clothing, bade their farewells to the *Aroostook*, and boarded Nancy One and Nancy Three. It had been so cold the previous night that steam lines had been rigged from the *Aroostook* to the two planes to keep their engines warm. The crew members knew that the cold of Trepassey would be nothing to the cold in the planes, even at one or two thousand feet; the cockpits were open.

By 5.00 p.m. the two flying boats were taxiing up and down the harbour to warm the engines. There was a thirty knot wind from the west, six foot swells outside The Narrows.

With NC-3 in the lead, the two started takeoff runs toward the south. As they gathered speed, spray drenched the pilots in their cockpits. Richardson couldn't lift the Nancy Three off, nor could Barin and Mitscher take off in the One. By the time they had almost enough speed for takeoff, they were meeting the heavy seas whose waves threatened to damage the planes.

The two aircraft made several attempts. It was while they were on their last try that the Nancy Four appeared overhead. The plane had made it from Halifax despite another engine problem, a piece of rubber clogging a fuel line. The crew had repaired it after the Nancy Four had landed, with a sputtering engine, in the little Nova Scotian harbour of Musquodoboit. It had taken two hours.

Now, at Trepassey, with the Nancy Four coming in for a landing, Towers, waiting below, was probably encouraged to delay any further takeoff attempts by the Nancies One and Three. Besides, the crews' clothing was soaked.

That evening, Nancy Four received new propellers and had her engines tuned and cleaned. The next day, May 16, dawned grey, a not unnatural prospect for Newfoundland.

Lavender, Towers' radio officer, remembers that Gregg and Barratt, the *Aroostook* aerographers, were sending balloons aloft, "gazing out into the distance and remaining non-committal."

But as the local sky lightened that Friday morning, favourable weather reports were received from the destroyers *Upshur, Walker, Meredith, Hopewell, Philip,* in the chain to the Azores, and from the battleships *Utah, Florida, Arkansas,* positioned at varying distances north of the line, and the battleships *Wyoming* and *Texas* to the south.

By noon even the *Aroostook's* meteorologists were beginning to cheer up. The six foot swells in Trepassey Bay, which had prevailed overnight, had now reduced to choppiness.

Towers gave the order to leave.

At 5.00 p.m. he assembled his entire air division on the deck of the *Aroostook* and thanked Captain Tombs for the ship's hospitality.

Tombs then bet Towers his ship would beat him to Plymouth, England. It seemed a foolhardy wager, even by the aviation standards of 1919 but, minutes later, Tombs probably thought he had won. With the rails of the ships around Trepassey harbour lined with men, one of Nancy Four's engines refused to start. That was normal. It needed fifteen minutes to fix the ignition.

The three planes, to the salutes of the surface vessels, then moved over choppy water to their starting point.

Towers signalled to his pilots and the Nancy Three made a first attempt at takeoff. It didn't make it. The Nancy Four tried, and became airborne, climbed, and started circling Trepassey. The One made a run – unsucessfully. The Four continued to circle, but then, after fifteen minutes, it landed.

Meanwhile, the Nancy Three was taxiing back to a launch, several miles over the windswept water. As it did so, its crew was ripping up much of the floor planking. It weighed fifty pounds, and was contributing to the Nancy's refusal to become airborne. So were extra tools, drums of spare oil, radiator water. All of these were placed in the launch.

So was the plane's emergency radio transmitter. It weighed twenty-six pounds. It would be the Nancy Three's only means of communication if the plane were forced down on the sea. Lavender, the radio officer, protested, but not for long. He knew Towers was right.

There was an even harder task facing the commander.

He went back to talk to Ensign Braxton Rhodes. The young officer was a big man. He knew what was coming. There was no need for two engine experts aboard. In the event of a breakdown, it was true that repairs could be made more quickly with two, but that was hardly enough reason to take him.

He clambered aboard the launch.

Nancy Three now taxied back to the start of its previous run. It was 6.00 p.m. The engines were given full throttle. The plane lumbered along with increasing speed, appeared to shiver, and then, as unwillingly as the schoolboy's gum being torn from the desk, it slowly lifted off.

Five minutes later the Four was airborne again, and in another five minutes the One was away too.

They were still only 100 feet high when they crossed their first destroyer marker, the *Greer,* many miles out to sea.

By the time they reached the next ship, the *Aaron Ward,* darkness was setting in. This destroyer therefore followed the orders which would be the pattern of that night. As soon as the planes' engines were heard, two searchlights on the ship's fantail pointed in the direction of the next destroyer, the *Buchanan.* Another searchlight was pointed in the direction of the wind. Starshells were fired to 10,000 feet to illuminate the ocean. The ship's siren was sounded and, as the planes passed overhead, the next ship was informed by radio of their latest position.

So the planes were passed from ship to ship. It is ironic that there were no hitches through the night.

But the Nancy Four was having a problem by the time she reached the second ship, the *Aaron Ward.* She was the faster plane, and her pilots were having difficulty holding her back. Every few minutes Read would realize his plane was creeping dangerously up on the Three. It was the first time the three planes had flown at night, trying to keep in formation. Thin scattered cloud made visibility difficult.

The Nancy Four had its running lights on, and after getting too close to the One, Read asked that plane to turn on its navigation lights. Lavender radioed back that they weren't working.

The Four, no longer the Lame Duck, kept creeping ahead. Eventually, Read told Elmer Stone at the controls to give up the attempt at formation flying. They passed the dark shape of the Three.

At the same time, it was apparent that the Nancy One was the real lame duck. Damaged by gale and fire, patched with parts from NC-2, she was struggling along.

Once, while looking for the destroyer *Boggs*, Mitscher and Barin, the One's pilots, saw a light flashing dead ahead. They were to learn much later, in the Azores, that it was a flashlight being waved by Lloyd Moore from the Nancy Three to wave them away from a collision.

Following this experience, the One decided it would go its own way too.

So the U.S. Navy's first air division became three individual planes trying to make the Azores, a group of nine small islands, with mountains, set in the vastness of the Atlantic.

CHAPTER 19

Nancy One

Bellinger's Nancy One had trouble from the beginning. Overloaded, she stumbled, rather than rose, into the air. Once up, she had a hard time keeping pace with the Nancy Three.

The rough air of the night crossing made conditions especially difficult for Mitscher and Barin, piloting the One. The wing which had been transferred from NC-2 created imbalance. So it took all the efforts of both men, hour after hour, to keep the flying boat level. Barin had injured his wrist. Mitscher was the smallest of the pilots. Both had to wrestle with the controls; neither was able to rest during the flight.

They saw the first destroyer station off the port wing, and there was no difficulty spotting the starshells of other ships through the night. With dawn, the situation changed. They ran into cloud and fog.

By daylight, all crew members were tired; several destroyers had been missed. The *Stockton*, on Station 17, was sighted through the mist, but she had been driven fifteen miles north of the line of ships. Bellinger searched the sea, through fog, for the destroyer *Craven*. Sadenwater, the radio man, was having no luck picking up signals.

The weather worsened and Nancy One went down to a few hundred feet above the sea. Twice, it nearly went out of control. There were times when it was difficult to see as far as the wingtips.

Bellinger decided, about 11.00 o'clock, that the strain of flying in fog was too great for his pilots. So he ordered them to take the plane up. At 2,500 feet, the Nancy One climbed above the fog and cruised on.

Bellinger figured they must be in the vicinity of the Azores. But for two hours they had flown without seeing the ocean and they'd missed many of the ships which were the navigational markers.

They had to go down again, to seventy-five feet above the sea, in a knuckle-whitening glide through thick fog. Only when they were at the

102

height of a six- or seven-storey building were they clear of the fog. Then the visibility was only half a mile.

Bellinger talked over the situation with his pilots. He frankly admitted they were lost. There was plenty of fuel left, but they decided that, if the weather worsened, they would land on the sea rather than risk running into a mountain. A little later the fog did become thicker and Bellinger made his decision. Mitscher was told to set the plane down. It was hoped that when they were on the water, Sadenwater could use his radio direction-finding set to get them bearings which they would be able to plot on charts to provide a position. Then they would go off again.

But Bellinger misjudged the state of the sea.

From seventy-five feet, it looked relatively calm. In fact, seas were running twelve feet high, with some waves of twenty feet. In addition, the wind was twenty knots, too high for a safe takeoff. The plane, moving at about forty knots, hit a large wave, shook itself, crashed down into the trough with such force that the lower section of the tail plane was ripped away. Bellinger's Nancy One was now useless and its position was unknown. As the Commander was to describe it later for New York *World* readers: "The outlook was exceedingly gloomy."

The plane had become a piece of jetsam. In these huge seas, it was being driven backward at ten miles per hour, its stern skidding into the waves.

The two machinists, Kessler and Christensen, rigged a sea anchor, but its cable snapped. They replaced it with a large metal bucket on a rope. This held, and at least helped to prevent the Nancy One from swinging aimlessly.

But a storm was building up. Within an hour the ailerons and elevators were carried away by the ravenous seas.

There was every danger of the plane capsizing, so Bellinger kept a centre motor running in a bid to give the aircraft forward taxiing motion and some stability. The situation had changed drastically: they had planned to find their position, then take off for the Azores: now it was a matter of survival.

Several crew members were seasick, vomiting, nauseous, as they bailed water from the rolling hull, cut away trailing wreckage from their wingtips and tail assembly, and made holes in the wings so the water could run through, rather than help drag down the flying boat even further.

Sadenwater had a single chore with his radio during all this time – to get the destroyers to listen to the Nancy One's predicament. But there was just too much chatter on the Atlantic that day.

For four hours, Sadenwater sent out their call sign. At last a destroyer picked it up and asked for a series of signals so it could get a bearing on the plane. At that moment the batteries of the One's transmitter went dead. The generator worked only when Bellinger started the forward centre engine, and then only for minutes. One wing was so damaged that the generator propeller which was on it, was broken. This meant no more radio communication was possible. And that dragging starboard wing meant that the plane could capsize unless it was counter-balanced.

Four men, Bellinger, Christensen, Kessler, Sadenwater (all the crew except the pilots, who were trying to steer the craft) clambered out on to the port wing so their weight would bring the other wing up.

Five hours after landing, they spotted a ship's smoke. Barin and Mitscher headed the plane in its direction, but as they got closer, the ship turned and was lost to view.

Hopes died. Everybody was soaking wet, many were ill: there were only five gallons of fresh water and some soggy sandwiches. If the port wing float was ripped away by the waves as the starboard float had been, the wings would be permanently under water and it would be only a matter of time before the entire flying boat broke up.

However, within a few minutes the fitful fog lifted and, a few hundred yards away, there was a ship.

It was the *Ionia*, typical of John Masefield's dirty little "tramps" but more welcome than any quinquereme from Ninevah. The *Ionia*, under Captain B. E. Panas, was, in fact, carrying coal, taking it from Hampton Roads, Virginia, to Gibraltar. She carried no radio.

Although the ship was so close that its name could be read by the crew of the Nancy One, it was no easy task to transfer to her dry decks. The *Ionia* had difficulty launching one of its boats in the high waves. Altogether, it took nearly two hours before a lifeboat was safely in the sea, across to the plane for the crew members, and back to the *Ionia*.

The boat's crew not only rescued Bellinger and his men but attached a hawser to the plane. A downed flying boat in that Atlantic that May afternoon must have seemed like an apparition for Captain Panas and his Greek crew (who knew nothing about an American attempt to fly the ocean), but they quickly adapted to the situation – and decided to attempt to haul the plane to port for salvage.

However, two hours after starting the journey, the tow rope snapped. It was now night, and the *Ionia's* captain felt that he should stand by the derelict, which had become a menace to shipping.

While the *Ionia* was hove to, the U.S. destroyer *Gridley* happened by, communicated with the ship, learned that Bellinger and the others were safely aboard, and transmitted this information to the Azores.

This news arrived in the United States in time for a new day's newspapers – it meant another day's main headlines would be devoted to the exploits of the Nancies.

Captain Panas hadn't been ready to change his course from Gibraltar when the crew of the One was picked up. But once the *Gridley* had arrived he had no chance of the spoils of salvage so he was easily talked into taking the crew of the Nancy One to Horta in the Azores. The *Ionia* arrived there shortly after noon the next day, May 18.

The remains of the Nancy One were still floundering in the seas, near the island of Faial in the Azores. Another American warship, the *Fairfax*, had taken over salvage duties. It managed to get a line on to the battered flying boat, but, when it pulled, the Nancy One turned turtle. Two days later, upsidedown, it sank.

CHAPTER 20
Nancy Three

When John Towers, the commander of the Nancy Three, returned to the United States, he said of his Atlantic flight attempt: "Those who think that having destroyers fifty miles apart made navigation as easy as walking down Broadway should have been with us that evening."

As the Nancy Three headed out over the Atlantic, it had a problem not faced by the others – lack of light. As soon as it was dark, Towers realized there were serious defects in the lighting system. The navigational "riding lights" didn't come on, so the plane couldn't be seen by the Nancy One and the Nancy Four. The lights were out on the instrument panels of the pilots, Holden Richardson and David McCulloch. Towers had limited light to plot his charts. But when his pilots took the plane up to 4,500 feet, they had a beautiful night which everybody, Towers especially, enjoyed. Stars were visible easily for navigation. The moon provided enough light to see the instruments. There were occasional gaps in the cloud below, through which they spotted some of the destroyers' star shells, and two lighted passenger ships.

For Towers, those night hours over the Atlantic always remained the most impressive of his life. The air was relatively smooth. Richardson and McCulloch took turns coming forward to the commanding officer's compartment for a coffee or a sandwich. Lavender, at his radio sets in the rear of the plane, was picking up the destroyers' signals.

But dawn brought an end to euphoria.

The destroyer *Cowell* was spotted from 4,300 feet, just before thick, higher cloudbanks were encountered. The Nancy Three glided down to 2,000 feet to get under them and spotted the *Maddox,* fifteen miles to the south. Towers had expected to see this ship to the north, and he ordered a change of course in the hope it would bring them through gusty rain squalls over the next destroyer.

He did not see the *Hopewell*, nor the *Stockton,* fifty miles onward. For more than an hour they flew without seeing a ship. Towers realized that possibly the last ship they had seen, fifteen miles away in the mist, was not the *Maddox*. His course correction had in fact moved the Nancy Three away from the line of destroyers. So Towers ordered a change of course again, this time to run a line parallel with the chain of ships.

Towers knew from radio messages passed him by Lavender that both the One and Four were having difficulty locating the destroyers. He told Lavender to transmit a message saying that the Three was off course somewhere between the *Stockton* and *Craven* on Stations 17 and 18. Ships at sea began to hear this message. Then there was silence. Vibrations from the Nancy Three's engines had shaken loose the generator's ground connection. For the next four hours a very frustrated radio officer transmitted messages without anybody receiving them, because no one noticed this loose connection.

The weather was deteriorating too. The plane flew low, only to meet fog. It tried going higher, but got into cloud. At other times, rain drove into the faces of the pilots.

Richardson had now been handling the aircraft for much of thirteen hours. Suddenly, he collapsed.

The medical officer at Rockaway had warned Towers this could happen to a pilot – and forearmed him with a medical kit which included strychnine. Richardson was given two injections. An hour later he went back to his post to help his fellow pilot, McCulloch.

The Nancy Three was now, without doubt, lost. The plane had flown for more than fifteen hours; everybody aboard feared they must be among the mountains of the Azores.

Towers managed to get a quick sun "shot" with his sextant. At least it gave him his approximate latitude. Based on this, he ordered a 60° turn to the north to get away from the mountains.

Lloyd Moore came forward to inform the commander there was enough fuel left for only two more hours of flying.

Towers went into conference. He crawled to the pilots' position. There they talked over the possibility of landing in the sea, switching off the engines, taking a steady radio compass bearing on the *Columbia* in Horta, thus finding their position precisely. Afterwards they would take off and fly to the nearest port.

The plane was flying only about 100 feet above the sea. They looked down and believed that a landing and take off were possible. Like Bellinger, they were wrong. Richardson took the plane down. The Nancy Three hit the first crest hard, and wouldn't stay down. It plunged into a trough, climbed the far side, went into the air, crashed back onto another wave-top. Struts buckled, wires snapped, hull seams split. Although none of the crew was hurt, the Nancy Three was terribly injured. Two metal supports for the centreline engines were so badly bent that the engines tipped crazily down toward the pilots' cockpit. And the hull began to take in water.

The plane obviously would never take off, even in a dead calm.

The emergency transmitter had been left behind to lighten the load, so the plane's ability to let its whereabouts be known suffered greatly. And that was all-important because the Nancy Three had ended up where the American Navy didn't expect it to be. It had overflown Flores, the westerly island of the Azores, and was forty-five miles southwest of Horta.

But the Three had one ace in the hole – seamanship.

John Towers had been a fine sailor before taking to the air. Now he applied his experience and used his flying boat like a ship. There were difficulties with this transformation. In the rough landing, control wires had been broken so it was hard to manoeuvre the bulky Nancy. In addition, the direction of the wind and current tended to control the progress of the crippled plane-boat. Consequently, much of its eventual journey was backward.

The first task was to secure the safety of the "ship." There was a bad leak under the pilots' cockpit, and a pump had to be set up to remove the water which had already seeped through the hull.

Lavender was able to receive radio messages on a main set, which established their position. Then he received disconcerting news. The various destroyers judged that the Three must be down on the ocean, and had started a search – but nowhere near where the Three was bouncing on the waves.

Despite these circumstances, Towers expected that they would be picked up within a few hours. Lavender wasn't so sure. He had a niggling thought. With all the signals he had sent out giving their position, including the one that announced they were going to land. Why were the warships concentrating their search far to the west? Could it be that none of them had received any of his messages?

He checked over his set again; only then was the loose connection discovered.

The ships he heard indicated that the search would be concentrated 300 miles from where Lavender was feverishly trying to make himself heard.

The plane's port engine was started so it could turn the generator and send a signal. But the engine could not be run at full speed because this turned the plane in circles. Nor could the starboard engine be run at the same time; with both engines working, the plane's nose dipped into the high waves, causing the hull to ship more water.

Again, there was a lot of inter-ship radio chatter. Nobody, Lavender grumbled bitterly, seemed to be listening. And if they were, he reckoned, they would have to be within thirty miles. He wasn't sure his signals were reaching beyond that.

But he could hear a storm warning!

Towers had already decided that if the Nancy Three could survive a storm, drift would take it eastward to Ponta Delgada in the Azores within two to three days.

He now took a commander's stock of men and materials. After fifteen hours in the air, three or four on the sea, all were weary, but only Richardson, older than the others, had suffered from a mixture of fatigue and nervous tension.

Food consisted of jelly sandwiches, mostly wet, and dry emergency rations, together with five small cakes of milk chocolate. Towers had decided to put the fresh water supply ashore at Trepassey to ease weight. So the men had to drink water from the radiator; it was a little rusty and oily, but that was the least of their worries.

One of the plane's elevators had been so badly damaged in landing that it threatened to increase the yawing of the aircraft and capsize her. So the crew clambered out and, in heavy seas, managed to cut it away.

The fabric covering of the lower wings became saturated as the waves sprayed them, and they began to sag and form depressions in which pools of water formed. These were dragging the plane down. Again crew members climbed out, clinging to struts, and cut holes in the wings to let the water drain through.

During the evening, the wind increased. By then everybody was wet.

A system of watches had been set up. Those off watch tried to curl up and sleep.

McCulloch was especially concerned that his mother would be worrying about him; he realized that now the New York newspapers would be reporting that they were missing. McCulloch was the emissary for the three planes. Wanamaker, the store millionaire, had given him a letter for delivery to the King of England. But McCulloch had no place to put it in the open pilots' cockpit, so he gave it to Lavender to tuck above his radio desk.

The Nancy Three was to be on the sea through parts of three days, Saturday, Sunday and Monday, May 17, 18 and 19. On that first evening, the hull had been pumped dry in an hour. On the Sunday, pumping went on for four hours. On Monday it went on steadily.

Lavender, an amateur student of psychology, was interested in the reaction of the various crew members to their predicament. He was also interested in his own behaviour. When pumping bilge water one time, for instance, Lavender saw a crust of bread floating by. He rescued it and put it in his pocket. In retrospect, he remembered the words "finders keepers" going through his mind. Later, he took the crust out gently from where he'd placed it, dried it, and ate it. Moreover, he recalled, it tasted good.

It was a miserable first night for everybody.

Towers was up through most of it, keeping those on lookout company, bolstering the spirits of his men.

Lavender, when off-duty, could only find one spot where he could stretch out full length, and that was between a gasoline tank and the hull. When he crawled into this narrow space, he found that the pressure of the sea squeezed the hull's wood in and out. It kept him awake.

McCulloch was seasick.

About four o'clock on the Sunday morning the storm was at its height, with winds of gale force and a driving rain.

All the men now had to take posts as a matter of survival.

The two pilots had to try and keep the plane headed into wind, though, without power, it was being driven backward.

The pump was manned.

A close watch was kept on the sea anchor which had been created out of two large canvas pails, and on the wing pontoons. At one stage, Towers decided to pour oil on the sea to calm it. However, the flying boat was being driven so fast over the ocean that it quickly moved out of the oil slick which was being created.

Between 7.00 and 8.00 a.m., on that grey, rainy Sunday morning, May 18, the Nancy Three slowly, piece by piece, began to break up.

The first blow was when a particularly heavy sea poured over the port lower wing, shattering ribs along its rear edge. Then the tail assembly dipped down into the sea and the lower elevator broke.

The wind was gusting to 60 miles per hour. In this gale, Richardson and Moore, with ropes tied round them, went out of the cockpit to walk a strut, seven-eighths of an inch wide, for fifty-six feet along the wing, so they could cut new holes in the fabric to let the water run through.

Sometime between 9.00 and 11.30 a.m. (the records and memories differed), the worst structural blow of all came. Without warning, a cross-sea caught the port wing and tore away the float at its tip. This made the craft lopsided. There was every possibility the plane would capsize. Towers had only one choice: to create a human counterbalance. If a man weighing up to 200 pounds could stay at the end of the opposite wing, he would act as a lever and bring up the wounded port wing.

So each crew member took it in turns, two hours at a time, going out to the end of the starboard wing in a harness. There they stayed, the sea often breaking over them, uncomplaining ballast, hanging onto a spar. It was an exhausting, lonely vigil, especially in the night – and there was still another night to go.

In the early afternoon preceding that second night, Richardson had a glimpse of that feared 7,500-foot mountain of the Azores – Pico. The wind was driving the plane away from this island, which Towers estimated to be thirty or forty miles away.

The commander and his pilots discussed whether they should try to reach it by taxiing, but it was agreed that, if the engines were turned on and an attempt was made to make forward progress through the churning seas, the aircraft couldn't stand the strain and would disintegrate quickly.

However, one engine was started so that Lavender could twice get off an SOS. The single engine drove the plane in a full circle, in buffeting cross-seas, and almost upset it.

Lavender didn't know whether his latest efforts had met success.

Every naval vessel near the Azores was searching for them – but hundreds of miles from where they were. (Several destroyer captains told Towers later that they did not believe the flying boat could survive such a gale: even their ships were having difficulties in the hunt.)

The second night on the sea was something, Towers later said, to try to forget. He knew that not one of his crew expected to live.

Toward dawn, the hull was so deep in water that Towers thought the Nancy was sinking. But six hours of continuous pumping finally lowered the level. It was miserable work; one man had to remain in the water to keep debris from getting into the suction inlet.

It was Towers' finest hour. He not only kept his men going, he set a course for Sao Miguel, the island on which was Ponta Delgada. He had to risk letting the disabled plane drift somewhat across the wind and it took careful manipulation of the controls by Richardson and McCulloch.

At 10.15 on the Monday morning he was rewarded. There, about forty miles off, was the shape of the island he had been heading for, or rather, backing for.

The effect was to galvanize every crew member. The gale had slackened somewhat, but there was still a heavy sea running, and strong winds. They drifted toward the land. Now there was hope. Towers celebrated by rescuing his uniform hat from the bilge water.

By the early afternoon, gunners at a battery on this largest of the Azores spotted them, and informed the *Melville* at Ponta Delgada. The duty officer on this American warship didn't believe the news, and told the gunners to look again. The marines replied that the flying boat had large 3's all over it.

Immediately, Ponta Delgada came alive. The destroyer *Harding* raced out of the port toward the crippled flying boat.

111

It arrived at a speed of fifteen knots, nearly enough to turn the plane over.

Instead of sending a string of oaths, Lavender picked up a signalling lamp and, on Towers' instructions, asked the destroyer to lower a boat which could be put under the Nancy's broken wing to help hold her up.

Back came the reply that it was too rough for a boat! The crew of the Nancy Three didn't mind. The truth is that they, at this moment, were a trifle independent. They had endured so much: they had navigated a crippled aircraft through a storm for 53 hours, travelling 205 miles – backward. They didn't want to miss reaching their objective now they were within hailing distance.

Not that they were without problems. They were off the breakwater of the outer harbour of Ponta Delgada when a wave smashed against the lower starboard wing and took off a second pontoon. Now the Nancy was really dragging.

Towers saw the danger, motioned to Lavender to run out to the starboard wing. The plane now had a 45° list and could go over at any moment.

The bulky Lavender made his way up the sloping wing, reached the end and leaned out as far as he could while hanging on to a strut. Gradually, with this leverage, the plane levelled. As soon as the plane reached the entrance of the harbour, boats were put under the wings, and the little port went mad with ships' whistles, sirens, the bells of the town's churches.

A petty officer in one of the ship's boats which had approached started pulling away pieces of the Nancy's wooden ribs and putting them in his pocket. He was a souvenir hunter.

Lavender exploded: "My dear sir, if you will only get that line around this ship, I'll be glad to see you get any part of it."

As the Nancy Three was brought to its buoy by McCulloch, the noise of welcome doubled. Sailors lined ships, which had been dressed overall, to cheer: the Portuguese shouted as they waved scarves or flags from the rooftops.

As Towers, the commanding officer of the naval air division stepped ashore, a twenty-one gun salute boomed out. Rear Admiral R. H. Jackson, representing the Navy; the Governor of the Azores; the mayor of Ponta Delgada; all stepped forward to welcome them. None of the Nancy Three's crew could move. They were so weary, and so unstable from pitching in the plane, that at first they found they were unable to walk unassisted.

However, like characters in a puppet show, they had to fulfil their roles. They were taken to the Governor's palace, marched out on a balcony so that the populace could see them, and then asked to take the salute as a parade marched past.

Then Towers, Richardson, McCulloch, Lavender, Moore were allowed to wash off their grime and brine and get a few hours' rest before going that evening to a formal dinner. Portuguese hospitality, they were finding out, could be punishing.

CHAPTER 21
Nancy Four

When the three Nancies took off from Trepassey, night clouds were forming and the wind was about forty knots. Then it dropped and "Putty" Read and the other crew members aboard the Nancy Four began enjoying what seemed like an unusually smooth flight.

There was some early haze and they used flashlights to read instruments. Then the moon rose above the horizon and gave more light. Read in his forward compartment kept his charts and log. From time to time, he crawled to the other compartments to check with Walter Hinton and Elmer Stone at the pilots' controls, with James Breese and Eugene Rhoads at their engine instruments, or with Herbert Rodd and his radio sets.

The Nancy Four was behaving like a dream. Each destroyer was sighted in turn. The night became so clear that some of the star shells they sent up were seen from forty miles away.

Rhoads slept on a pile of lifejackets. Hinton and Stone were able to spell each other while one or the other had a drink from his thermos or a sandwich. But there was little rest for Rodd at his radio.

J. S. Howell, a radio operator on a merchantman bound westward across the Atlantic, remembers that night of May 16-17. Once into the open Atlantic his watches were remarkable for their inactivity. Usually, the mid-Atlantic, for a radio op., "was as silent as the grave." But this trip had been different. Day after day he'd picked up messages from American warships. Finally, it dawned on him that this was the bridge of ships he had read about before leaving Britain.

Now, this night, the air crackled with messages. Rodd, on the Nancy Four, was picking up his fair share. Rodd was a veteran of Great Lakes ships (he had sent an SOS from one when it had run aground). He was fascinated by radio and, once nestled in the radio compartment of the

114

Nancy Four, was never idle for a moment. He has been described as the "eyes" of the plane that night. Later it was discovered that, while the other two planes were receiving radio bearings from a distance of fifteen miles, Rodd would get them from fifty miles away – and once he picked up the destroyer *Crosby's* radio from 350 miles. Nor did Rodd communicate only with ships. At least once in the night he spoke to Sadenwater, the radio operator of the Nancy One. (Sadenwater told him he was eating a sandwich at the time.)

Five hours and forty minutes after takeoff, the crew of the Nancy Four saw the light of dawn. Read was buoyant. It looked as though the crossing would be a cinch. He decided he would celebrate with his flask of coffee and some chocolate. They had spotted the first fourteen destroyers without difficulty. But they overflew the *Maddox* on Station 15 because of fog. It didn't matter. The fog changed to drizzle, and they spotted the *Hopewell* on Station 16. There was now only 250 miles to go; three quarters of the distance to Ponta Delgada had been covered. The Nancy Four had been averaging ninety knots.

Then the weather deteriorated. First there were rainclouds which the Nancy Four tried to fly around. Then rain. Then fog – thick fog.

It was so dense that the pilots had difficulty making out the bow of the flying boat. Previously, when there had been scattered cloud, the Four had climbed over it. Now it couldn't escape it.

Read and his crew were unable to spot the destroyer at Station 17.

Then Read, surrounded by the cottonwool clamminess (it was still only about 8.00 a.m. GMT), sensed that something was wrong. His head began to swim. Direction became confused. Suddenly he felt the strength of wind against his face increase. This could mean only one thing: the plane was in a dive.

Stone, who had been at the controls, had been flying blind – without the benefit of those blind flying instruments still to be developed for aviation.

The problem with flying in thick cloud or fog is that there is no horizon. Direction becomes confusing. This is why the Nancy Four went into a spiral dive. Stone, like his commander, knew it was happening because of the feel of wind on his face. Fortunately, the plane was up a few thousand feet and this allowed for manoeuvring. Stone coolly, gradually, brought the diving flying boat back under control. For a few moments he flew it level at 1,200 feet, and then started to climb again. A few minutes before 10.00 a.m. GMT on May 17, when they had been in the air for nearly thirteen hours, the Four broke through the top of the fog bank into bright sunshine at 14,000 feet. This would have brought great joy except that Read discovered immediately that, in getting out of the dive, the plane had turned around so that it was now flying in the wrong direction, back toward Newfoundland.

Three hours had passed since the crew of the Four had seen the destroyer *Hopewell* on Station 16; other destroyers' radio reports indicated the weather was thickening to the east. Read was to say later that the Nancy Four simply was "running out of ships."

Read changed course slightly to the south. He knew he was near the Azores, and he didn't want to tangle with Pico, the 7,000-foot peak.

Fortunately, within minutes, Read spotted a gap in the fog. Looking through the hole, he thought he saw a riptide, near land, because of two shades of colour in the water. Then he realized that the darker colour wasn't water at all, but land. It was the southern side of the small westerly Azorean island of Flores.

Read at once ordered Stone to throttle back so the plane could descend through the lucky hole.

The plane went down to 200 feet above the sea. Read, with Flores as his checkpoint, was now able to order an eastward course for the islands of Faial and Sao Miguel.

The fog was erratic. One minute it would thin, the next it would thicken.

A few minutes of this kind of flying and the Nancy Four saw the smoke of the destroyer *Harding* ahead. The flying boat flew past the warship at masthead level, so close that each member of the crew could see clearly the sailors on the decks.

The plane was now less than 200 miles from the port of Ponta Delgada on the main island of Sao Miguel. But the ceiling was lowering; Stone was flying the ship only fifty feet above the sea.

When the fog lifted slightly so that the green, rugged shore of the island of Faial could be seen, Read decided he'd better not take chances. He would land at Horta. They followed the shoreline for a few minutes, rounded a point, headed into a small bay with a port. Down came the Nancy Four. It touched the water and slowed. Read and his men looked around. They bay seemed remarkably empty of American ships. They had landed in the wrong bay.

Stone turned the plane round, took off, and within minutes had rounded another point to find the familiar four smokestacks of the *USS Columbia* moored off Horta.

Nancy Four landed again, fifteen hours and eighteen minutes after leaving Trepassey, and Herbert Rodd, who had been cramped close to fuel tanks, unable to smoke, decided to celebrate with a cigarette. He moved away from them, and lit up. As he did so the fog started to worsen. By the time the plane was moored to the *Columbia*, it was dense.

Another five minutes, and they would have had the greatest difficulty finding the harbour.

Captain Harry Brinser of the *Columbia* had time only to welcome them aboard before the cruiser was besieged by Portuguese villagers. They came in every conceivable craft, bringing flowers – and even musicians to serenade the heroes.

Horta was larger than Trepassey, but they had run neck and neck through the centuries in the race for an uneventful history. Now, the little community was in the spotlight (messages were already going to Washington, telling of the Nancy Four's success).

"Putty" Read was never more deserving of his nickname than in these celebrations. His accounts are without emotion. His official report reads: ". . . landed near the *Columbia* off Horta at 1.23." His next entry is "We were held at Horta by fog and then a gale . . ." No mention of flowers or kisses there, or the sunny way of the islanders.

CHAPTER 22
The Unexpected Entry

Among all those exciting days in Newfoundland, days of planning and preparation, of rumours and arrivals and false-starts, one day, May 16, stands out as probably the most exciting of all. This was the day the three Nancies had taken off from Trepassey, bound for the Azores, but it was also the day the people of St. John's welcomed a giant American airship, the C-5.

About a week earlier, the C-5, tested and proven, had arrived at the U.S. base at Montauk on Long Island. There, final preparations had begun to fly it to Newfoundland where it was to be readied for a separate American attempt at an Atlantic crossing.

In Newfoundland, negotiations were made for a landing ground in St. John's. One farmer had wanted to sell the Americans a field for $3,500. He was turned down. (Some Newfoundlanders realized that, if they were fortunate enough to own flat land, somebody might want to land some kind of flying machine on it.) Eventually, the Americans were loaned some buildings and an old cricket field, for nothing. Two neighbouring farms were also offered.

A huge, grey, American cruiser, the *Chicago,* eased into St. John's harbour and moored at Shea's Wharf, within sight of the Cochrane Hotel; for a week, American ships had been putting into Trepassey, to get ready to launch the Nancies on the way, but this new American ship, right there at St. John's, so close to the operations of the British flyers, seemed to heighten the rivalry and the tensions.

Again, Lester, the man who owned the slovens, was needed. He transported a thousand iron bottles containing hydrogen from the *Chicago* to the cricket field, where Lieutenant R. F. Tyler, a gas expert, arranged their storage. At the same time, fifty men from the *Chicago* built a landing platform for the C-5.

Magazines such as *Flying, Aeronautics, Scientific American, Aerial Age Weekly, The Aeroplane, Aviation,* on both sides of the Atlantic, were full of articles such as "The case for the airship," and "Nature favours the airship." Not one of these was too concerned with the large numbers of men required to manoeuvre them on the ground.

When the C-5 was ready, in Montauk, to start its journey to Newfoundland, 300 men were required to walk it out of the hangar. Although there was a wind of only 15 miles per hour that morning, the blimp was hard to handle. It was 192 feet long, was the height of a four-storey building, about the same width, and held 180,000 cubic feet of hydrogen.

When it was in the air, along the route previously taken by the Nancies, it cruised a thousand feet above the sea at a speed of 55 miles per hour. Hanging underneath the gas bag was a gondola, the "bridge" of this particular ship. Into it were crowded the captain, Lieutenant-Commander Emory Coil, and the crew, Lieutenant John Lawrence and Ensign David Campbell, co-pilots; Lieutenant Marcus Easterley; Chief Machinist's Mates T. L. Moorman and H. S. Blackburn.

Officially, the Navy Department was calling the cruise a test "of the practical radius of this type of airship," but the press wasn't fooled. Coil let the cat out of the bag; just before takeoff he told newsmen, "We'll beat the seaplanes yet." The Montauk commanding officer wished him luck, and suggested that when he arrived in England "he might shake hands with the king for me."

In Newfoundland, already beside itself with excitement over the Nancies down at Trepassey and the flyers based at St. John's, the word spread that a blimp might be the next to arrive.

One of the afternoon papers that May 15 said that if the C-5 approached St. John's the next morning, as expected, Mr. Stone, on Signal Hill, would herald its coming by firing a gun. This cannon was the city's main form of signalling major news before radio was in common use. If Mr. Stone fired his charge, hundreds would hurry out to Pleasantville.

One who did so was Mrs. Augustus Lester. This remarkable chirpy octogenarian was able to remember that day vividly for the writer fifty-four years after the event. As the daughter-in-law of Charles Lester and sister-in-law of Rupert Lester, the two Lesters who ran the slovens, she was close to the developments of 1919, and knew several of the flyers well, especially Alcock and Brown. It wasn't her first brush with the famous. When she had immigrated to Newfoundland as a child, Marconi, the inventor, had been on the same ship and, she recalled, she had danced for him.

In May of 1919, Mrs. Lester went in her horse-drawn fly to Pleasant-ville in the east side of St. John's. She was headed to the old cricket field where the American airship was expected to land. She wasn't alone. Hundreds went on foot, some on bicycles, many in wagons such as hers, a few in cars. Nobody, of course, had seen an airship before. And that included her horse; Mrs. Lester's most undimmed memory was how the horse shied when he got near the gently swaying, giant balloon on the ground.

The C-5 had fine weather for its flying during the daylight hours of May 14 and that night there was a full moon and the first part of the evening's flying was good. But then there was some cloud, a little fog, and – after Cape Breton – a severe storm which made some of the crew airsick. The winds made steering difficult and rolled the ship so much that there were times when the engines stopped temporarily. The wind diminished at dawn, but there was fog off the Newfoundland coast. The island of Miquelon was spotted but, after crossing Placentia Bay, the airship lost its bearings. However, it was now in radio contact with the *Chicago,* which suggested the crew look for the railway line across Newfoundland.

When the C-5 landed three or four hours later than anticipated, one of the crew members blamed the delay on the fact that "they had been jazzing about all over Newfoundland." They might have continued to do so had not a gap in the fog shown them a railway junction below. They were then only sixty feet above the ground and were able to shout out to some people they saw below, "What is this place?"

"Placentia Junction," came the reply. Out came the charts again, and with them and the railway line they were able to fly into St. John's landing field, and meet the distinguished guests who were there. Among these were Newfoundland's Governor, the American consul, Admiral Spencer Wood from the *Chicago,* and Morgan, who had come across from the Quidi Vidi hangar.

The ship nearly hit a house in which supplies were stored beside the field, but scores of sailors managed to grab trailing ropes and bring the C-5 to a standstill. The journey had taken twenty-five hours.

The time was 1.50 p.m., and in a 20 miles per hour wind, the airship was frisky.

Commander Coil, once through the pleasantries with the "brass," told the press that he and his crew were ready to start on an Atlantic crossing as soon as they had a little sleep.

Members of the crew were not only tired but almost deaf from the noise of the two Union engines beside them in the gondola. So they were quickly taken to the *Chicago* where meals, showers, and bunks awaited them. Theirs had been a notable flight. They had covered 1,177 miles non-stop, which was a record for an airship; they had used only 200 of their 500 gallons of fuel. It looked as though they would be able to cross the Atlantic easily. Coil was not being too specific when he landed but he certainly gave the impression that, with the right weather conditions, he would take the C-5 across the Atlantic the following day.

Meanwhile, there was work for the young officers who had been sent to St. John's. They had to organize refueling the C-5, replenish her hydrogen, make repairs. All of this was carried out in the open; there had been no time to build a hangar.

When the C-5 landed, she had been tied down with earth anchors. Those were sufficient for a 20 miles per hour wind, but within half an hour the wind was nearly 10 miles per hour stronger. Lieutenant Little and 100 men from the *Chicago* were having difficulty controlling the swaying, elephant shape. The hemp lines were three inches thick, but they were in danger of snapping.

As the wind continued to increase, the young ground officers faced two choices: they could take the airship up and ride out the storm or they could pull out her ripping panel, which would deflate her quickly. This explains the meaning of a message sent to the *Chicago*, about three miles away, before 5.00 o'clock that afternoon: "Can't Control Machine. May Have To Rip." Coil and his crew were informed, borrowed a car, and drove toward the field. They were too late.

In fact, there was no choice: the carburettors of the C-5 had been removed for servicing, so the airship couldn't have taken off.

But if the ripping panel were removed there could be no chance of an Atlantic flight; its replacement was a tricky job that had to be carried out inside a hangar.

The wind screamed through the streets of St. John's, whipped up white-caps on Quidi Vidi Lake, and reached sixty knots in gusts at Pleasantville.

Little decided to save the C-5. The ripping panel cord was pulled–but it broke. Almost simultaneously, two steel mooring cables snapped.

By now many of the Newfoundlanders who had come out to Pleasantville that warm morning found themselves helping to try and save the airship. Among them were boys who had been there most of the day, waiting because the airship had been expected early in the morning; after the late landing they had stayed on because they had never seen such a sight.

As the wind strengthened, these spectators realized that something was dreadfully wrong. Quickly, they found themselves helping.

Thus, when the steel hawsers broke, there were casualties. Two boys were hit by the whiplashing wire; one, fifteen years old, the son of James Cleary, had a broken collar bone; the other, a son of Garrett Kavenagh, received such a severe concussion that it was thought he wouldn't recover (indeed, early reports said he had been killed).

There was one other casualty that day. Lieutenant Charles Little, who was in charge of the blimp on the ground, Lieutenant Preston, and a machinist were in the control car of the C-5. Around them were hundreds of St. John's men and Americans, trying to hold on to the airship, and being dragged across the field as the wind pulled the C-5 upward. A small group had dropped away to aid the two stricken boys. The last half-inch lines were being broken like thread. Already the control car was thirty feet above the ground. Little gave the order to jump. Preston and the machinist did so, Little followed. He fell awkwardly and received a badly swollen ankle.

The C-5, now lighter than ever, soared to 200 feet, bounced back to earth so that the car broke away from the bag, and then, with mooring lines trailing like streamers, went out to sea over Signal Hill.

It still wasn't six o'clock. A half an hour later the lighthousekeeper at Cape Spear, reported seeing the big bag dipsy-doodling eastward. He was the last man to spot it.

As soon as word that the ship had broken loose was received on the *Chicago*, the destroyer *Edwards* was ordered to sea, to search for it. She remained out in the Atlantic all night, but saw no sign of the airship.

The C-5's captain, Lieutenant-Commander Coil, didn't see the airship which had stood him and his crew in such good stead, at her wildest moments. He returned to the *Chicago* and immediately radioed a report of the incident to the Navy Department in Washington, ending with a request that a sister ship be readied at once for a non-stop flight from the U.S. to Europe.

Washington had other ideas. Two days later, on May 18, Coil and his crew left St. John's aboard a destroyer to make a fuller report.

CHAPTER 23
Hawker Away

Harry Hawker heard a report in St. John's that all three American Nancies had made it to the Azores and he decided, then and there, that he had to take off. He soon learned that, in fact, only the Nancy Four had flown to the Azores – it didn't matter; he had made up his mind to go. The Nancy Four had a head start but his own flight would be direct to Britain and he could still get there first.

By starting, he prompted a controversy which lasted for weeks. Some said it was a rash decision.

One, Geoffrey Taylor, the weather man for the Handley Page team, maintained Hawker would never have begun if he had known accurately what the weather was over the latter part of the route.

But Alan Hawley, president of the Aero Club of America, welcomed Hawker's takeoff, "after the Navy had completed the worst part of the trans-Atlantic flight" because "it developed the greatest race the world has ever seen."

Hawley claimed the race was not merely between aviators of the two largest English-speaking nations, but between representatives of two schools of flying: "The first is convinced that the large aeroplane with multiple power plants is best suited for trans-Atlantic flight, while the second is just as firmly convinced that the small machine with only one motor is best suited for the severe test."

Major Arthur Partridge, the official referee for the *Daily Mail* contest, had an agreement with both Hawker and Raynham that they would give him plenty of warning when they intended to take off. It was only one of the many unwritten pacts among those at the Cochrane.

Partridge, even if he hadn't been told, would only have had to be at the airstrips in the late afternoon. All the flyers wanted to take off then so they could limit the hours of darkness in any crossing.

On that weekend in mid-May, Hawker at first thought he might get away on the Saturday. But the weather reports were mixed.

Both he and Grieve were out at their airstrip, had lunch and then posed for a stiff photograph. On Saturday afternoon, all the flyers returned to the Cochrane – Hawker from Glendinning's Farm, Raynham from Quidi Vidi, Alcock from one of his first jaunts by car searching for an airfield – and they learned that Read and the Nancy Four had made the crossing to the Azores.

If Hawker was depressed by the news of Read's success, he was comforted very early the next morning: reports indicated that the storm over the Atlantic was dying out. Hawker and Grieve were up early that Sunday. So were Raynham and Morgan.

By breakfast time there was a feeling that this was the day the two British planes would leave. Agnes Dooley ordered kitchen help to cut sandwiches again.

It was an unusual May day for St. John's. The sky was cloudless. Hawker, deceived by meteorological fool's gold, was buoyant.

There of course would be many people later, gifted with twenty-twenty hindsight, who said he should never have started. But there was nobody that May morning to snatch his sleeve and hold him back.

Monty Fenn, the manager of Hawker's Sopwith entrant, and the last man to speak to Hawker before his takeoff, said he was absolutely confident of success: "But I don't say that the news of the Americans did not influence him because he is so intensely patriotic a man that he wanted the honour to go to England," Fenn told a newspaper.

The London *Times* had already reported that Grieve, Hawker's navigator, planned a course for the first 600 miles which would bring the little plane, Atlantic, over the main west-east shipping lane. Then he intended to change course and follow the lane. Grieve was also quoted, later, as saying of the start: "We had been waiting so long that we felt callous (sic) about the whole thing."

The plane was readied all through that Sunday morning, May 18. Gasoline was filtered into the tanks. Letters from a mail bag, which had been divided between Hawker and Raynham, were put aboard. The more important were addressed to King George V, England's Prime Minister Lloyd George, and "to the people of Britain from the people of Newfoundland." Some chocolate, dates, and brandy were among emergency rations good for three days, which were stored away.

By now Raynham had been informed that Hawker would definitely leave that afternoon.

The people of St. John's knew by noon that both flyers really would take off. It was the climax of a hectic weekend for Newfoundland. Yet only about 200 went all the way out to Mount Pearl to witness Hawker and Grieve go.

As soon as Hawker's plane had left the ground, those at the Glendinning Farm air stip gathered a large pile of debris ready for a bonfire. It would have two purposes. If the Atlantic had to return that night for any reason, it could be lit to help guide it to the ground. Alternatively, if it crossed the ocean successfully, the fire would become a beacon spreading the news of Hawker's success.

Grieve's parting words were, "I'll see you in London."

Hawker lifted Grieve's bag in the cockpit, and asked whether he couldn't dispense with his pyjamas as he would "soon get a long night's sleep in London."

"Tell Raynham I'll greet him at Brooklands," Hawker added.

The engine was warmed up. There was a final wave. The plane picked up speed, ran for 300 yards, hit a bump, and lifted. Even so, it only just cleared a fence. It was about a quarter after three, local time.

Three minutes later the Atlantic was climbing steadily over St. John's. As far as Hawker was concerned all the Newfoundland messing around was at an end. By the time he was over Quidi Vidi, he had the plane at two thousand feet. He could see Raynham and Morgan's plane below, surrounded by a large crowd. "As we flew over, we kissed Raynham goodbye," Hawker said later.

The Atlantic crossed the coast and then, soon, was flying over icebergs. A little way from shore, Hawker dropped the 450 pound undercarriage, and speedily climbed to 4,000 feet. Down below, Fenn and the others in Hawker's Sopwith team had plenty of work. Flares had to be prepared to mark a landing strip in case the plane had to return. There was an advertisement to be written, offering a reward for the return of the two aeroplane wheels and undercarriage. Still, it was time to ease off a little. Ten minutes after starting, Hawker and Grieve were out of sight.

On the ground, over at Quidi Vidi, everything in the Raynham-Morgan effort was mounting to a climax.

As two thousand people gathered, the biplane was loaded with 350 gallons of fuel, some food, letters.

That afternoon, their plane, the Raymor, was to take off, in defiance of all the laws of aerodynamics, with a wind somewhat behind it. Raynham said it was the only course. It was a run of desperation.

All the flyers' new-found friends, the elite of St. John's were there, the crowd which had gathered was bigger than for the annual Regatta Day.

Shortly after four o'clock the plane was started. Handshakes all round. A cheer from the crowd.

In its test, with a strong facing wind and light fuel load, the Raymor had risen from Quidi Vidi in thirty-seven yards.

Now it went a hundred, two hundred, three, and was still down. Finally, it hit a bump, rose into the air jerkily, more than a hundred feet, wavered, and plummetted down so hard that the undercarriage buckled. It ran forward into a soft spot at the end of the runway, and tipped forward.

Raynham cut off both the engine and the fuel supply, to avoid fire.

Some of the crowd surged forward to pull Raynham and Morgan from the wreckage. But, by the time they reached it, Raynham was already out.

Morgan had to be extricated. His artificial leg made it more difficult for him to get in and out of the plane in normal conditions, and now he was the more severely injured of the two.

Raynham had received a blow to the abdomen, had been bruised, slightly cut, and partly winded. He had a badly bleeding nose.

Morgan was not as lucky. At the time of the impact he had been looking over the side of the plane, and struck the left side of his face with terrific force. He had to be supported as he walked from the plane. Dr. Will Parsons, who had been medical officer of the Newfoundland Regiment overseas, and Dr. Fred Burden were at the field. They and Mrs. Gladys Job, a housewife who knew first aid, treated the men at the roadside.

Once his bloody nose was stanched, Raynham was too annoyed to lie peacefully. He stalked off to look at the damaged plane.

Morgan, in shock, could hardly move. He was put in a car and taken to the home of a friend, Gerald Harvey, where he fainted.

Raynham was rounded up and driven to the Cochrane.

A more careful examination of Morgan followed, once he was in bed. Four stitches were put in his left cheek, two over the eye. His left shoulder and leg were badly bruised. He was in intense pain, and was given morphine. Then he cheered up, chatted with his friends, bemoaned his bad luck, and fell asleep. He was blind in one eye, but the doctors felt this was caused by the bruising above it. He had had a small piece of shrapnel enter that left eye during the war. Specialists in England had been afraid to remove it for fear of blinding him. The Newfoundland doctors didn't know this when Morgan went to sleep that night. If they had, they might have been more concerned.

Raynham was also examined. There was little damage and, after a late tea, he was able to drive his borrowed car out to Quidi Vidi to look at the Raymor. The fuselage behind the pilot's seat was undamaged but the engine was so strained that it would have to be replaced, as would the undercarriage. It was all going to cost thousands of pounds: the Martinsyde company would have to be consulted. As far as Raynham was con-

126

cerned, he was willing to try again. However, it appeared he would need another navigator.

By Monday morning, Morgan was feeling considerably better, but he was still blind in the left eye. The doctors looked at it again, and were perturbed. They told him to rest another day.

People in St. John's were sorry for what had happened to the Raymor. Admiral Spencer Wood, aboard the *USS Chicago,* disappointed at what had befallen his C-5, sent condolences. People left notes at the Cochrane. Others went up to Fred Raynham on the street to sympathize. Morgan, the most popular of all the flyers, was deluged with messages.

On Tuesday, Morgan was talking of going to Britain to clear up his affairs, but said he would return to live in St. John's and start an air service between that city and Montreal. He was allowed to go out, and was taken for a drive around the city by prominent ladies.

It was a bold front. The doctors first had told Morgan that it would take a long time to recover from the shock and his injuries, then that he would never fly again, then that he would have to return to England for more specialized treatment – a sliver of glass had penetrated his skull; it had come from the compass, broken in the crash.

Morgan, though weak, remained cheerful. He started to make preparations to leave.

Within three days of the crash, the St. John's doctors had definitely prohibited Morgan from ever flying again.

A week later, Morgan left St. John's.

When he did, he left a letter which was published in the *Evening Telegram.* It read:

> "I take this opportunity of saying farewell to my friends in Newfoundland. Unfortunately, it has not turned out to be the way of leaving I prayed for, namely, waving to you all 'au revoir' as we sailed over the hills on the long trip east.
>
> "It is said that a sailor can never leave the sea, and the man who said that was fairly right, and the good old sea will take me away.
>
> "It is now almost four months since I came to St. John's. Many wonderful things have happened during that time. Newfoundland and St. John's have become centres of attraction.
>
> "Although your country is far, far from being an ideal place for flying, no better place in the world could have been chosen for the kindness given to an airman. It was even said in Halifax papers some time ago that an Atlantic flight wouldn't take place for a few days since the airmen had several social engagements. If that was true, who knows? But it is true that none of us airmen was ever in want of hospitality.

"Yet it was a very big strain, always thinking of what the weather would be, and with all the disappointments. Perhaps at some times we may have answered abruptly, but I think most people of average intelligence would understand.

"The doctors have rung the death knell on my ever flying again, but the Raymor will fly again, and a better man than I am. You will be blessed by seeing her rise again. My heart and thoughts will always be with her, and perhaps I shall have but the greater pleasure of seeing her land safe in England – the air conqueror of the Atlantic."

The rival *Daily Star* ran a piece by "an admirer," and entitled "A Gallant English Gentleman." It noted Morgan's boyish looks, his courteous manner with crowds, his war record, and the fact that he looked upon crossing the Atlantic by air rather like "a schoolboy playing a great game."

Raynham and Morgan had crashed but Hawker and Grieve had made their successful departure. The day after their takeoff, on May 19, The St. John's *Evening Telegram* was running a seven-column headline:

BRITANNIA RULES THE AIR

Underneath, also over seven columns, was "Halifax, N.S. – Flash – Hawker has been sighted off Ireland."

For a day, for the people in Newfoundland, and for many in Britain and other parts of the world, the Atlantic race was over. The British had won.

But, as with the first reports on the Nancies, the "flash" about Hawker was wrong.

1 A bust of Santos-Dumont serves as a memorial in Petropolis,
   the former summer capital of Brazil where the pioneer-flyer
   lived.

2 Encantada, the home of Santos-Dumont, in Petropolis, Brazil.

3 Alcock, second from right in shorts, with other pilots at Mudros wartime base in Aegean Sea.

4 A German plane, believed to have been shot down by Alcock over Gallipoli in 1916.

5 Jack Alcock, at Mudros while on war service in 1916.

6 U.S. Navy airship C-5 being walked from hangar for takeoff.
   Note the two upright engines with props and crew's gondola
   slung under the "gas bag" of the airship.

7 U.S. Navy blimp C-5 about to leave U.S. Air Station at Cape May, New Jersey.

8 The C-5 airship coming in to land at Pleasantville, a suburb of St. John's, Newfoundland.

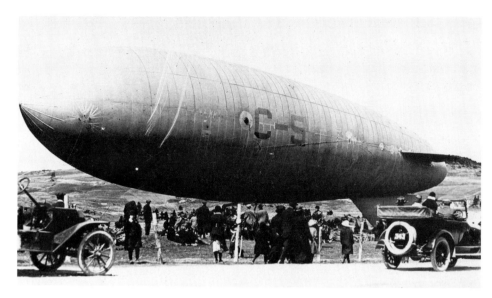

9 The C-5 airship shortly after it had landed outside St. John's.

10 The Cochrane Hotel, in St. John's, Newfoundland,
    headquarters for the Atlantic flyers, is little changed today.

11 Four of the 1919 Atlantic race contestants on the steps of the
Cochrane Hotel, St. John's, Newfoundland: left to right,
Mackenzie-Grieve, Raynham, Hawker, Morgan.

12 The Raymor, with Freddie Raynham as its pilot, surrounded by
well-wishers immediately before its attempted takeoff to fly the
Atlantic.

13 A dog (bottom) is curious onlooker at St. John's after the
Raymor, piloted by Freddie Raynham crashed on takeoff at
start of attempt to fly the Atlantic.

14 Mackenzie-Grieve (left) and Hawker dressed in tweeds, the type of casual attire in which people like Hawker often went flying in 1919.

15 Hawker's plane, the Sopwith product, named the Atlantic, being held back for takeoff from Mount Pearl, Newfoundland.

16 Packing cases containing the broken-down Handley Page
    bomber had to be unloaded from *S. S. Digby* in St. John's, then
    moved by rail to Harbour Grace for assembly.

17 British-built Handley Page bomber, assembled at Harbour
    Grace, Newfoundland, for bid to fly the Atlantic.

18 Eighteen crew members of the three Nancy flying boats,
photographed at Rockaway naval air base on Long Island, prior
to the Atlantic attempt.

19 NC-4 flying boat of U.S. Navy at Rockaway air base on Long
Island.

20 The NC-3 and NC-4 shown close to U.S. warship at Trepassey, Newfoundland, prior to main leg of Atlantic flight.

21 Ground crew working on Nancy Four flying boat.

22 The NC-4 taking off from Trepassey, Newfoundland, bound for the Azores.

23 The NC-4, commanded by Lt. Cdr. A. C. Read, arriving at Lisbon on May 27, 1919.

24 The NC-4 taxiing after landing in Tagus River at Lisbon.

25 The unsmiling Putty Read, commander of the NC-4 flying boat
which flew the Atlantic, is second from right, with his crew
members. Man at right is unidentified naval officer.

26 Horses owned by the Newfoundland carter, Charles Lester, haul
a sloven containing part of Alcock and Brown's plane to airfield
on outskirts of St. John's.

27 Pleasantville, beside Quidi Vidi Lake (background), was used as
an airfield by both Raynham and Alcock. The tent hangar was
headquarters for the erection of Alcock's Vimy.

28 Four of the Vickers ground crew relax with refreshments in
Newfoundland.

29 Alcock in Newfoundland.

30 Assembly of the Vickers Vimy in Newfoundland.

31 Assembly of the Vickers Vimy was carried on in Newfoundland outdoors.

32 Mechanics and riggers in front of the Vickers Vimy at Lester's
    Field, Newfoundland.

33 Holiday atmosphere prevailed at Lester's Field on the Sunday
    afternoon prior to Alcock and Brown's departure for Britain,
    with Newfoundlanders gathering to have their photograph
    taken in front of the plane. Arthur Whitten-Brown's signature
    shows on right hand corner of photo.

34 Jack Alcock (left) and Arthur Whitten-Brown look more
suitably dressed for a shooting expedition than flying the
Atlantic when they posed before their Vimy at Lester's Field in
Newfoundland.

35 Twinkletoes, one of the mascots presented by Kathleen
Kennedy to Alcock and Brown, and carried on the flight across
the Atlantic.

36 Artist's impression – by T. Drover – of Alcock and Brown in
low flight in their Vimy over the Atlantic.

37 The Vickers Vimy of Alcock and Brown nose-down in a bog
near Clifden, Ireland, after flying the Atlantic.

AIRCRAFT. **VICKERS VIMY** DATE **14–15 June 1919** ___ NAVIGATOR **Lt. A.W. BROWN** SHEET No. **1**

GMT X	TRUE TRACK	W.V. U/MD	TAS/HDG	VARN	DEV.	HDG COMP	COMP	OBSERVATIONS	AIR ALT.	R.A.S.	ALT. TEMP	TAS	G.S.	DR	TIME	E.T.A.
1612	260/35							A/B St. JOHNS Message to B2M Windy strong and gusty								
1620	078	220/30		078	30		108	S/C GALWAY Weather Cloudy	70	1000			120			
1628								Posn. 47·30 N. Over coast 52·30 W.		1200						
1654										1600			120			
1700								Pre-computed Could not get sun Sun alt. 56·14 as over starbd. wing								
1720	078				30		124	D.R. posn 47·52 N. Impossible to get 50·00 W. obs. of sun between fog and high clouds	70	1600			104			
1820	078			084	31		124	D.R. posn. 48·16 N. Cloud above and 47·00 W. below readings impossible.	65				120	224		
1920	078	J/R		089	31		120	D.R. posn 48·37 N. Climbing but still 44·32 W. no chance of sights	65	3000			100	324		
1940								Wireless busy no message for us yet. We have 4 hours yet to climb (to darkness)								
2020	078				31		120	D.R. posn. 48·54 N. Too cloudy for 42·32 W. drift obs. vations	65	4500			80	404		
2031								FIX. 49·30 N. By Sun Obs at 17·50 38·35 W. and D.R.					143	680		
2120								Dense cloud above and below. Sun obs. shows that D.R. is badly out.								
2220	078				29		120	D.R. posn 50·23 N. This seems to be 32·00 W. too far awards stars No obs. and D.R. apparently out.		3600			140	834		
2260								Someone is trying to talk but is being jammed.								
2320	078						116	Climbing to get above clouds for star fixes. No sights up to present	65	5200						
June 15 0017								Vega Obs. alt 67·30 Sky cleared. Polaris ✓ / 49·40 : Q = +27 Practically no dip as cloud horizon not far below								

QFS REC / E 351.1952   Signed *A.W. Brown* .... Navigator

38 The complete two pages of Brown's navigational log for the first successful non-stop flight of Atlantic.

AIRCRAFT _VICKERS VIMY_   DATE _15ᵗʰ June 1919_   NAVIGATOR _Lt. A. W. BROWN_   SHEET No. _2_

	TRUE TR'K	W/V USED	TRUE HEADING	VAR'N W	DEV.	V.S.C. COMP HD ALL ERROR	COMP. HD ALL'G	OBSERVATIONS	SAFE ALT.	R.A.I. mph	ALT. TEMP °C mph	TAS mph	G/S mph	DIST. TO RUN	TIME	E.T.A.
0720	077		23				120	D.R pos. 52.30N This does not agree 12.00W with sun P.L.		65	11000	80		140		
								Occasional glimpses of sun still climbing Thick cloud and sleet D.R shows north of track								
0765								Dropped to 1000 with starboard engine popping. Drift sights on waves gave W/V26/30K along track of 075 at 110 T.A.S.			1000					
0800							160	A/C Don't be afraid of S, we have too much N already								
	126			20			170	From star sights we must be about 64.00N. 10.30W S/C for GALWAY								
0820								In sight of land ESHEL and Jurat Isles								
0826								Crossed coast probably N. Ireland. Can you carry on and go further S? Follow rly						103		
								Coast to coast time 15·57 hrs.								
0840								Landed CLIFDEN						1830		
								Flying time 16·28 hrs.								

39 Alcock wears cap and ill-fitting suit, Brown his air force
uniform, after flying the Atlantic. Brown holds a bag of 192
letters – the first trans-Atlantic air mail.

40 Garden party given at the home of the chairman of Vickers
aircraft company, Lord Dawson, to mark successful flight of
Atlantic. Both Sir John Alcock (left) and Sir Arthur Whitten-
Brown are in the uniform of the Royal Air Force.

41 Some of the contestants in the Atlantic race gathered at the Cafe
Royal in London in the autumn of 1919 for a special dinner.
Among them: Alcock (extreme left), Hawker (third from left),
Brown (fifth from right), Raynham (right foreground).

42 At luncheon given by *Daily Mail* at London's Savoy Hotel,
Winston Churchill presents Alcock and Brown with prize
money of £10,000 for crossing the Atlantic.

43 Alcock is lionized in London after successful flight, and is
carried on shoulders through the streets to a special reception.

44 Two commemorative first day covers honouring Santos-
    Dumont and the Alcock-Brown flight.

45 Replica of Alcock and Brown's Vickers Vimy, built by the
    Vintage Aircraft Association, and standing beside the Concorde.

Captain JOHN W ALCOCK
Pilot

LESTER'S FIELD TO CLIFDEN · 1800 AIR MILES
IN 16 HOURS 12 MINUTES IN A VICKERS VIMY BIPLANE

CLIFDEN IRELAND

NEWFOUNDLAND ST JOHN'S

Lieutenant A WHITTEN BROWN
Navigator

ROSE CRAFT

COMMEMORATING THE
50TH ANNIVERSARY OF THE
FIRST NONSTOP TRANSATLANTIC FLIGHT
14-15 JUNE 1919

OTTAWA ONTARIO
13 VI
1969
CANADA

CANADA

DAY
OF ISSUE

, JOUR
D'EMISSION

FIRST NON-STOP TRANSATLANTIC FLIGHT.
LE PREMIER VOL TRANSATLANTIQUE SANS ESCALE

46 Monument to Alcock and Brown beside the bog where they
landed near Clifden, Ireland.

CHAPTER 24
The Mary's Rescue

Within fifteen minutes' flying from the Newfoundland coast, Harry Hawker ran into what those seas are famous for – fog. Before he climbed through it, Grieve got one wind drift reading. Here was a navigator without illusions. Before the flight he had told the *Daily Mail's* Fred Memory in St. John's that navigation of the Atlantic "must necessarily be of the rough and ready type." Grieve, nothing if not honest, said he was relying on the fact that Ireland was large and "without any high dangers in the air. . .to keep clear of."

For the first four and a half hours it was peaceful enough. They were above cloud. Grieve was able to take sextant shots every half hour. At the end of that time, after flying an easterly course, they reckoned they had averaged 91 miles per hour and reached the shipping lane. So they changed course to 75° to follow it.

The weather worsened. First, heavy cloudbanks caused the visibility to decrease. Then they were in rain squalls. Strong northerly winds buffetted the Atlantic off course. Navigation was almost impossible.

Hawker climbed higher through the darkness, to 10,000 feet. Except for the first ten minutes off Newfoundland, they had seen the sea only once in six hours' flying.

The pair flew through bitterly cold temperatures.

A cane ring forming the collar of Hawker's flying suit kept riding up, threatening to strangle him. Grieve had to force it back, taking off his gloves to fit the cane back into the fabric. In doing so, his hands were slightly frostbitten several times.

This was a minor problem. What was really worrying was the temperature gauge reading for the radiator. It started to rise after they had been in the air five hours. Once it rose from 168° to 176° Fahrenheit in a few minutes – then stayed constant for a couple of hours.

An even greater problem was the degree of their drift. Sextant shots were impossible because of cloud and lack of an horizon. When Grieve finally got a "fix" he found the plane was 150 miles south of their desired course.

By now Hawker realized that the high readings on the temperature gauge meant that his radiator water was boiling away. Some foreign matter must be clogging the cooling lines around the engine. The only way he could think of to clear it was to switch off the engine, go into a steep dive, and so dislodge it.

It worked and for a time the temperature was normal. But when he was about 800 miles east of St. John's the trouble was back. He tried the same tactics, but this time the obstruction was not dislodged. Worse: he lost height in the dive and, when he climbed back to his original altitude, the engine overheated further.

Hawker went up to 12,000 feet and later to 15,000, to avoid high clouds. He flew with the throttle back a little to ease the overheating. Of course, this didn't help the speed.

The overheating vexed the pilot: "We could have let down a bucket on a rope, if we had had a bucket and a rope," he was to say. "There was the whole damned Atlantic beneath us."

So the Atlantic went on hour after hour, with Hawker nursing the plane so that the temperature of the nineteen gallons of coolant water did not get up to the 212° Fahrenheit, where it would boil away.

Yet this was a minor problem compared to what was to come.

In mid-ocean they were suddenly faced with a vast castling cloudbank which they could not bypass. They went down to 6,000 feet, but it was blacker than ever.

Almost immediately, Hawker had to put the plane into a dive in another attempt to cool the water. He turned off the engine.

At about a thousand feet over the sea, he opened the throttle but got no response.

He shouted to Grieve to get busy on the hand gasoline pump. Nothing happened.

Hawker tried to hold the plane in a low, flat glide. But it was still going down "at a pretty good speed."

Hawker could see the ocean. It was very rough. He knew there was "going to be a crash of sorts and that if Grieve remained where he was, trying to pump fuel into the engine, he would be shot forward head first into the petrol tank."

Hawker yelled at his navigator that he was going to land, simultaneously clapping his hand on Grieve's back.

The pilot, in a later "ghost written" book, claimed that they were, at that point, ten feet above the "particularly uninviting-looking waves."

This was romantic hyperbole. Few aviators are ever ten feet above the ground or sea, except for an instant after takeoff and before landing. But the plane may have been only a hundred feet above the Atlantic. In any case, it was a narrow squeak.

At that moment they had the biggest stroke of luck – "thanks to Grieve's pumping, the engine fired. I gave her a good mouthful of throttle, and she roared away with the best will in the world."

Soon (continuing in Hawker's words) they were back at a four-figure altitude.

Harry maintained later that if the plane had hit the water, "we would probably have been hurt because of our speed, the plane would have been badly damaged, and it was ten to one that if we had sense enough left to launch the boat we shouldn't have been able to use it, and there was every probability of it being all over with us very quickly."

He declared that he never wanted "a narrower shave." There was no doubt that he was shaken by the incident, perhaps even more than the phlegmatic Grieve. In any case, moments later, they agreed there was no sense in trying to go on to Ireland, and that they should start looking for a rescue ship.

They went down to a low altitude in worsening weather. They were below a thousand feet, and it was bumpy. They flew diagonally across what they thought was the shipping lane. Hawker would fly a few minutes on a southeasterly course, turn ninety degrees, fly a few more minutes, then return to the southeasterly course.

This went on for two and a half hours.

Hawker became seasick, a situation he described as "not very merry and bright."

It was like being in a small motor boat in a heavy sea as their plane was buffetted by rain squalls under low cloud.

Grieve sent out SOS messages every quarter of an hour, but he really didn't expect to be heard, because the range of their messages was limited by their low altitude.

It was Hawker who first spotted the ship, the *Mary,* a small Danish "tramp" carrying sacks of cottonseed cake. She had a crew of forty-one men, under Captain Adolph Carl Duhn. She was not a fast ship. She was only 1,800 tons and it would take her twenty-seven days to make her journey from New Orleans, where she'd taken on her cargo, to a Scottish landfall.

What was unusual about Captain Duhn's route was that it was not in the main west-east shipping lane. The ship had had a quiet voyage. Then, about 7.00 o'clock in the morning of May 19, First Mate W. Schubert, who had the watch, saw a plane which, according to his later written account, "let a bomb drop."

He continued: "We assumed it was a signal that it was in distress, and shortly afterward we saw that the plane hit the water. We launched a boat at once, manned by three sailors, the second mate (Christian Hoy) and me. When we reached it we saw two pilots aboard. At first they refused to leave it, thinking that they could set it up again and get the motor working.

"We stayed close by, and as the plane began to sink and the weather got stormy, they consented to come on board with us. Soon the storm increased and the plane went down. Some time afterwards I was presented with a silver bowl, 500 crowns in cash and a life-saving medal by the Lord Mayor of Newcastle on behalf of the English Government as a reward and token of recognition for the rescue."

Those cryptic words covered a difficult rescue lasting one and a half hours.

Hawker said later that he fired three Verey flares. Then his plane circled low over the ship until someone on deck waved their arms to indicate the plane had been spotted. Hawker decided to land about two miles ahead.

"We were almost on top of her (the *Mary*) when we spotted her," said Hawker. There was fog and low cloud. The seas, by the pilot's estimation, were running twelve feet high.

Hawker made a good landing. Neither of the flyers was hurt, and they were able to release their boat part of the fuselage. It rode the waves well, but the motion compounded Hawker's nausea. Both he and Grieve were seasick, but he suffered the most. The seasickness lasted for the hour and a half they were in the plane-boat, then, for Hawker, for another two days when he was aboard the *Mary*.

They were up to their knees in water in their small convertible boat by the time the *Mary* steamed to within 200 yards of them and hove to. An attempt was made to launch a ship's boat. It was no easy task.

Hawker and Grieve were near enough to watch all the attempts. They also watched as the Atlantic began to devour the plane which had been named after it. One huge wave carried the trailing edge of their top wing clean away. Other seas spun the aircraft around like a cork.

The flyers lost their belongings. All of Grieve's log, except for a page of rough notes, was washed out of the navigator's pocket. When they came to board the *Mary*, they had neither boots nor caps.

Eventually first mate Schubert and second mate Christian Hoy managed to get a boat into the sea. A helmsman called Schwartz, a seaman named Fred Johnson and the ship's carpenter, Christian Larson set out to cover the 200 yards to the British pair.

Captain Duhn of the *Mary* said that when he was called to the bridge after the plane had been spotted, it was already blowing hard. If it had all been an hour later, a rescue might have been impossible, he added; half an hour after Hawker and Grieve were aboard, a full gale was raging.

As it was, the ship's boat had difficulty manoeuvring near the plane. At first, the sea drove it into the plane. Finally, a rope was thrown to Hawker and Grieve; their lifeboat was pulled to the ship's boat; and they were hauled aboard.

A few minutes later they were climbing on to the deck of the *Mary*. It had been fourteen and a half hours since they took off from St. John's, which was 1,050 miles away. The time was 8.30 on a grey morning.

The flyers were surprised to find they were on a Danish ship because Captain Duhn spoke such good English. He, for his part, expected them to be Americans.

Hawker asked whether an attempt could be made to salvage the plane, but Duhn said it would be impossible to tow it.

Both Hawker and Grieve were wet and exhausted. Hawker could hardly stand on the rolling deck.

He was given warm clothes, went to a bunk, and stayed there for two days and nights, seasick, not wanting anything to eat. It meant that in seventy-two hours of travelling by air and sea across the Atlantic he had only one sandwich and four cups of coffee, and those had all been at the start of the flight.

The storm was so bad the first night the flyers were aboard the *Mary* that the ship only averaged a speed of one knot. But at last the gale abated, Hawker was able to get up, and both he and Grieve were able to chat with the Captain. Captain Duhn had many books in English that might have whiled away the hours for another man, but Hawker was already restless.

And there was another problem. The *Mary* had no radio. There was no way of telling the world they were safe.

CHAPTER 25
A Wife's Faith

Muriel Hawker was at home on the Sunday night of May 18 when she received word that her husband had started his flight. Her first reaction was to go outdoors and string up Union Jacks around the front door to welcome him home. She expected Harry the next day.

That done, she tried to busy herself. But time dragged. Harry had written down, before he left, a scrappy timetable showing where he should be after each hour of the flight, and as each hour passed she ticked it off.

The Monday morning papers were full of the takeoff. She went down to Brooklands, expecting his arrival later in the day. Various friends from the Sopwith Company looked after her. But there was no plane and no news until she was home again that evening. About 10.00 p.m. there was a phone message: Harry had landed in the sea about forty miles from Ireland.

Other people had this news too, and although it wasn't a completed crossing, Muriel's phone rang for the next four hours as she accepted congratulations. Muriel's brother, who was at the house, stayed up all night, in case there were more.

Muriel went to bed, but was too excited to fall asleep. Finally she did so – but she was the first one awake to bring in the newspapers. What a shock! *The Daily Mail's* main headline read: "Hawker Missing – False Report of Fall in the Sea."

For a few minutes Muriel Hawker's spirit wavered. Then she remembered Harry's words just before he left: "If things don't go quite right, never give up hope." She was later to recall that it was these words which helped her cling to the belief that he was alive.

But by Tuesday, two days after Hawker's departure from Newfoundland, the rest of the world realized that Harry Hawker hadn't crossed the Atlantic.

Two squadrons of R.A.F. planes started a hunt. Two destroyers, a sloop, a naval patrol boat and three paddle steamers were brought out of Irish ports to search.

Outside London, Mrs. Sopwith hurried to be with Mrs. Hawker. From Tuesday on, each day, Muriel Hawker found someone to look after her baby, and, after reading the morning newspapers, went up to the Admiralty in London to get more news.

On Wednesday, May 21, three days after Hawker's takeoff, the London *Times* said that "the only faint hope is that Mr. Hawker and his companion may have been taken aboard a vessel that has no wireless installation, a deficiency seldom found now in trans-Atlantic ships."

As hope for the flyers diminished, so indignation grew. For the rest of the week it spread. When a demand was made for a sizeable search force to be despatched from Plymouth, the Admiralty made a mealy-mouthed reply that it had too many commitments to allow this to be carried out for "an unofficial undertaking." (Grieve's father, the ex-naval captain, had gone to Plymouth himself to see how he could help and was kept informed of R.A.F. operations.)

This type of official treatment raised the hackles of Englishmen. They couldn't help comparing the vast force the U.S. Navy had mounted in support of its flying boats.

As a St. John's newspaper noted, "the British Air Ministry did not bestir itself."

Questions were asked in the House of Commons. Captain Elliot, a Member of Parliament for Lanark, said the government had been "lamentably remiss and desperately careless of the honour of this country and the life of a very gallant gentleman."

Major-General Seely, the under-secretary of the Air Ministry, had to answer (most thought weakly) when hard pressed by Perry Williams, M.P., and Captain Wedgwood Benn, M.P., about the lack of gumption by the services in providing navigational aids in the first place, and pushing on with the search in the second.

Through it all, a few people were optimistic, and one had faith.

In Newfoundland, where Newfoundlanders were consoling Monty Fenn and others of Hawker's Sopwith team, one member of the remaining crews believed that Hawker and Grieve had been picked up.

This was Tryggve Gran, the man who had been lost many times in the blizzards of Antarctica. Now, as navigator for the Handley Page, he was waiting to fly the Atlantic himself. He believed Hawker's plane had gone down right on the route of Scandinavian ships carrying food from the U.S. to hungry post-war Europe. He had word, he said, without revealing from where, that there were at least sixty Scandinavian ships of this type on the route at the present time, and that "a large majority do not carry wireless."

Gran had a hunch; for Muriel Hawker it was far more than that.

Close relatives, friends, neighbours were amazed by her demeanour. She was sure Harry was safe.

Her appearance and behaviour struck Northcliffe forcibly. Despite his failing health, his many aberrations, his feud with Lloyd George, the *Daily Mail* was his baby and the Atlantic race his creation. He felt involved, responsible. So he went to see Muriel Hawker to sympathize with her at the time of her anxiety.

He came away so impressed by her faith and courage that he ordered the *Daily Mail* to announce that the £10,000 prize money would be divided between the next of kin of Hawker and Mackenzie-Grieve if they did not return.

Northcliffe, who was still often a better reporter than his staff men, said, "Mrs. Hawker is one of the most remarkable people I have ever talked to.

"When I went to see her Wednesday to advance the question of a prize for her husband, I could not get near the topic.

"Her attitude was one of perplexity at the ignorance of the public of the airman's personality. 'They don't understand what a man of resource my husband is,' she said.

"Mrs. Hawker has no doubt whatever as to his safety."

Muriel Hawker also wrote a letter to the *Daily Mail* when the announcement to provide the prize money was made:

"With a firm faith in the power of God to succour my husband and his companion, wherever they may fall, but with a lowly heart, I thank you for your most generous offer.

"Whenever the time comes for my trouble to be relieved, among my happiest duties will be that of teaching my little Pamela that her father did not hesitate to venture all for the honour and glory of his country."

"But," she added, "I cannot and will not believe that my husband is not alive."

At this point, there was hardly a person who did not know of Muriel Hawker. She was the ideal of all brave English women. But few could still believe her husband was alive. Not even in the highest circles.

On Saturday, May 24, Empire Day (and six days after Harry Hawker's takeoff), she received a telegram: "The King, fearing the worst must now be realized regarding the fate of your husband, wishes to express his great sympathy and that of the Queen in your sudden and tragic sorrow. His Majesty feels that the nation has lost one of its most able and daring pilots, who sacrificed his life for the fame and honour of British flying." It was signed Stamfordham, a peer and a senior royal aide.

It was perhaps as well that she had a premonition that day: only one more day, she believed, and there would be good news.

She was right.

The Sunday papers were gloomy. They reported that all hope had been given up. Muriel recalled later how silly the phrase "all hope" sounded. She went across the road to the little church, which practically faced the Hawkers' house. There special prayers were said for Hawker and Grieve.

After the service, she hurried home, expecting news. There was none.

Then, after about an hour, the phone rang.

It was the *Daily Mirror* on the line. It had "scooped" the *Daily Mail*. It had a message: Mr. Hawker and Commander Grieve had been rescued by a Danish ship, and could the *Mirror* send a representative down for a private interview?

CHAPTER 26
Triumphal Procession

It was sunny and perfectly clear that Sunday morning on the Butt of Lewis, that most northerly point of the Outer Hebrides, off Scotland.

Chief Officer of the Coastguard William Ingham and Leading Seaman George Harding were on duty at the signal station there.

Coming in from the west was a small steamer. As the ship came closer, it started sounding its siren.

Ingham thought this peculiar, seeing that visibility was so good. He and Harding had discussed Hawker and Grieve "but had given up hope, like everybody else."

Then, as they watched the little tramp come closer, they saw that flags of the international code were broken out.

The wind was blowing the flags nearly at right angles to the coast-guardsmen, making it difficult to read the message. First, the ship gave its name:

M – A – R – Y

Then the next flags came up:

S – A – V – E – D   H – A – N – D – S

Next a flag came up indicating they would spell out words in their next signal.

It came: S – O – P   A – E – R – O – P – L – A – N – E

Grieve, who could read the international code, was on the deck of the *Mary,* an interested witness to all that was going on.

By now the ship was getting out of signalling range on her way to Denmark. Captain Duhn, with better weather and only a day or so's journey from port, was anxious to get home to his young wife, Irene.

Ingham began signalling to the *Mary:*

I – S   I – T . . . and Duhn turned his ship so the next two hoists could be read: H – A – W . . . K – E – R?

Then the flag was sent up by the Mary:

Y - E - S

It was just after 10.00 a.m. A message was sent to the naval base at Scapa Flow.

The *Mary* continued on her way. Off Loch Erribel, a destroyer, the *Woolston,* came alongside. Hawker and Grieve said farewell to Duhn, Schubert, Hoy, the men of the *Mary.*

Duhn said the flyers were amiable men, and he had delighted in their company.

The *Woolston* sent up her rooster waves, showed her tail to the tardy *Mary.*

In London, special editions of Sunday newspapers were being prepared. When the placards appeared on the streets, reading "Hawker Saved. Special," the papers were torn from the vendor's hands.

All Britain went wild.

Where there were public meetings, announcements of the rescue were made. At London's Albert Hall, in the middle of a concert of Wagnerian music, the audience stood and cheered the news for several minutes. In smaller centres without newspaper extras, notices of the rescue were posted on town halls and outside post offices.

In Newfoundland, the news that Hawker and Grieve were safe was received by radio a week after (almost to the hour) of their departure. At first the news was greeted with skepticism, but when the Shipping Record had been checked to find that there was indeed a ship named *Mary,* Union Jacks which had been at half-mast were raised. Out at the airfield at Glendinning's Farm the bonfire was lit. Raynham at the Cochrane sent off a cable to Grieve in Britain, asking him to be his new navigator.

As soon as Muriel Hawker had put the phone down after talking to the *Mirror,* she told her brother the news. With feet as light as wings, they were then off to the neighbours to spread it further. Those people, in their turn, came out to put up flags and tell others. Rev. T. J. Wood, the clergyman across the street, now planned a thanksgiving service that evening.

The Hawkers' phone started ringing off the hook as people, friends, relatives, in tears, laughing, tongue-tied, choking, tried to spreak to Muriel. Telegraph boys came up the path with messages. Cars began arriving with reporters from London. Many were from Northcliffe's newspapers. "The Chief" himself sent a message to Mrs. Hawker: "Please let me express my delight at the accuracy of your prediction of Wednesday last."

By mid-afternoon Londoners were getting the news not only from the special editions of newspapers, but from each other. They would shout the latest developments from one open double-decker bus top to the other. The Admiralty was thronged with people seeking more news. Lloyd's of London, the great shipping agency, normally maintained only a small staff over the weekends. It was hard put, that Sunday, to answer the questions which came by phone from all over the country.

As soon as she could, Muriel Hawker went to the bungalow of Fred Sigrist, the Sopwith works manager, and his wife, where she had spent the previous day. They had already heard the news of the rescue when she arrived. As she came up the path, Fred came rushing down the steps and mocked, "What can I do for you?" Muriel, nearly in tears with relief, retaliated: "Oh, jump in." Which he promptly did, running fully clothed into the Thames. There were other people at the Sigrists', and they returned in a caravan of cars to the Hawker house, where there were dozens of newsmen.

By now, Muriel had calmed down; the hostess was beginning to prevail over the wife. There were drinks and tea, but she hadn't found time to supervise shopping in the past week, and now she was concerned that there was so little food.

In the early evening everybody went to the thanksgiving service in the little Surrey church. Then Muriel, her brother, others of the family, the Sigrists, the Sopwiths, and friends, went off, thirty in all, for dinner at the Piccadilly Hotel in London; the men in boating flannels, the women in summer frocks. They were stopped by the police for speeding. But the constable recognized the enormous Aussie flag, draped across the radiator of the Sunbeam, and waved them on. At the hotel, the band struck up "For He's A Jolly Good Fellow" when the party came in.

That night when Muriel returned home, there were more messages. From George V: "The King rejoices with you and the nation on the happy rescue of your gallant husband. He trusts that he may be long spared to you." From Queen Alexandria, the widow of King Edward the Seventh, who had been a princess of Denmark: "With all my heart I wish you and the nation joy at the safety of your gallant husband and his companion. I rejoice that a Danish ship rescued his precious life."

Tuesday was the day of Muriel's reunion with Harry. It was such a happy day that she decided to enjoy it from the start – by staying in bed late. When she was finally ready, someone in the house asked whether she would like the mail brought up. There were 2,000 letters of congratulation.

It was two days earlier that the ship, the *Mary,* had signalled the good news about Hawker and Grieve. They had been taken by the destroyer *Woolston* to the flagship of the home fleet, the battleship *Revenge*, where they had been met by Admiral Fremantle and cheered by ships' crews.

Hawker made an odd hero. He was wearing an ill-fitting civvy suit.

There were drinks in the wardroom, an elaborate meal, and a long night's untroubled sleep aboard the battleship.

The next morning, a destroyer took the pair to Thurso, the most northerly mainland Scottish town. It was low tide so the heroes had to be rowed ashore to Scarbster Pier.

Provost and Mrs. McKay and the members of the Thurso Council were all drawn up to greet them. After the cheers of the Scots as Hawker put his foot on land, the provost read an address of welcome "not only to Thurso, but to the shores of Britain." He added: "Throughout the length and breadth of the land, and of every land, today the news of your safe deliverance is ringing and hearts are rejoicing. . ."

Great crowds were at the Thurso railway station to see them off.

A triumphal procession, the like of which might have been the envy of the Caesars, had started. At Brora, most of the population crowded the railway platform. At Invergordon there were more crowds. At Alness there were pipers. At Dingwall and Beuly there were women throwing bouquets. At little stations in the Highlands children shouted "Good luck" and some adults said, "You will do it yet." This was all rural Scotland.

Even in the night, as their train headed toward Edinburgh, there were tiny knots of people on village platforms, hoping to see them.

They were out of their "sleeper" at Perth at 5.00 a.m., with thousands cheering and bouquets being presented.

At Edinburgh, three hours later, the crowds broke through police lines, and carried off the flyers, shoulder-high, to the Station Hotel for breakfast.

Hawker, tremendously impressed, enjoying every minute of it, looked fit. Grieve enjoyed it too, was proud of his countrymen and appreciative of their reception, but was very tired.

At Newcastle there were more huge crowds this Tuesday morning. Replying to the Lord Mayor and Sheriff of that city, Hawker made reference to Muriel: "I have been loyally backed up by my wife, and when a man embarks on an adventure of this kind the spirit in which it is taken by his wife counts for a great deal."

At York, Hawker received a message, a royal command from Buckingham Palace to meet the king.

Late that morning, Muriel, T.O.M. Sopwith and his wife, Grieve's parents and a few others, had taken the train north to Grantham, where it was arranged that they would meet Harry and return to London with him on the same train.

Hawker managed to scramble out of the train, at Grantham, through the crowd to a small room on the station. In it was Muriel. His first words were: "Don't cry." Then he kissed her.

From Grantham south, the train had an escort of planes. When it had been realized, late Sunday night, what the effect on the public had been, it had been decided to hold a welcoming parade for Hawker and Grieve in London, followed by a reception at the Royal Aero Club.

So it was that at 5.00 p.m. Tuesday, after work, large crowds began to gather, especially outside King's Cross railway station. By 7.00 p.m., when the train pulled into King's Cross, all the streets of the parade route were packed.

A platform had been cleared so that an official welcoming party could meet Hawker and Grieve. But almost before the train had stopped, three hundred of Hawker's fellow Aussies, all in uniform, all waiting to return home after war service, swept through the barricades, picked up the small pilot, carried him outside.

They put him in his own Sunbeam car, let his wife in, then started to drag the car through the streets of London at the head of a frenzied procession of near relatives and officials. Thousands cheered from the sidewalks.

By now, Hawker was beginning to fear for his vehicle so he decided to leave it. He began to get out, and found himself being handed over heads by upstretched arms. Eventually, a mounted policeman seeing his predicament, pulled him up so that he could ride pillion behind him. Then, when this became too uncomfortable, the policeman climbed down. From a journey that started by plane in Newfoundland, Hawker had passed to tramp steamer, destroyer, battleship, express train, car, and now to horse to make his last progress through a rapturous London.

At the Royal Aero Club's rooms on Clifford Street, the crowds were bigger than ever. After a reception inside, Sopwith went out on the balcony to make an appeal for the crowd to disperse. For there was still another party, this time at the Sopwith factory in Surrey. The party included an impromptu supper, and went on past midnight. The Hawkers were then able to go home – and another reception.

As they drove up the street, all the neighbours were out, and a firework setpiece exploded into "Welcome Home."

There was little sleep and little peace. The next morning, at 10.30, Hawker and Grieve had to be at Buckingham Palace to meet the King.

They were invested with the Air Force Cross. In Hawker's case, it was the first time it had been awarded to a civilian. Then the Queen and Prince Albert joined the King to listen to Hawker and Grieve describe their flight.

After that, it was time to move to the Savoy Hotel for a lunch given by the *Daily Mail*. There was a wire from Australia's Prime Minister who said he, "greatly regrets that fate denies me the opportunity of paying my tribute to one of Australia's most noble sons and his estimable navigator."

Northcliffe did not attend because he was about to have an operation. He sent a message, read to the assemblage: "War has shown us that the courage of the sister nations of Australia, Canada, South Africa and Newfoundland is every whit equal to that of the small motherland from which they sprung. The partnership of Hawker the Australian flyer and Mackenzie-Grieve of the Royal Navy has proved what can be achieved by the unity of members of one British Commonwealth.

"The lessons that they have learned will help forward the time when a direct Atlantic flight will be almost as easy as, and even more useful than, that across the English Channel.

"As remarkable as the exploits of our two heroes is the immutable confidence in Divine Providence of Muriel Hawker, who not for one instant faltered in her absolute belief that her husband would be restored to her.

"Were I present I should like to raise a glass in congratulation of our American friends on their careful and characteristic preparations for their fine record-breaking flight to the Azores and Lisbon. They have still left to us the problem of a direct flight from America to Europe.

"Personally, I have no doubt but that, with the lessons and experience gained by Hawker and Mackenzie-Grieve, a direct flight will be soon accomplished, and that by a British aeroplane with a British motor, manned by Britons."

Major-General Seely, the under-secretary for air, awarded the consolation cheque of £5,000 which Northcliffe had now decided to give the flyers. Then it was the turn of the flyers.

Hawker spoke briefly, but it wasn't brief enough. For in his speech was the only sour note. He deprecated the Americans' effort, saying that if you put a ship every fifty miles, it only showed a lack of faith in your motor or your machine.

The three hundred prominent guests, all British, received the words in stunned silence. This was bad form, unsporting. The British never criticized their competitors. Especially the Yanks. They might think that they had overdone it a bit, with all their money, but one didn't say those things. Unless one was a "colonial," a bit brusque, from Down Under.

But Hawker made amends. A few days later he said that he didn't intend any criticism of the Americans, to whom he wished the best of luck; he had simply been attacking the British government for not supporting the British flyers more.

That was all right, of course; everybody attacked the government, and soon Hawker was back in everybody's good books.

When the flight was being planned, Hawker and Grieve had agreed that if they won the *Daily Mail* prize, Hawker would get 70 per cent of it, Grieve 30 per cent. Now that it was a £5,000 consolation prize, however, Hawker decided that Grieve should get half of it.

Grieve, the unknown, had been somewhat overshadowed by Hawker, the popular hero. But on the afternoon of the May day which had started with investiture by the King, Lieutenant-Commander Kenneth Mackenzie-Grieve, alone, stood in the limelight of the little Hampshire village of Droxford, which was his home.

He went down by train. The villagers knew he would – so the booking office on the little platform was covered with flags and flowers for his arrival.

The schoolchildren were lined up to sing a special song for the day. Written by a thirteen-year-old, Annie Merritt, it was sung to the tune of "It Is The Navy, The British Navy," and the refrain went:

> "It was the airmen, the British airmen
> Who for England's glory tried
> To Fly right across the Atlantic Ocean
> And win for England pride."

Canon Stephenson, the local clergyman, made a short speech in the station yard; and Grieve thanked Droxford for its welcome. There was a service at the parish church where, outside, Sir Graham Bower (the best little Droxford could do in the way of a squire) stood on a chair to make a speech. It was Droxford's official welcome, and it was followed by thanks to God for Mackenzie-Grieve's safe deliverance. Then, of course, there was a call for three cheers and, almost as an afterthought, another three cheers for Mr. and Mrs. Hawker.

There were more cheers for Hawker a couple of days later. It was planned that on the Saturday Hendon would honour Hawker and Grieve. However, some work was expected of Harry. Specifically, he was asked to do a few stunts.

Grieve feigned illness and didn't attend. But the Hawkers did, in style. Harry and his wife flew over from Brooklands in his own plane. Muriel climbed out of the cockpit wearing a pink summery dress and a picture hat.

The great crowd loved it. The Hawkers were driven up and down the field to cheers, then there was an auction, to sell the privilege of flying as a passenger with Hawker. The first chance went for sixty guineas; forty guineas was paid to go on the second and third flights.

It was typical of the exaggeration which found expression everywhere that week of Hawker's return. It wasn't only in England either.

Editorialists had a heyday.

The London *Times* said, "There is more romance in this flight of Hawker's, failure and apparently disaster though it has been, than in the voyages of the Argonauts and in all the wanderings of Ulysses."

The New York *Globe* wasn't to be outdone: "Hawker and Mackenzie-Grieve have done better than make a sober addition to the science of flying – they have given a lesson in the art of living and dying ... they have not only glorified a country, they have enriched mankind."

Canada's Prime Minister Sir Robert Borden called the flight a "magnificent gallant attempt." Lieutenant-Colonel Barker, the Canadian V.C. winner, congratulated his friend Hawker "on his fine effort and failure, which is glorious."

Heady stuff, but Hawker would have better appreciated the honest opinions of other flyers. Like Towers, who said, "Even if he had arrived in Ireland, it would only have proved he was a great flyer with wonderful luck."

And there were thousands of poems, nearly all bad.

The august New York *Times* had Elizabeth Newport Hepburn writing "To The Brave." It began:

"Across the world the wireless flashes fast
They're found, our bold adventurers, at last ..."

This was followed by a male contribution. It was called, "Danish Mary."

" 'Twas Danish Mary picked them up
Out of the air and sea;
A shoddy, trudging lollypup
A-traipsing slatternly.
The cry rang north, the cry rang south
'The vanished – where are they?'
But Danish Mary shut her mouth
And shuffled on her way."

And the poem shuffled along itself stanza after stanza.

CHAPTER 27
First Across

On the day that Hawker took off from St. John's, "Putty" Read and the Americans' Nancy Four had been weatherbound at Horta in the Azores. It was not until two days later, May 20, that the Four was able to leave and fly the 190 miles to Ponta Delgada, on the larger island of the Azores, Sao Miguel. Now the Four was the only hope America had of making the first aerial trans-Atlantic crossing.

With all the Nancy crews reunited in the Azores, there was relief but, almost instantly, tension. John Towers, the Commander of all the Nancies, was pleased with the success of Read. But he was haggard, weary, from his own ordeal.

That evening of reunion, there was a large formal dinner. Towers may have known, as the toasts were being drunk, that the spotlight of the operation was going to be moved onto Read.

Towers wrote later for *Everybody's* magazine that he expected to fly on himself to Lisbon, with Read. He had historical precedent for such a belief. It had always been the custom of the American Navy that a commander-in-chief of a fleet, no matter how small its numbers, had the right to transfer his flag to another ship if his own was disabled.

But Josephus Daniels, Secretary of the Navy, thought otherwise. The arrival of Read's Nancy Four at Horta had brought out the largest type in American newspapers since the armistice. And Daniels had been a publisher. He thrived on publicity, and felt the U.S. Navy would too.

Now the American newsmen and, through them, the American public, had taken Read to their collective hearts. Daniels thought Read was too good an asset to drop. He wanted him to complete the flight as commander. It would not only add to the prestige of the U.S. Navy, it would help recruiting, and aid the cabinet minister in his demands to Congress for continued big budgets for men and material.

Towers was informed he would not take over command of the Nancy Four. He was bitterly disappointed. His orders, signed by Franklin Delano Roosevelt, had specifically noted that, as commander of the NC Division One, his "status was the same as the commander of sea-going ships of the Navy."

Now Towers saw his own plane, the Nancy Three, being taken apart for carriage back to the United States aboard the *Melville,* and he learned that he and all the crews of the One and Three would proceed to Lisbon aboard the destroyer *Stockton.*

Read and the Nancy Four expected to leave Ponta Delgada for Lisbon the day after arrival, but again the weather was against them.

It remained that way for some days so that when Towers arrived in Lisbon by ship and transferred to the cruiser *Rochester,* he learned that he had not only lost the glory, but also his bet with the captain of the *Aroostook.* The *Aroostook* had already reached Plymouth from Trepassey before any of the planes.

On Monday, May 26, the cloud over the Azores disappeared. By the evening, a meteorologist, Lieutenant Anderson, was predicting good weather on the morrow.

Read's crew members wakened early, but again there was engine trouble and two hours were lost while a carburettor was changed. At 10.18 local time on May 27, Nancy Four was again airborne, and by 11.00 a.m., Read had Herbert Rodd send Admiral Jackson aboard the *Melville* at Ponta Delgada a message: "We seem to be on our way. Thanks for your hospitality."

The Four overflew the destroyers *Sampson* and *Dupont,* missed *Cassin,* spotted the *Wilkes* on Station 4. Then it ran into squalls and didn't see another of the marker ships until it flew above *Wadsworth* on Station 9. After that, there were sunshine and light winds all the way. The lighthouse on Cabo da Roca, the westernmost point of Europe, came into view. Read looked at it for some minutes. He said he knew that at that moment, "no matter what happened – even if we crashed on landing – the Trans-Atlantic flight, the first one in the history of the world, was an accomplished fact."

He went down to his little navigational table to write his reports of the flight for Towers and the Navy Department.

Thousands stood at the Lisbon waterfront to watch the landing. At about 11.30 that morning, the *Rochester's* whistle and siren had been sounded repeatedly. This was a pre-arranged signal, publicized in the Lisbon press, to indicate that the Four had left the Azores.

The U.S. Navy, egged on by Daniels, was determined to get every mile of publicity out of the Four's crossing. A signalling system was devised to keep the Lisbon people informed of the plane's progress.

The heart of Lisbon is the large Black Horse Square, beside its historic river, the Tagus, from which Portuguese explorers had sailed to new worlds and on which flyers from the New World would now land.

On the seawall beside this square, sailors had erected blackboards. As messages were received in the radio shack of the *Rochester,* they were transferred by semaphore flags to the seawall. Thus, the Lisbon populace was informed of how the aircraft was proceeding.

At five minutes past eight that evening, the *Rochester* blew her whistle again. This time it was joined by all the whistles and sirens of all the ships in the harbour. The quays were all dressed with flags. The sun was going down blazingly. The crowds were excited. There was a U.S. Navy artist on hand to record all this. So was well-known reporter Walter Duranty for the New York *Times;* it reminded him of the happy ending of a Broadway musical.

The destroyer *Shawmut's* searchlight went on in the gathering dusk as the Nancy Four was spotted. The plane swung into the line of the wind.

Read, somewhat uncharacteristically, let his pilots make a few flourishes with the plane, rather like the flicks of the toreador's cape. Then it was down to business, and the Four flew straight up the Tagus River at a height of 1,500 feet, to the Tower of Belem from whence Vasco da Gama set sail. Then the plane began its letdown. At 9.01 it landed. As it touched the water, the *Rochester* gave a twenty-one gun salute (usually reserved for heads of state) and a Portuguese warship followed with an equal number.

No sooner was the flying boat moored to a buoy than it was surrounded by small craft. Read boarded the *Rochester.* Towers stepped forward and shook his hand. Just as he was about to shake Stone's, the ship's band struck up the Star Spangled Banner, all came to attention, officers saluted, a searchlight was very ceremoniously trained on the Nancy. As Duranty said, "it made a wonderful picture."

Portugal's ministers of foreign affairs and marine then approached, congratulated Read, and decorated him with the ancient Order of the Tower and Sword, a decoration subsequently given to every member of the crews of the three Nancies.

The cruiser's radio room was an even busier place than the quarter deck. There were messages for Read from President Wilson and Secretary Daniels, who, after referring to "Navy genius," said "now there will be no stopping the Navy." It didn't matter in the excitement that the Four's flying time from Rockaway to Lisbon had been forty-two hours and forty-three minutes and that it had been nineteen days since a start had been made.

Had the Nancy Four won the first air race across the Atlantic? As far as the American press, and most of the public, was concerned, there was no doubt about it.

The U.S. Navy had never said it was making a non-stop flight. Now a plane had reached the European mainland. The *New York Times* pulled out all the stops. Its headline, across page one, read:

NC-4 Wins First Ocean Flight For America
9½ Hours From Ponta Delgada To Lisbon

The nationalistic rivalry over the first plane crossing of the Atlantic was epitomized in the press. The Americans got a few half hidden inches of type in the *Daily Mail,* not much more in the London *Times.* At the same time, column after column in those English papers was devoted to Hawker, the hero who had flown only half-way.

The reverse was also true. American newspapers went wild over the naval flyers; some hardly mentioned that there were English flyers in Newfoundland.

It was a little difficult to know whether Josephus Daniels, the Secretary of the Navy, was taking his cue from the newspapers, or *vice-versa,* by the time Read had landed at Lisbon. The Washington *Evening Star* bawled from the rooftops for everybody when it said in an editorial: "American ability, American ingenuity, American thoroughness, American nerve have again come into their own. Epitomizing these inherent qualities of the American Navy, Lieutenant Commander Albert Cushing Read of Washington, D.C. has blazed an air trail from the new world to the old, adding honour to his country, prestige to his service and fame to his name."

Two more days of functions followed the Four's arrival in Lisbon. Read and his crew met the President of Portugal, received medals from the Lisbon city council, were guests at a banquet given by the Portuguese Navy, toured the city.

Towers, Bellinger, and their crews slipped away, almost unnoticed, on the *Rochester,* for Britain. On May 30 at 6.29 a.m. it was Read's turn. With Hinton at the controls, and the usual salutation of bells and whistles, the Four lifted off from the Tagus River. The ship turned round, flew low over the river to simulate landing conditions for those photographers who, three nights before, had not been able to get "shots." Then it left on the flight to Plymouth, England.

There were five U.S. warships between Cabo da Roca and Cape Finisterre, and another six across the Bay of Biscay. Elmer Stone, who did much of the piloting, said it was a "joyride" all the way, and that all the crew "felt like fighting cocks." But there were problems. There was a leak in a water jacket, noticed shortly after the first ship, the *Connor,* had been overflown, and Read decided to land.

The plane was brought down in the estuary of the Mondego River, which was full of sandbars, and it went aground. With all hands running back and forth on the lower wing to rock the plane, it was refloated.

The leak was quickly repaired as the plane floated, an unexpected apparition, before hundreds of citizens of the small town of Figueira da Foz. From the port captain, by means of sketchy French and gestures, Read learned that high tide wouldn't be for another five hours. So Rodd was instructed to ask the destroyers for a port to the north where the Four might land and stay overnight.

At half past one that afternoon, the plane took off, and ninety minutes later it was over the destroyer *Yarnell,* which informed Read that Ferrol, in northern Spain, would be the best place for the night. Two other ships, the *Tarbell* and *Harding* signalled that they were leaving their stations to steam there.

The Spanish were pleased the Americans could drop in. The captain of the Ferrol port and the local British consul both came aboard the *Harding* to pay their respects, as did all the city's dignitaries. But there were no official functions, and Read's crew was able to get a night's sleep.

The next morning the weather reports weren't too encouraging. Locally, there was sunshine, but there were unfavourable forecasts. Read decided to take a chance. There was another takeoff around 6.30.

Some in the Nancy didn't agree with Elmer Stone's assessment of this leg. For most of the way the weather was wretched. Only two of the six destroyers were sighted. But, by Brest, the skies were brightening. The pilots decided to fly the plane low over the French port for a couple of orbits so the "doughboys" there, awaiting shipment home, could see them.

"The Great Yankee Triumph," as one American newspaper had already called it, was near an end.

Three British flying boats escorted the Four across the Channel into Plymouth.

The Nancy came over Plymouth, circled Drake's Island, and hit the water at 2.30 p.m., with the British planes, in formation, 500 yards behind.

It was Lisbon all over again. Ships sounded their sirens. Bells rang. Shore crowds cheered. Aboard the *Rochester,* Read and his men were greeted by Rear Admiral Plunkett, the U.S. flag officer in charge of the entire trans-Atlantic operation; the Commander-in-Chief of the Royal Navy's nearby Devonport dockyard; a Colonel Shepherd of the Royal Air Force who represented the British Air Ministry, the mayor and corporation of the city of Plymouth, and, again, the crews of the One and Three.

An hour later, Read was ashore at the Barbican, from which the Pilgrim Fathers had originally set sail. There, crowds broke through on the procession to the Grand Hotel, where there was to be an official reception. Another crowd besieged the hotel itself.

The pattern was the same the following day when a train brought Read's crew into London's Paddington Station.

Harry and Muriel Hawker had arrived a little earlier in his car to welcome the adversaries. He was given a great welcome by the crowd and was asked to make a speech. Feeling it was the Americans' day, he stood up and shouted, "You're wasting your energy, and you'll want it presently. Save it up and really do it properly. Make yourselves hoarse so that you can't talk for two or three days." Muriel carried a small American flag.

When the train drew in, the Nancy crew was met by Admiral Robinson of the U.S. Navy, others from his London staff, a guard of marines. But again protocol didn't stand much chance. Read was grabbed by a number of American troops, lifted onto their shoulders, and carried out of the station to Hawker's car. It was Hawker who drove Read to the Royal Aero Club for yet another reception.

"We are safely across the pond. The job is finished," "Putty" Read had said. But the "job" of receptions was almost as arduous.

After the Royal Aero Club's welcome, they were taken to Hendon for a display of aerobatics. Then they were sent to Paris to meet President Wilson, Prime Minister David Lloyd George, Georges Clemenceau–the "tiger" of France, and Italy's Prime Minister Orlando.

Back in London there was lunch at the House of Commons.

Then Towers, Read, and other officers of the Four's crew were given the Air Force Cross. There were more luncheons, and then a week's leave in Paris, before they could go home.

CHAPTER 28

"Lucky if we get a Languid Hand"

During that third week of May, Newfoundlanders were too concerned over Hawker and Grieve, agitated by the crash of the Raymor, and interested in the progress of the Americans, to give much time to Alcock and Brown.

There were exceptions. Joey Smallwood, rushing off for a first chat, found Jack Alcock big, rosy-cheeked, easy to talk to; he saw Brown as smaller in stature, but about the same kind of man in temperament – a misjudgement which may have shown how brief was the interview.

Thomas Dalton worked for Reid's Newfoundland Railway, at the offices of the St. John's railway station, which served as an unofficial public relations and information sorting centre for the flyers. Mr. Dalton remembered Jack Alcock and Teddy Brown for their casualness, their courtesy and general pleasant attitude.

A taxi driver named Harry Burgess remembered them. There were no taxi companies, only liveries with horse cabs. These were hardly suitable for touring the rugged Newfoundland roads outside St. John's, looking for a patch to take off a plane. However, there was one city garage that would rent out a car and it was Burgess' job to drive it. So he drove them down to Ferryland in the southeast corner of the island, toward Torbay, and to the west of St. John's in search of an airstrip. At the start, Alcock joked about the countryside, although Brown was his usual sobersides. After a day or so, there were few smiles from either man. Not only was level ground almost non-existent, but the canny Newfies who had some, found it had become an eminently marketable asset.

Raynham had offered the use of his Quidi Vidi site for Alcock's Vimy plane which was still crated and somewhere at sea. In exchange, Alcock arranged that some of his Vickers' Vimy ground crew already in St. John's should help with repairs to the rival Raymor. But the arrangement was a stopgap. Alcock's Vimy would be hauled by those ponderous slovens to Quidi Vidi for assembly and for a test flight. But the field was too short for the start of a twin-engine plane weighing 12,000 pounds. Another field had to be found.

Alcock and Brown became angry at the inflationary prices. Out at Mount Pearl, a rent of $2,000 was being demanded for one field – but only to June 15, after which it would cost an additional $200 a day. A meadow at Harbour Grace was offered for $30,000. This was on an island of rock where often an acre of land could be bought for 35 cents.

Jack Alcock was thoroughly fed up when Charles Lester, the man who owned the slovens, finally came to the rescue. He provided a combination potato field and grazing pasture about a quarter mile square. It was rolled flat by thirty men.

If the field was a problem, the weather and the plane weren't. The Vimy was easily unloaded, on May 25, as easily moved to Quidi Vidi.

The fuselage was in a crate fifty feet long, so a couple of bridge parapets and some fencing had to be removed to get it out to the hangar at Quidi Vidi. The fuselage was too large to be assembled in the hangar. Only canvas screens could be put up as any form of weather protection as the thirteen men of the Vickers' crew worked ten to twelve hours a day, often in cold, raw weather, to put the plane together. But at least there weren't the blizzards that the Hawker or Raynham crews had experienced.

The engines were mounted four days after the ship docked, the wings were in place a day later. Every day the work went on steadily while Alcock and Brown continued their search.

Alcock occasionally saw his rival, Admiral Mark Kerr when he came in from the Handley Page base at Harbour Grace to stay or have a meal at the Crosbie Hotel. Once, he remarked on the coincidence that they each had a type of plane which was being prepared, when the armistice interceded, to bomb Berlin.

On June 9 the Vimy was ready for its first test flight. It only had to be "gassed." The first of twenty-three large steel gasoline drums was opened. The contents were contaminated by a rubber compound, which served as a lining for the drums, but dissolved in the gasoline. A second drum was opened; same thing. And a third – all of the drums had suffered the same fate. Again Raynham was the Samaritan, loaning some of his own aviation fuel. The Vimy took off.

It was almost too easy. The plane lifted smoothly, flew over Signal Hill, turned over Conception Bay, back across the city, banked above the Atlantic Ocean, returned toward the coast at Cape Spear and headed for Lester's Field. The landing was as simple as the takeoff. The flight had been observed by several thousand people. The interest in Atlantic flying had waned a little as the papers told of the complexities of Versailles, and of "bolshie" riots in Canadian cities. Now it was renewed.

Hawker had been rescued, Read and the Nancy Four had crossed the Atlantic. But nobody yet had flown to England in one hop. That's what it was all about – at least that's the way the St. Johnsmen felt.

In the evenings, at the Cochrane Hotel, Alcock and Brown shared their own feelings about the flight. Jack Alcock admitted to Brown that "their (Englishmen's) hands are so blistered clapping Harry Hawker, that we'll be lucky to get a languid hand."

A few days earlier, Brown had written to Kathleen on paper with the letterhead of the Cochrane Hotel. It was hardly the missive of a star-crossed lover. This is the letter, *in toto:*

> "Dear Miss Kennedy,
> Just a line by aerial mail as a souvenir of the flight – which should take place at an early date now. Everything has gone well so far, with the exception of a little trouble with the wireless.
> Kindest regards to Major Kennedy and Eileen.
>
> > Sincerely,
> > Teddy."

Although it was June, the Newfoundland weather had reverted to its usual inclemency. Even a visit to the plane, and a blessing, by His Grace Archbishop Roche hadn't helped. After the plane had been landed at Lester's Field on June 9, it clouded over, rained, and then, for nearly forty-eight hours, the wind on this exposed height was at near-gale force. The Vimy was anchored with extra ropes. Its ground crew, in watches, looked over it day and night.

Still, each morning Agnes Dooley presented the pilot and navigator with new sandwiches and flasks of coffee for the flight. She did so on Friday, June 13, although there was a strong wind, heavy rain clouds, white-caps in the harbour. It was a dismal prospect, unrelieved by weather forecasts. The wind would continue at strength all day and likely through the next, they said.

There was nothing much to do. Harry Couch, the rigger, found a discarded shoe from one of Lester's horses and tacked it under Alcock's seat for luck. He knew the pilot was superstitious. He had heard about the rabbit's foot and coffee flask Alcock always carried, the Lucky Jim and Twinkletoes mascots that Kathleen Kennedy had given the flyers before they left England.

Although the wind was still high, it was decided to fuel the Vimy. So through Friday afternoon the gasoline was pumped by hoses, filtered through chamois, into tanks behind the cockpit. Alcock watched carefully; he did not want a speck of dirt to end his flight.

As the job was nearly finished, Bob Dicker looked at the wheel on one side of the plane, and noticed it was no longer straight. A shock absorber had gone. All the fuel had to be removed. The shock was taken off and a stronger one installed. Then, once again, 865 gallons of gasoline, forty gallons of oil, six gallons of water had to be fed to the plane.

The storm continued through the evening, but Alcock and Brown didn't know this because they had gone to bed early.

The weather change was so dramatic that it woke Jack Alcock shortly before 3.00 a.m. on June 14. He looked out of his window over the roofs of St. John's. There were no clouds, only a gentle breeze. After the roar of the wind of the past couple of days, the silence took a little getting used to. He woke Brown, announced his intentions. By 3.30 a.m. they had left the Cochrane. The sandwiches and hot flasks were sent out to Lester's Field.

It was still dark, but the ground crew, Lieutenant Clements, the weather expert, and Major Partridge were all gathered around the plane. Clements was more optimistic. Reports being received from ships showed that the conditions might be reasonable.

But the takeoff didn't take place until Saturday afternoon. By then, many in St. John's knew it would happen that day; some had made their way to the airfield.

The newsmen were there. So were others, to wish them luck – the Right Honourable Michael Cashin, the new Prime Minister of Newfoundland, Mayor Gosling of St. John's, other cabinet ministers, friends who had helped the flyers.

About noon, Jack Alcock pulled a flying suit over his ill-fitting blue civvy suit, Brown put his over an airforce uniform. Now the reporters were ready for the last words. Lowell Thomas was to report that Brown said, "Our objective is Ireland, we shall aim for the centre of the target." Another reporter wrote that Alcock blithely quipped, "We shall hang our hat on the aerial of the Clifden wireless station as we go by."

A bag of mail carrying special stamps was put aboard. It included a rare letter from Alcock to his parents which read: "This letter I am sending by the first trans-Atlantic airpost, which I am going to carry."

The aviators' personal belongings for the flight ran to toilet kits. In addition there was a bottle of whiskey, given by a Dr. Campbell, some bottles of ale, flasks of malted milk, Oxo, coffee, some chocolate bars, and the sandwiches.

The wind had not only slackened. It had changed direction. This meant that the plane had to be moved from one end of the field to the other.

Couch, the rigger, said this was done with the help of thirty "locals."

The fully loaded aircraft weighed about six tons so that it could be moved only four or five yards at a time. The new takeoff direction, into wind, had another disadvantage; the length of run was cut from 600 to 400 yards.

So "we all stood in front of the wings, holding the plane back," said Couch. "Alcock revved up the engines to full power. Then, on a signal, we all sat down on the ground, and the plane shot forward."

But not upward. The *Daily Mail* man at the scene wrote "the engines roared out and immediately the machine moved forward. One hundred, two hundred, three hundred yards and the machine still moved forward, but showing not the least desire to rise."

There were many that day who thought for a moment that the same fate would befall Alcock as Raynham.

Alcock's plane, nearly at the end of the roughly levelled stretch, skimmed above a rock. Then it flew over a hollow, partially out of sight of the spectators. Many thought it had crashed. But when it came into view again it was a little higher and waddling upward. By the time it crossed the coast it was 200 feet high. Brown turned to Alcock to say "Hey, Jack, I'm going to send St. John's a few words of greeting."

"Tell them we shall be across in sixteen hours if this wind keeps us in his lap," Alcock suggested. But as Brown sent out the Vimy's call letter, the tell-tale spark of the radio transmitter grew dimmer. Soon there was no flashing blue light at all. The generator propeller for the set had somehow been carried away or damaged on takeoff. Brown said that he at once told Alcock of this condition. Alcock later said that if he had known they were without radio while still near St. John's he would have turned back.

Anyway, ships on the Atlantic knew they had started. As soon as they were in the air, messages were sent asking all shipping to keep a watch for them.

CHAPTER 29
Nose down in a bog

Alcock's Vimy took off from Newfoundland before two o'clock. It was already after Saturday tea time in England. It was the beginning of what Alcock was to describe as a "terrible trip."

After throttling back, the pair were able to shout to each other and still be heard above the engines as the Vimy climbed gradually upward for half an hour. Brown was able to use his navigational instruments to advantage.

Then they were in cold fog, and for an hour could hardly see their wingtips. Alcock held the controls tightly, keeping the plane steady to the compass needle reading which Brown had set. Ireland is a big island. The "centre of it," as a bullseye, allows for a little leeway, but only a degree or two. They didn't even have enough fuel to reach Scandinavia.

They had flown for two hours when the first incident occurred to help make it a "terrible trip." An exhaust pipe, with its silencer, on one of the engines, burned away. This meant that the roar of the engine was intensified. Speech became an impossibility; they had to start writing notes to each other. The heat of the open exhaust was also a fire danger.

After four hours, Brown was able to see the sun long enough to get a "fix." It showed that his mathematical skill – his "dead reckoning" – had placed him on the chart only a few miles from the true position, now confirmed by the sun and his sextant.

Within minutes cloud had surrounded them again.

Soon, it was night, colder – and it was uncomfortable, because the heating in their suits had failed. Their legs were getting cramps.

But there were compensations. As Sunday (on Greenwich Mean Time) began, Brown estimated they were almost half-way across, travelling at 120 miles per hour, helped by a backing wind of 30 m.p.h.

The comfort from these statistics didn't last long. They were already dead tired, slightly frostbitten, their hearing affected, their nerve ends frayed. And, as the first streaks of grey dawn appeared, they saw before them that nightmare of early flying, towering cumulo-nimbus cloud which could toss a light plane around like a feather, even destroy it.

Up, up, seemingly endless, went the wall of cloud. There was no way the Vimy could climb over it. And in the poor light there was no knowing how far it extended downward. In any case, Alcock decided it would be madness to fly under it.

He was hardly master of his decisions. In an instant, the plane was inside the cloud. It was black as night again. Hail beat against the fabric, the engines, the exposed upper torsos of the flyers. The plane was lifted mercilessly and cast down. Brown thought that Alcock looped the loop in this cloud. It would have been unlikely, if not impossible. But neither flyer, in the first seconds of the nightmare, would have had control over the plane, or even their own senses. The situation was worsened by ice, weighing down the wings and covering the airspeed indicator. There was no horizon, and no way to tell the pilot which side was up. If Alcock, in those moments, had pulled the controls hard the wrong way, it could have meant disaster.

Seconds later, air rushing against their faces told the flyers they were descending fast.

They were in fact in a steep, spiral dive.

The plane plummetted seaward, corkscrew fashion. The flyers saw nothing.

Then, suddenly, the plane broke out of the base of the cloud into dim daylight, almost upside down. The sea was only a hundred feet away.

By some miracle, Alcock turned the aircraft right side up, instantly pushed the throttle forward, and started to climb away from the sea.

It was a miracle, or it was luck, or it was great piloting.

Whatever it was, it affected both men.

Alcock said it was the nearest he ever came to death in his flying career.

For Brown, the imprint was more lasting. He never flew again in a plane as a crew member. The dangers of the whole flight scarred him, but the near-fatal spin had the most telling effect.

After falling nearly 4,000 feet, Alcock patiently took the Vimy back up to 6,500 feet. Like all airmen then and thereafter he sought the safety of space.

As the plane ascended, the pilot and navigator took swigs of various drinks to fortify their spirits, and they ate their sandwiches. Then more "thunderhead" clouds were ahead.

Alcock, whatever he did, wasn't going to enter such a cloud again. He decided to go over it.

The plane went steadily upward, through rain, then snow, then freezing rain. The Vimy's ailerons began to freeze up and clog so that control became difficult. And, as the wings and fuselage became more coated with ice, there was danger that the Vimy would stall and go into another dive.

Instruments on the engine casings were also ice-covered; they could not be read. Worse, the air intakes for the engines were being blocked.

Both flyers realized how serious this was, but it was Brown who took action. Thus was born one of the great epic stories of flight.

Brown, the cripple, clambered out of the cockpit, hauled himself up gingerly on to the slippery wing which was coated with ice, made his way out in semi-darkness, holding on to the struts while the plane was a mile above the Atlantic.

Then, with the slipstream rushing past him, balancing on a plane moving at around 100 miles per hour, in somewhat bumpy conditions, Brown used a knife to hack away the ice.

Next, he crawled back along the wing, got into the cockpit, climbed over Alcock, hoisted himself out again on to the other wing, and walked along it so he could hack off the ice from the other air intake, an operation which meant hanging on to a strut with one hand yet managing to keep balance.

None of this is shown in the gothic penmanship of Brown's logbook. He covers the entire trip in two facing pages and the writing looks as though it were done in a club, between tea and dinner, at a desk, quietly.

The plane was still heavy with ice but, according to Brown's navigation, Ireland should be just ahead. Alcock decided he could go lower to get thawing air. However, the Vimy hadn't been descending long before the engines began to stutter because of the ice still blocking the intakes.

So Alcock decided to switch off the engines and glide through the cloud. They broke into the open, with the engines restarted, about 500 feet above the sea. They began to peer forward, searching for the coast.

About 8.15 a.m. they spotted two dots in the sea ahead . . . and then a mass behind.

A few more minutes and the specks became identifiable as islands.

Beyond them were the low mountains of the mainland.

A few seconds more and Brown recognized the islands as Eashol and Turbot, the mountains as belonging to Connemara.

And by now they could see a town. It was Clifden.

At 8.25 they crossed over the coast.

There was a hurried exchange of notes. Should they go on to England?

There was no doubt about the answer. Both were tired, shaken by their experiences. They had flown the Atlantic; they had won the prize; they were the first to fly the ocean non-stop.

All they had to do was land. Alcock took the plane round the radio masts at Clifden. Flares were dropped.

Alcock had spotted a level field, brilliantly paddy green. It looked ideal. Alcock had to bring the plane down in a long gliding approach, clear a stone wall, and land. He and Brown carried out the proper drill, and the plane came in, crossed the wall safely. But then, with the undercarriage wheels nearly touching, both men realized it was not the pasture they had thought, but tussocks interspersed by water–that most Irish of terrains – a bog.

The Vimy slowed; its wheels skimmed tufts, splashed into water, and were suddenly braked by mud. Rapidly the plane was brought to a standstill, tilted, and ended up, grotesquely, nose-down, in peat.

Neither flyer was hurt. But they could have wished for a less ignominious ending. For already they must have known their position would be photographed, sketched, painted, written about, described for posterity.

During sixteen hours they had been alone, their fate unknown, without a link with the rest of mankind. Now they were victors and not alone.

People were coming, running, tumbling, splashing, toward them.

CHAPTER 30
Controversial Walk

Anyone who visits London's Science Museum can see the Vimy in which Alcock and Brown became the first men to cross the Atlantic nonstop, the endeavour which prompted another flyer to say, on arrival in Paris nearly eight years later, "My name is Lindbergh. I have come from America. Alcock and Brown showed me the way."

Inside the Science Museum is not the place to appreciate hardships. There, no rain beats down into the cockpit. There is no howl of wind, no cold, no noise, no bumps, no darkness, no mystery, no fear.

But it is worth standing beside that cockpit to look at the old fashioned brass switches, the dials (the biggest of which is a clock), the polished woodwork. Look carefully at the controls. There is no automatic pilot, as in today's aircraft. That steering column had to be held rigidly by Alcock for sixteen hours. Members of Britain's Vintage Aircraft Association, which flew a replica to mark the fiftieth anniversary of the flight, carried out many tests. One showed that what Alcock did with the control column was equivalent to holding a fifty-pound weight in his arms for two-thirds of a day.

Now look at the two engines set a few feet from the heads of the pilot and navigator, then imagine the noise from them. A motorcyclist can sense this most easily: he knows that, after an hour, he can be numbed by noise when travelling at high speed. Alcock and Brown heard engine drone for sixteen hours. No wonder that, for minutes after landing, they couldn't hear.

Finally, regard the wire elbow guards on either side of the cockpit, designed to prevent the flyers extending their arms, to prevent them from being cut off by the whirling propellers. These are an important clue to the resolution of a controversy: did Brown really crawl out along the wings?

Some accounts over the years, repeating the legend into the seventies, had Brown do it, not once, but six times.

It was glorious, heroic stuff.

But the Vintage Aircraft Association made a test to determine whether it was possible. One of its members, at Brooklands (that home of so many scientific advances) tried to stand on the wing of a rebuilt Vimy when the engines were throttled forward. And he couldn't do it, for more than a few seconds, even if he held on to the spars with both hands. This was when the plane was on the ground, by day, not in half-darkness. It was on a wing that was dry, not covered in ice; when the plane was level, not climbing.

And Brown, so the story goes, didn't even do it that way. He would have had to climb up over that elbow guard, the one you can see in the Science Museum. Yet the guard was built as part of the plane because the propeller came within two inches of it and there was no way that anyone, with unsure footing, hampered by ice, could climb over it without being seriously injured, possibly decapitated.

How did the story get started?

No one can tell precisely. Some suggest it was Alcock, trying to share the glory with his navigator. Others believe it was due to the creativity of reporters.

However, it began, the story grew, was embroidered, became schoolboy legend and, finally, an integral part of every description of the first trans-Atlantic flight. It is so much part of the flight that, when the Vintage Air-craft Association tested the real possibilities of such a feat, it made them quietly, with no publicity. Britain doesn't like doubts thrown at its heroes.

No matter how remote the idea of Brown's wing-walk may be, there are many who stick with the theory, including the younger brother of Jack Alcock. He is Captain E.S.J. Alcock, a commercial pilot, and the only doubt he will concede is that perhaps Brown had a rope tied around him.

It really doesn't matter; whatever did happen in those storms above the Atlantic, the flight certainly was not as easy as it sounded in the headline in the New York Herald:

Two British Flyers Make 1,900 Mile Dash
Across Atlantic To Ireland In 16 Hours;
Alcock And Brown Win $50,000 Prize

CHAPTER 31
Knights of the Air

Many claimed they were the first to offer the hand of welcome that Sunday morning when Alcock and Brown dropped down in Ireland.

Tom Gallivan was at the Clifden station that day with five others. Only when the noise of a plane became more persistent, overhead, did he go out from the station to see one dropping flares. He knew it must be Alcock and Brown, safely across.

The Vimy landed only a couple of hundred yards from where he had been standing. He was beside the plane as Alcock climbed down.

"We've made it," Alcock said, and laughed. The pilot's blue civvy suit surprised the radioman, as did six cigarettes, unwrapped, sticking from its pocket. "I never had time to smoke them," Alcock explained.

Frederick Teague, working with Gallivan, claimed he sent the first message giving the news that the pair had crossed the Atlantic.

The Right Reverend Monsignor MacAlpine was one of the first to reach the flyers with congratulations – another was Edward King, chairman of the local district council.

One newspaper claimed an Australian soldier, on his honeymoon, looked out a small hotel window, and was the first to see the Vimy.

Details differed. A small boy was the first to reach the plane in Derrygimia Bog, said another reporter, and Alcock threw him something from the cockpit, shouting, "Here, have an orange from America." And the man for the Manchester *Guardian,* reported that Alcock said that he was the first man ever able to say "yesterday I was in America."

"We looped the loop, I do believe," Alcock was quoted next day in the *Daily Mail,* and "we did some very comic stunts for we had no sense of horizon."

There was conflict in these accounts. At one stage, Alcock is reported to have said that an hour and a half before landing, they had no idea where they were. Then, in praising Brown, he said (hardly waiting a moment to catch his breath), "but we believed we were at Galway or thereabouts."

Brown, laconic, managed to send a message to Kathleen. It read:

LANDED CLIFDEN, IRELAND SAFELY THIS MORNING. WILL BE WITH YOU VERY SOON.

TEDDY

After breakfast, Brown went to bed, but could not sleep.

Clifden was besieged by newspapermen. Alcock went over the trip in detail, praised Brown's work: "Brown knows his job as well as any man. My part's simple enough. It's my trade. The navigation's the ticklish part." This wasn't for Boys' Own Weekly, but a daily newspaper.

The world knew of the successful crossing gradually.

King George the Fifth was leaving chapel at Windsor when he was informed. He ordered his congratulations to be sent.

It wasn't long before Newfoundland knew. Because of the time difference, it was very early morning there but word was passed along by churchgoers.

Northcliffe was one of the first to send congratulations: "A very hearty welcome to the pioneer of direct Atlantic flight. Your journey with your brave companion, Whitten-Brown, is a typical exhibition of British courage and organizing efficiency." He had no doubt, he said, that, when he offered the prize in 1913, "it would soon be won" and he looked forward with certainty to the time when London morning newspapers would be selling in New York in the evening, and *vice versa.*

Kathleen Kennedy found newspaper reporters at her parents' door, and described how she was "almost beside myself with joy when I heard of the safe arrival of the plane."

It was after four o'clock in the afternoon before Alcock and Brown set out by car from Clifden for the nearby city of Galway.

There was an official reception there, as there was the next day in Dublin. Civic officials wore their badges of office. Troops formed guards of honour.

All the British editorial stops could be pulled. In Newfoundland, the St. John's *Evening Telegram* on Monday labelled the two flyers in their main headline as "Lords of the Air."

In Britain, the *Daily Despatch,* printed in Manchester, started its main editorial with, "Two Manchester men have set an imperishable record."

The London *Morning Chronicle* said the two had won "the greatest sporting event of all time."

Nor were the Americans poor sports. The newspapers of the larger U.S. cities all made the successful flight Page One news.

Henry Woodhouse, vice-president of the Aerial League of America, declared Alcock and Brown's crossing "the most stupendous feat of the age." He thought "the flight advances the science of aviation at least five years."

Alan Hawley, of the Aero Club of America, termed the flight "magnificent," and noted that it proved land planes could fly to any part of the world.

Apart from the plaudits and platitudes, there were confidences. Kathleen Kennedy, interviewed in her now flag-bedecked home, told the *Daily Mail* that "the suspense of waiting for the news was terrible." The reporter, noting that she was "a tall, vivacious girl, who looked charming in her cool tennis costume," also quoted her as saying, "I shall sleep sounder tonight, you may be certain."

Meanwhile, up in Manchester, Jack Alcock's home was besieged by visitors who had to wait in queues. "I had faith in my son," his mother said. "He told me he would make the flight safely."

There were more welcomes when the pair boarded a ship across the Irish Sea, others at Holyhead, and at rail stops on the way to London.

Newspapers continued to make hay – 1,880 mile flight for a bride, was one headline.

Congratulatory messages followed the flyers to London – from Britain's Prime Minister Lloyd George and from American President Woodrow Wilson.

The New York *Times* began its editorial on the achievement with: "Like Alexander, the record-making aviator will soon weep because he has no more worlds to conquer. After such a flight what is a small voyage like death, across a peaceful river, to a fate determined. For human daring our hats are off to this Englishman who fought the sun, the stars and Sir Isaac Newton's best theory and beat them all."

But nowhere did the newsmen find such good "copy" as from Brown's bubbling fiance, Kathleen Kennedy. Teddy Brown might be a dour old stick, but she was a reporter's delight.

"Oh, it's just ripping, isn't it? Don't interview me please. I am sure I shall say such a lot of silly things. Teddy's safe. He's done it. He said he wanted to so much. I guess this is the proudest moment of my life. I am the happiest girl in London today," was one contribution to go with the kippers and marmalade at breakfast on the Monday morning.

In another newspaper, she discussed her wedding: "I am very keen on having an aeroplane honeymoon and I think Teddy would like it too."

Teddy probably hadn't given it a thought. He found the whole trip to

London confusing. He may have been still suffering some degree of deafness. He had endured a frightening experience. He was in, for him, an unnatural situation: being looked at, photographed, forced to keep up with the ebullient Alcock.

"Ireland is wonderful," Alcock said. "Our reception was wonderful. Y'know, it was a bigger strain than the flight." He was a man of twenty-six, but as agog as a schoolboy.

At Holyhead, ships and jetties were dressed with flags, and there was a welcoming party from Vickers.

At little stations and railway crossings knots of people greeted the heroes. Kathleen had come up to meet the train at Rugby, and had sent a telegram to Brown to say she was coming. As he hung out the window he caught a glimpse of her on the platform. She saw him, and raced toward his carriage while the train slowed. They kissed (you can be sure, with Brown, very primly). Then she gave Alcock a peck. He left the compartment for a few minutes to let the engaged couple be on their own.

Twenty miles from the capital, a couple of planes appeared over the train to escort it to Euston station.

Police were determined there wouldn't be the disorder of three weeks earlier when Hawker and Grieve had arrived. But there was a little trepidation when Harry Hawker and Muriel drove up, to cheers. He was still so much the hero that there was a moment of anxiety. Would the crowd break police lines? Would Harry steal the show?

It was just after 6.00 p.m. when the train pulled in. The mayor of the borough of St. Pancras, in his robes, was there; so were Brigadier-General Sir Cavel Holden, for the Royal Aero Club; others from Vickers and Rolls Royce; the Kennedy family; Alcock's father and thousands of ordinary Londoners.

Outside the station, after the official greetings and the handshakes between Hawker and the flyers, they entered the Rolls Royce which was to take them to the Royal Aero Club. There were crowds, bands, confetti, Union Jacks, thrown flowers. The car was halted several times. It was the Hawker procession all over again – except that Alcock didn't have to ride a horse.

At the club, there were speeches and a balcony appearance. Finally, Alcock was able to leave – and typically he went to watch a heavyweight championship fight.

Brown, worn out, wasn't so lucky. The Kennedys now lived at Ealing Common, and the Kennedys (especially Mrs. Kennedy) were social climbers. So they were in their glory and almost edging Brown and Kathleen out of the front row when the Mayor of Ealing and his council gave a reception for him. The mayor noted that Freddie Raynham also lived in

Ealing, as had Mrs. Hawker at one time. A band of the Middlesex Regiment played. Cadets were lined. Kathleen received a bouquet. The local weekly newspaper had a field day.

Finally, Arthur Whitten-Brown could escape the attention that is fixed on the newly famous. But not for long.

He, with Alcock, was summoned to a Savoy Hotel luncheon on the Friday. It was given by the *Daily Mail*. The flyers would be the guests of honour and Mr. Winston Churchill, the Secretary of State for War, would present them with the £10,000 prize.

Northcliffe was ill and couldn't be there. Everybody else in government and aeronautics seemed to be.

The menu started with ouefs poches Alcock, moved to Supreme de sole à la Brown and ended with Gateau Grand Succes.

It was Churchill who won all the attention. He did so, as he was to do in his prime, a quarter century later, with his descriptive powers, his human quirk of being confused, and his relish for the dramatic gesture.

The confusion came as he referred to Kathleen Kennedy as though she were already Brown's wife, and had been for some time.

The description came when he asked his audience to "think of the broad Atlantic, that terrible waste of desolate waters, tossing in tumult in repeated, almost ceaseless storms, and shrouded with an unbroken canopy of mist. Across this waste, and through this obscurity, two human beings, hurtled through the air, piercing the clouds and darkness, finding their unerring path in spite of every difficulty, to their exact objective across those hundreds of miles, arriving almost on scheduled time, and at every moment in this voyage liable to destruction from a drop of water in the carburettor, or a spot of oil on their plugs, or a tiny grain of dirt in their feed pipe, or from any other of the hundred and one indirect causes which in the present state of aeronautics might drag an aeroplane to its fate.

"When one considers all these factors I really do not know what we should admire the most in our guests – their audacity, their determination, their skill, their science, their Vickers Vimy aeroplane, their Rolls Royce engines, or their good fortune."

Then he presented his dramatic coup: "I am very happy to be able to tell you that I have received His Majesty's gracious consent to an immediate award of the Knight Commandership of the Order of the British Empire to both Captain Alcock and Lieutenant Brown."

They went to Windsor the next morning to see their King.

Alcock wore uniform. Brown was nervous. They travelled from London together by train, Alcock reading the newspapers.

At Windsor railway station, a horse-drawn carriage was waiting to take them up the hill, through the castle gate, for the investiture. So were about a hundred Eton schoolboys, all hiding. As the carriage started, the boys in their shiny top hats and long black coats ran out in the street to accompany it to Windsor Castle.

For Alcock especially, the son of the horse dealer, who had left school to become an apprentice mechanic, it was a signal distinction. These were the sons of the rich and powerful, pupils of Britain's most privileged school, running after him.

Alcock and Brown met the Prince of Wales, were invested with their knighthoods. They presented one of the trans-Atlantic airmail stamps to King George, signed a royal autograph album, and had lunch with the Royal Family.

When they returned to London, Sir Arthur Whitten-Brown headed for Ealing and Kathleen.

Sir John Alcock, who everybody called Jack, took a taxi to Hendon to see the end of an Aerial Derby. He was a little annoyed; he had put his name down to fly in it, but now it was too late in the day.

PART THREE

CHAPTER 32
Later Attempts

It was only a month after Alcock and Brown had fought their way across the Atlantic that a British airship, the R-34, took off from East Fortune, in Scotland, and flew to New York. It made the trip non-stop, easily and smoothly. Its crew was entertained in New York, then the airship flew back to Britain.

Admiral Kerr and the big Handley Page aircraft, as well as Raynham and his plane, were still in Newfoundland. Kerr had already decided there was no point in following the wash of Alcock and Brown.

Raynham was still determined. He invited Hawker's navigator, Mackenzie-Grieve, to make the flight with him but Grieve declined. Raynham found another navigator, Lieutenant Conrad Biddlecombe, a master mariner and pilot.

Raynham got a new engine to replace the one he'd damaged on his first Atlantic take-off attempt and the plane was almost completely rebuilt in a garage on the outskirts of St. John's.

It was given a new name, Chimera, and, on July 17, it was fueled and the pilot and navigator took their thermoses and food aboard, along with a sack of mail. Word had gone around that the popular Raynham, unlucky in his first attempt, was trying again. Hundreds of people came out for another look.

The plane rode along the ground, managed to skip into the air after about 300 yards, shuddered, and was caught by a side gust of wind. It was not high enough. A wing dipped, touched the ground. Raynham righted the aircraft, but it was too late. The plane pancaked down. Undercarriage, propeller, under wing, part of the fuselage were badly damaged. Neither flyer was hurt. Raynham gave up, and caught the first ship back to Britain.

The remnants of the Chimera, alias Raymor, arrived in Britain, a sorry sight, on the steamship *Grampian.*

Freddie Raynham was bitter. His sister, Mrs. Underwood, remembered how he came home, flung the bag of mail into a corner, and would not do anything about it for days.

Now there was only Kerr's Handley Page left in Newfoundland.

The little admiral was the soul of conviviality, and tried to keep his crew happy. However, there were minor abrasions.

Geoffrey Taylor, the weather specialist, shared "digs" with Tryggve Gran, the Norwegian navigator, and found him a bit of a trial, "forever playing the hero. I think he had won too much renown as a skier when young."

The social activities continued. Taylor went on a walking expedition and to parties at the Crosbie Hotel. There were less organized occasions in Harbour Grace, and Kerr, Brackley, Stedman, and others, dashed between the capital and the smaller town in the Rolls Royce loaned by Reid.

Air tests had been made in June.

Finally, orders came from the Handley Page Company in England; Kerr and his crew were to fly in the opposite direction – to the United States. The company hoped it might sell some planes there.

The plane, weighing nearly fifteen tons, took off at 5.55 p.m. on July 4. It carried 1,300 gallons of fuel, plus Kerr, Brackley, Gran, Wyatt (the radio man) and two mechanics.

About twelve hours later, while they were over Nova Scotia, a starboard engine began to give trouble. Then the pilots heard a loud crack, and the engine stopped. Pieces of metal came through the fuselage. Kerr and "Brackles" decided they couldn't fly on to New York. They came down at a place called Parrsboro, in Nova Scotia.

Kerr describes what happened in his book, *Land, Sea and Air:*

> . . .at 5.50 a.m. we landed in a field which looked as though it contained an old bicycle race-track. In my notebook, in which I used to write as I went along, I find the entry: 'Found wire fences, jumped two, hit bad hollow and crashed.' The machine stood on her nose, which concertina'd a bit, but not quite enough to squeeze us.

Kerr found the people of Parrsboro notably friendly and helpful: ". . . nobody seemed to do much work and every one appeared to have two or three motor-cars; all the girls were pretty and charming, and all the inhabitants seemed to think we were doing them a favour when we accepted their hospitality."

It was a good thing the admiral found Parrsboro so congenial. The

Handley Page plane would remain there for several months. But, as far as Kerr was concerned, there was all the time in the world. He went off to New York City, then visited friends on an island in the St. Lawrence. Gran and Wyatt went back to Britain. Stedman and his crew crossed to Nova Scotia by ship, from Newfoundland, and started repairs.

On October 9, the plane set out for New York with quite a load – five mechanics, three newspapermen and a movie cameraman. It was but another act in an increasingly hilarious saga. After twelve hours' flight, they were lost, although Kerr thought they were near New London, Connecticut. In darkness, they searched for a suitable landing space, with the fuel counters registering empty. Finally, flying low, they found a small field in which Brackley made a fine landing. It turned out to be near Greensport, on the eastern end of Long Island, about fifty miles from their destination of Mitchell Field, at Mineola, N.Y.

Kerr's next flight was on behalf of the American Express Company, which had decided to publicize itself by starting an "air express" service. The Handley Page would be filled with valuables, such as furs, and fly to Chicago.

It took off, still with Kerr and "Brackles" alternately at the controls. It ran into gale headwinds over the Catskills and, after eight hours' flying, one of the radiators was boiling madly. The plane had to land in a field near the small town of Mount Jowett. Fortunately, it was close to a railway station because American Express officials had begun to fear for their valuables and they were able to send the cargo on by train.

It took two days to fix the plane, and it was approaching 2.00 p.m. on a wintry November 16 before it took off again, this time for Cleveland. Again there were headwinds so that it was nearly dark when the plane was over Cleveland. The sun was setting, and there was this plane which had, like Hawker's, been named the Atlantic, stooging paradoxically above Lake Erie, looking for Glenn Martin Field.

Nobody could see it. What they did see was a race track, and Kerr and Brackley decided to land on that.

"Brackles" brought the plane down, using the flat, unobstructed, if narrow, track. It was a fine landing, right down the "stretch," – with the wings running along above the rails. But there was no time to stop. The plane rolled to the winning line.

One wingtip was smashed off by the judges' box, the other, reaching out over the opposite side of the track, was caved in by the winning post.

The Handley Page, built to attack Berlin, would never fly again.

CHAPTER 33

A Foggy Day in France

Only one man was killed during the 1919 attempts to fly the Atlantic. Chief Machinist's Mate James Welch was aboard the U.S. destroyer *Stockton* in the "bridge of ships" when a turbo-generator exploded. He died of burns and injuries caused by the fractured metal.

Others, better known, were to die more slowly, if more dramatically.

Alcock and Brown each had taken £4,000 from the £10,000 *Daily Mail* prize. The rest was distributed among Vickers' workers. Brown knew how he was going to spend his share. He planned a leisurely honeymoon, and a trip round the world. None of it by air. There was no hurry. Four thousand pounds, plus other savings meant that Teddy Brown was relatively comfortable.

He and Kathleen set out for the United States in October, 1919.

Alcock was working full time again at Brooklands, testing planes. On Saturdays he returned to competitive flying. On December 15 he was present at the Science Museum in London when the Vimy, hauled from the Irish bog, was presented to the nation. Three days later, he had to deliver a new Vickers plane, the Viking, to Paris, for the first aeronautical exhibition there since the war.

Low cloud, rain, and strong wind made the morning miserable. Alcock's colleagues suggested he delay the flight, but he left – with no navigator.

Over the English Channel, the weather was blustery; when he reached the Normandy coast, the plane was in fog. Alcock must have taken it low in an attempt to see a town or a railway line he could identify.

About one o'clock that afternoon, a farmer named Pelletier was in his fields at Cote d'Evrard, near Rouen. He saw a big plane "become unsteady, make a big sway and fall to earth." Although it didn't catch fire, the Viking was wrecked. Pelletier found Alcock, "a terrible mess," unconscious in the cabin. From papers in a pocket of Alcock's civilian suit, and from an engraving on his diamond-studded wristwatch, the farmer identified him.

The farmer and another worker carried Alcock to the farmhouse. The other man was sent to the road, where British Army vehicles often passed, to flag one down. A priest was called.

No army truck went by that afternoon, but eventually contact was made with No. 6 British General Hospital at Rouen, which sent doctors.

By then Sir John Alcock was dead.

Alcock's parents were notified, as was the world. Brown heard about it in San Francisco. His statement was a cliche: "Alcock's death was a true sacrifice for humanity."

The coffin, with a military escort, crossed the Channel from Le Havre, was received at London's Waterloo Station by Alcock's parents and representatives of the Vickers company. The procession reached Manchester on Christmas Day and the coffin was taken to the parish church of the parents in Fallowfield. Then a service was held in Manchester Cathedral. Among those present were representatives of all the companies which sent planes to Newfoundland.

A few weeks after Alcock had been killed, Harry Hawker was suffering from an increasing pain in his back. X-rays showed tubercular damage to his spine. Doctors recommended an operation but Hawker refused; the post-operative treatment involved lying on his back for months. Even at that, the doctors told him, part of his spine probably would be unbendable. He would have to give up flying and the car racing to which he was addicted.

Harry Hawker had limited interests. He could never settle down with a book. He never tried gardening. Walking through the woods bored him. He lived for speed.

So he decided against the operation. Instead, he drugged himself with speed. His cars (there were several) were seen at the major aerodromes; his photo was often in the papers. He took foolish risks, such as flying at 25,000 feet for a few minutes without an oxygen mask.

He had many escapes. In 1920, for example, while testing a new car at Brooklands, he swerved and crashed into iron fencing. The car was demolished, but Harry managed to scramble out and hang around until a photo was taken.

Harry turned more and more to motorcycles, motorboat racing, and cars. He formed a new company with Sopwith and Sigrist – the H. G. Hawker Engineering Company – to make two-stroke motorcycles and aluminium bodies for cars.

Harry tinkered with his own mechanical joy, a 450 h.p. Sunbeam. He also tested high-speed boats.

Muriel rarely left him. She knew about the tubercular spine, possibly realized that Harry wouldn't live long. She was pregnant.

She went to Brooklands and must have had moments when she thought the end had arrived.

Once, he left the track at 100 m.p.h., and she heard a spectator say, "Harry will need his luck now." But the car soared over the concrete parapet surrounding the track, and Harry was undisturbed – and unhurt.

The baby, a girl, was born on the anniversary of the day Hawker and Grieve had taken off from Newfoundland. In honour of the little rescue ship, she was named Mary. Her birth provided only an interlude: someone once had said that Harry's ambition was to get more from an internal combustion engine of given size than anyone else had succeeded in getting.

He went flying at the meets in the summer of 1920, and returned to the sport in 1921, though his hands had begun to twitch.

That summer, he was planning to enter the British Nieuport Company's Goshawk plane in the Hendon Aerial Derby. Four days before, on the morning of July 12, he left home early, before 6.00 a.m., and drove – fast – on a motorbike to Hendon airfield.

There, he had the Goshawk started, climbed in, took off. He started climbing – also fast.

He was at a great height, probably more than 15,000 feet, when the plane burst into flames, went into a dive, turned over two or three times during the fall, and crashed into a field at Burnt Oak, a London suburb. Hawker was found dead some distance from the plane.

Did Harry Hawker die because of a mechanical failure, because of a sudden physical collapse, or because he chose suicide?

Reports of the accident were (as the magazine, The Aeroplane, noted) utterly contradictory. Eyewitnesses, including some of experience from Hendon, said there was a burst of flame under the plane. Others reported flame but no smoke.

The key witness at an inquest was a Dr. Gardiner of Weybridge, the small Surrey town near Brooklands. He related how Hawker had refused an operation on his spine eighteen months before.

Then he told how the injured vertebrae, examined after the crash, were found to be reduced to a shell. An abscess in the spine, the doctor added, had burst while the flyer was still alive. This would have paralyzed Hawker's legs so that it would have been impossible for him to use the rudder bar, and so land an aircraft that was in trouble. The abscess haemorrhage might have occurred while Hawker was driving his motorbike, or while the plane was climbing.

There was never much strength to the theory that Hawker killed himself. But, as the details of his death were discussed among flyers and in the aviation periodicals, there were many who believed that rather than die, lingeringly, bedridden, he might have chosen to kill himself, as he had lived in a plane, fast. The overwhelming counter-argument is that, by 1921, Hendon, Burnt Oak, the entire area northwest of London was built-up. Harry would never have risked the lives of other people.

CHAPTER 34
The Edge of Sanity

Among all the people involved in the Atlantic air race, Northcliffe's death was the most spectacular. In 1919, after the race, he wrote: "It is unlikely that I shall ever be able to return to the full tide of work." This was a shattering admission for a man who, in the spring of that year, was lambasting the British Prime Minister, Lloyd George, pouring out a stream of memos to his newspaper executives, and trying to keep an eye open for any new technical development.

Northcliffe's *Daily Mail* was the world's largest newspaper and he had immense wealth. But he could not control his body nor, eventually, his mind.

He had been offered several cabinet posts, including the all-powerful Ministry of War, but he had declined them all. He wanted to be prime minister – because it was the top job. As John Buchan said – he was a vain man.

When Northcliffe couldn't get what he wanted, both his megalomania and his hypochondria increased. Hamilton Fyfe, a senior aide, said Northcliffe's decline began because of "mystical belief that he was the man appointed to clean up the chaos into which the world had fallen."

He'd already had premonitions of an early death, claimed he was being poisoned by the Germans, complained about eye trouble, feared cancer, translated indigestion into a heart attack. So it was almost a relief to him when doctors, whom he saw frequently, recommended a minor throat operation for thyroid in 1919. It was carried out a few days after Alcock's flight. Northcliffe was forty-four.

In the summer of 1921 he set out on a world tour. He looked florid, overweight, and admitted he was troubled with "brain fag."

One night, while Northcliffe was cruising in the hot Indian Ocean, a secretary, William Snoad, had to take dictation for six hours. Snoad, one of the many flunkeys Northcliffe had taken along, transcribed all the notes; they ran to scores of pages. But Northcliffe never asked to see them. From that time on, Snoad had his doubts about "The Chief's" mental state. Six months of globe-trotting ended in France and he was soon complaining that his catarrh had returned, that he'd caught a chill, that his throat was giving him pain. All of these ailments were, mainly, imagined.

He returned to London, briefly, and there were more serious imaginings. He met Newman Flower of the book publishing firm of Cassell's. He didn't know Flower well but, within minutes, he was confiding: "I've been to my thirty-second specialist today. I'm going to die."

It was not just his view of his own well-being that now became extreme. He sent a "Strictly Private" memo to one of his executives – "Be very wary of B. P. (Baden Powell). He is not the inventor of the idea of the Boy Scouts." Rumours of his unsound mind grew. Wickham Steed had doubts about Northcliffe's sanity and had said his brain had worked "curiously." Hannen Swaffer, the columnist, repeated the claim that Northcliffe was insane. These rumours seeped through to Northcliffe himself. His reaction was volcanic. He phoned an editor. "I hear they are saying I am mad," he roared, "Send down one of the best reporters for the story."

Then he headed for Germany. He slipped off with, for him, a small retinue of assistants, his blue Rolls Royce, and a revolver to protect himself against the "Huns." From a Boulogne hotel, he sent a message to the London *Times:* "Have forgotten business want no figures fullstop reading French fullstop every time you wire causes me trouble fullstop very cold here." Later, from Boulogne, he wrote a six-page letter to Sir Robert Hudson. It started: "You have with you the most distinguished medical man in the world (Sir Frederick Treves). Will you kindly ask his opinion as to my sanity?"

Other missives were simply offensive. One wire to the directors of his Associated Newspapers Limited, read: "Telegraph me this morning whether my overpaid directors are carrying out my instructions." And he sent another cable later that same June day in 1922 threatening to return within forty-eight hours to "dismiss every relation fullstop."

Douglas Reed, later a well-known foreign correspondent, was sent out as a temporary secretary for Northcliffe in Boulogne. Reed wrote later: "He felt himself surrounded by treachery. He put his hand under his pillow and brought out a little black silk bag. 'Look at this,' he said, 'it was left here for me, for Mr. Leonard Brown, by a man who would not give the porter his name. How do they know I am here? You see the colour? It is the colour of death.' "

His obsessions grew. Still, Reed had a stream of telegraphs to send. One day, Reed was impusively sent to London to buy for himself, with £150, a possession Northcliffe thought imperative for every secretary: a silver-fitted, crocodile leather suitcase.

The madness even extended to sartorial injunctions. On June 9, Northcliffe commanded H. G. Price, a male secretary: "For God's sake give your dirty grey suit away."

Northcliffe went from Boulogne to Paris and was installed at the Hotel Plaza-Athenee, where the illustrious Wickham Steed met him. Steed noted that Northcliffe's tongue was black, his eyes wild, with a squint, and that he rambled illogically. Steed was at Northcliffe's bedside when he suddenly produced a Colt revolver from under his pillow and aimed it at his dressing gown hanging on the door: he'd mistaken the garment for an intruder.

Next, Northcliffe left for Evian-les-Bains, accompanied by Steed and a Sisley Huddleston. They travelled by train and, as soon as it had started, Northcliffe summoned Huddleston and told him he was no gentleman because he had a red silk handkerchief hanging loosely from his pocket, his teeth were bad, and his breath was foul. Huddleston, understandably incensed, left the train at the first stop.

Steed had to sit for nine hours in a darkened compartment listening to Northcliffe's gibberish. The only relief was when he called in another member of the party, Peter Goudie, and told him to go straight to London and dismiss 120 people on the *Times*' staff. Then a Miss Rudge, a *Daily Mail* telephonist who had been sent over to Europe to help out Northcliffe's staff, was called in—and was told dirty stories. Then Northcliffe was contrite. He asked Steed: "Did I go a little too far with that girl? Don't you think I am mad?"

At Evian he insulted the hotel manager, drove away an old friend, threatened the hall porter, and sent his wife away from his room by the viciousness of his remarks—all within an hour. The next day, the first of the telegrams to his mother began: "I am in a delightful place where intend to spend some time with my dear wife among wild flowers stop."

A Swiss neurologist certified Northcliffe as insane (though, later, many, including some of Northcliffe's physicians disputed that any certification of insanity was ever issued, anywhere).

Fleet Street was swept with rumours. The *Daily Mail* itself was forced to announce: "On account of indisposition, Lord Northcliffe has been ordered to abstain from work for the present. The publication of his articles on Germany will therefore be temporarily suspended."

He returned to London where a doctor found that he was afflicted with the "most insidious type of blood poisoning known to us." The British

Medical Journal, reviewing the illness later, said Northcliffe had been suffering from a streptococcal infection for at least a year. He was given blood transfusions, but started slipping into unconsciousness. His mother was brought from Kent despite her great age. She sat on his bed and asked the doctors, "Is it his head?"

He wrote two wills during this time, both full of delusions and recriminations. He gave two reasons for his fatal illness: "Indian jungle fever" and "Poisoning by ice cream supplied on the Belgian frontier."

By August of 1922, Northcliffe's doctor decided his patient should have fresh air, night and day. The roof of his home, Number One Carlton Gardens was inspected to see if a shelter could be created there. When this was found unfeasible, the Duke of Devonshire, who lived next door, gave permission for such a structure to go on his adjoining roof. Holes had to be cut through ceilings to allow Northcliffe to be hoisted to his new "ward" on a stretcher.

Northcliffe knew he was dying, and murmured into a doctor's ear: "In the *Times* I should like a page reviewing my life-work by someone who really knows, and a leading article by the best man available on the night."

On August 14, he died. Three days later, after a great service in Westminster Abbey, he was buried, as he had requested, in a north London cemetery. As the coffin was lowered, an aircraft dipped in salute.

CHAPTER 35
Decline

In 1922, Santos-Dumont was in Paris, a forgotten man. He had not piloted a plane for thirteen years and, in fact, he would not fly for the rest of his life.

In the first quarter of this century, aviation developed with such speed that the infant-pioneers had to adapt almost daily. Santos-Dumont simply abdicated.

Nobody knows exactly why. In 1909 he was flying his highly successful Demoiselle aircraft from Paris over the French countryside, offering its plans without cost to anybody who wished to build it (he claimed it had reached the phenomenal speed of 70 miles per hour). He was still dining at Maxim's, dressing fastidiously, writing letters. One of these, written before the war, congratulated Bleriot on flying the English Channel, and it prophesied: "One day, thanks to you, aviation will cross the Atlantic."

Then, overnight, *"Le Petit Santos"* gave up flying.

There was an announcement that he had suffered a nervous breakdown, that he was confined to his home, that he would not see anybody. He was retiring.

"I felt my nerves were worn out," he wrote – though he was only thirty-six years old.

For the next twenty-two years he was an invalid, melancholy, eventually mad. He began wandering from country to country. In the years before the Atlantic was flown, he went to the French coasts, to Brazil, to the United States, back to Paris, back to the Riviera, to Chile, to his native Brazil again.

He made speeches in the United States during wartime that were as confusing as some of Northcliffe's later mental zig-zags, at one time he advocated the airship for use in war, at others deplored the building of machines that would kill men.

He aged rapidly in these years but there were long periods when he was relatively active. He built a seaplane hangar at Rio de Janeiro, although never the planes to fill it. He created a home called *Encantado* (The Enchanted House), near the old royal palace at Petropolis, forty miles away from Rio, up in the cool mountains. There he had an observatory, and many gadgets. The small house, tucked into the hillside, appears to have been built for gnomes. The staircase to the house was constructed by Santos-Dumont so that an invalid could use half-steps. But they are so steep as to be almost unscaleable for any but the healthiest of persons.

Dumont wrote one of his muddled accounts of his earlier flying days, made his morning coffee, interfered with the household chores, and, wasted away his time.

In the year that Alcock and Brown flew the ocean, the Brazilian government gave him the house in which he had been born, with its extensive grounds. He tried, for a year or so, to farm it. But he wasn't capable of it, and he sold the land.

Then he went to France – impulsively. As quickly, he made a decision to return to Brazil. Over the next few years he moved around from town to town in his own country, returned to France, went to Spain, to Portugal. His despair grew, and his hands shook so badly that when, from a Swiss sanatorium, he wrote the Aero Club of France, declining an offer to preside at a banquet, hardly anybody could understand the letter.

The sanatorium was a stopgap. He left it for the home of a friend at Biarritz, and there, possibly recalling through his dim mind those soaring Brazilian birds of his childhood, busied himself planning an ornithopter, a device with a small engine which, when strapped to a man's back, would allow him to fly. Of course, like everything else in the last half of his life, it came to nothing.

He began feeling remorse over flying accidents. Every one was so much his personal cross that friends and relatives would not bring him newspapers telling of them.

He developed an obsession with the idea that he'd been responsible, personally, for the deaths of the cream of Brazil's scientific world. This came from an accident in 1928. Dumont had returned to his own country and, as the liner on which he was a passenger approached Rio, a large seaplane, carrying many of the country's intellectuals, took off to welcome him home. It had hardly left Guanabara Bay when there was an explosion, and it sank. All on board were killed.

Santos-Dumont, who had seen the disaster, insisted on working in salvage boats for days, looking for bodies, and repeated again and again: "How many lives were sacrificed for me?" Then he shut himself away in a hotel, unseen, for two weeks.

He left the hotel to return to "The Enchanted House" but he couldn't abide life there. He booked for France, moved to Switzerland, went back to Biarritz. There, he was found by a fellow Brazilian who cabled his family orders to come and fetch him.

The family took him to a beach house near Sao Paolo. A nephew stayed with him. It was a black task. Several times Santos-Dumont tried to commit suicide. The little aeronaut who was Brazil's hero would sit for hours at a time, crying out, his shaking hands holding his grey head and covering his ears from any noise – especially noise of the occasional aircraft.

On July 23, 1932, there was a civil war in Brazil and war planes happened to cross over the beach house.

That evening Alberto Santos-Dumont went into the bathroom and hanged himself with a necktie.

CHAPTER 36
Some Became Admirals

An American transport ship, called *Zeppelin*, sailed from France to New York in the summer of 1919, carrying more than 4,000 troops returning home to the U.S., about fifty war brides – and the crews of the Nancy flying boats. As the ship approached Long Island, a blimp, a C-4, appeared overhead and, with numerous Navy vessels, escorted the *Zeppelin* into New York harbour. The escort was in honour of the Nancies' crossing of the Atlantic – even if it had taken them twenty-two days.

The Nancy crews received no official welcome ashore. However, Glenn Curtiss, at considerable expense, gave a banquet at New York's Commodore Hotel; he had the dining room mocked up like a giant trans-Atlantic flying boat. Each crew member received a gold watch with the letters NC inscribed on it, while every other guest at the dinner was given a souvenir – a piece of fabric from the Nancy Four's wings.

Nobody appeared to mind the desecration of the plane. Perhaps they took their cues from Read, the commander of the Nancy Four, who said, "Crossing the Atlantic by seaplane will not be profitable commercially soon," and from Towers, overall commander of the Nancies, who thought: "Until the seaplane is made larger, the dirigible will have the advantage in overseas flight."

When the Nancy Four flew the Atlantic, the American composer Frederick Bigelow wrote "The NC-4 March," which has remained a popular piece of parade music. There were few other extravagances.

After the dinner at the Commodore, John Towers mustered his naval air division at New York's Penn Station for the trip to Washington, but nobody recognized them. At Union Station in Washington there was no fanfare. However, their great boosters, Secretary of the Navy Daniels and his assistant, Roosevelt, gave them a warm welcome, and told them that

Congress had ordered that a special medal be struck in their honour and awarded to each man.

Then, from Washington, the flyers went their different ways.

"Putty" Read eventually became a Rear Admiral. He retired in 1946 and died twenty-one years later in Miami.

John Towers became Commander of Naval Air Forces in the Pacific a year after Pearl Harbour. He was in the Navy for forty-five years, altogether, retiring, a full Admiral, in 1947. He died eight years later.

Pat Bellinger, became a Rear Admiral. He commanded the Norfolk Navy Yard, and later became commander of the Navy's Atlantic air forces, in the Second World War.

Elmer Stone returned to the U.S. Coastguard, set a world's speed record for an amphibian plane in 1926 (191.79 m.p.h.), rose to Commander. He died of a heart attack while inspecting a patrol plane in 1936.

Walter Hinton left the Navy to enter commercial flying. He was a member of the first flight from New York to Rio de Janeiro.

Bellinger's pilot, Lieutenant Louis Barin, was killed in a flying accident.

Marc Mitscher, the other pilot aboard the Nancy One, became an Admiral and was commanding the carrier *Hornet* when Jimmy Doolittle led a flight of B-25 bombers off its decks to make the first World War Two attack on Tokyo.

Holden Richardson died at the age of eighty-one. When in his seventies, he worked for the Smithsonian Institute as an advisor on aeronautical affairs.

Robert Lavender, the only crew member still living in 1974, was a patent engineer in connection with the development of the atomic bomb. Although eighty-five years old when interviewed in his Washington apartment, he was active and healthy.

Eugene Rhoads flew as a passenger from New York to Lisbon on the thirtieth anniversary of the Four's flight. But in 1949, the trip, aboard the Lockheed P2V-2 bomber, took only sixteen hours and fifty minutes which, coincidentally, was roughly the time of Alcock and Brown's nonstop crossing to Ireland.

Emory Coil, the commander of the C-5 airship that managed to get to St. John's was in another dirigible over England on August 24, 1921 when it burst into flames. Coil, with more than forty others, was killed.

CHAPTER 37
The Slipstream of Years

Some of the British flyers died in the Americas. Mackenzie-Grieve slipped so easily from the limelight that there were few in Victoria, British Columbia, where he had gone to live in 1929, who knew that he had been Hawker's navigator. They learned of his feat when they read his obituary in 1942. He was sixty-two when he died, after a long, painful illness. He left a widow and daughter.

Freddie Raynham was sour when he returned to England after his two failed starts in Newfoundland. He continued work for the Martinsyde company but, in 1920, that firm was in trouble. The palmy days of war production lines were over. Freddie decided to look around for another job.

Like Hawker, he went on with competitive flying. On March 21, 1920, he set a world speed record of 161.4 miles per hour over a kilometre course. The following year, he was back to second place – in the King's Cup race. Second place was his destiny even when he switched to gliders. For example, at one Sussex meet, in 1922, he set a gliding endurance record of nearly two hours, only to have it broken on the same day.

Raynham once was engaged to make a silent movie called "The Hawk." He had to shoot off a cliff in his glider, land in the sea, and rescue the heroine. Again he was number two: he was doubling for the film's hero.

He went to Asia where he formed the India Air Survey and Transport Company. After much flying in both India and Burma, he returned to England with his wife, the former Dodie Macpherson, whom he'd married after leaving Newfoundland. They then went to the U.S., bought a motor home and lived a wandering life for six years before he died in 1954, after suffering a heart attack. He is buried in the Evergreen Cemetery, Colorado Springs, Colorado.

"Brackles" also died in the New World. He was chief executive of British South American Airways and he was staying at the Copacabana Palace Hotel in Rio de Janeiro when, on a day in November, 1948, he wrote a letter to his wife in which he said: "I hope I can get time for a bathe tomorrow morning before we start the day's rounds." The following morning, he was caught in the undertow, and died shortly after being pulled to shore. He was fifty-four.

Admiral Kerr had no trouble finding a publisher from his vast range of friends and acquaintances for a whole series of books and poems he wrote through the 1920s and 1930s. They have such names as *The Sailor's Nelson, The Navy In My Time, Prayer of Empire*. He died at seventy-nine.

Tryggve Gran also wrote books and they had titles as impressive as Kerr's. *En helt: Kaptein Scott's siste ferd* (A hero: Captain Scott's last journey) was one.

Two years after his stay in Newfoundland, his left leg was so badly crushed in a car accident that doctors gave him little hope of walking properly again. But the following year, he was skiing the inland massif of Spitzbergen on an expedition and, by 1928, he was leading another in search of lost airmen who had tried to fly over the North Pole.

However, by 1940, Tryggve Gran was no longer a hero to the West, nor to many of his own people. After the invasion of Norway by the Nazis, he was made the first honorary member of the German-backed Quisling air corps in Norway.

In a speech to that corps, he said: "Many of my old friends have asked me: 'Why are you a member of the Nasjonal Samling (the group led by the Nazi puppet, Vidkun Quisling)?' I always answer that we aviators are founding everything on new inventions. We are all aviators who have backed the new national socialistic idea. We see them in Italy and in Spain, yes, even in England and America."

Such speeches brought Gran to trial and disgrace after the war. His name was rarely mentioned in the Norwegian press. He lived in the small southern Norwegian town of Grimstad.

In 1971, the controversy over his wartime role was forgotten and he was invited back to Cruden Bay, near Aberdeen, to stand on the spot from whence he had taken off fifty-seven years before, on his North Sea Flight. The Royal Air Force let bygones be bygones and provided a guard of honour as he unveiled a monument.

In 1974, Tryggve Gran was still active in spite of his eighty-five years.

When Teddy Whitten-Brown's Atlantic adventure was over, and he'd finished an extended, round-the-world honeymoon with Kathleen, he ended up in the South Wales industrial city of Swansea, going every day to the office of his employer, Metro Vickers, on Wind Street.

The job was a sinecure. Whitten-Brown, qualified both as a mechanical and electrical engineer, was tucked into a small office on a back street. Nothing was ever made there; it was simply a branch of a giant concern, mainly in the business of distributing electric light bulbs. The Atlantic hero was nothing but a glorified salesman-cum-office manager.

John Grey, who went to work in this plant as a stock boy during World War Two, recalls that he ran messages for Whitten-Brown. Grey started as a lad of sixteen and it didn't seem right, to a youth, using his imagination, that Sir Arthur Whitten-Brown, a knight, a former prisoner behind German lines in the First War, the first aerial navigator of the Atlantic, should be peddling light bulbs. Grey figured he might be a spy, working for MI 5, or in counter-espionage – Grey admits that he never did quite make up his mind.

Norman Clarke, who was a friend of Brown, recalled that Brown never moved far from the route between the middle class flat he shared with Kathleen and the downtown office and its nearby hotels. He liked to have a few drinks at lunch in hotels.

In 1939, Brown was a deputy lieutenant for the county of Glamorgan, in which Swansea was situated. The title is honorary, often given to ex-officers and heroes. It meant that he had to put in an appearance at the occasional function. Deputy lieutenants are the type of people presented to princesses when they lay a foundation stone or watch a horse show. A DL has to "fly the flag" and jump into uniform of some kind on the out-break of any war. In Brown's case, in 1939, it was first the uniform of the Home Guard, then that of an officer of an air cadet squadron. Teddy didn't think much of either role, and eventually faded out of them after handing out a lot of beer tankards to the cadets as prizes.

Teddy had no wish to fly; in fact, he avoided ceremonies in connection with his famous flight.

Kathleen, as vivacious as ever, worked more actively in the war, serving on various women's auxiliaries, as an officer in the female branch of the Army; and then with the Women's Land Army.

The Browns' only son, Arthur (nicknamed "Buster"), joined the Royal Air Force early in the war, trained for flying crew, married a local girl that both the Whitten-Browns liked.

In 1944, on D-Day, Flight Lieutenant Arthur Whitten-Brown, the son, flew over France but didn't come back.

For days, weeks, Teddy and Kathleen clung to each other, as if physical coupling could double the chances of his returning.

Then he was no longer in that half-land of the missing. It was con-firmed that he had been killed. The parents' world crumbled.

Kathleen was the stronger; she busied herself on the staff of the Women's Land Army. Teddy moped.

He did answer the letters of schoolboys and he agreed to one or two interviews with newspaper reporters. On a Saturday, in October, in 1948, he even agreed to be on a BBC show. After it, he and Kathleen returned to the Swansea flat and spent a quiet Sunday. On the Monday morning, she went to wake him. He was dead. He had taken veronal.

In Newfoundland, during that month, Joey Smallwood was involved in a battle to unite what had been Britain's oldest colony with Canada. He was to win a narrow victory and become the province's first Premier.

And in Newfoundland, on the fiftieth anniversary of the Alcock and Brown flight, another memorial was added to those already dedicated over the years – on the edge of the Irish bog near Clifden; at London airport; at other places.

This new one was unveiled on a rise which was surrounded by small suburban homes. The knoll and the houses were part of what once had been Lester's Field, the take-off point.

That June day in St. John's was a denial of all the climatic slanders hurled on that city. The sky was cloudless, the air warm. So everybody at the ceremony could see clearly an airliner on an east-west track, as if on cue, six miles above. It was one of scores which flew the Atlantic that day.

Thanks

This book was researched in many places – Newfoundland, Ottawa, Toronto, London, Manchester, South Wales, Washington, and Petropolis in Brazil among them.

But far more numerous than the locations where diaries and newspaper clippings, books and photos were studied, are the people who so willingly gave of their time and memories. Some went to considerable inconvenience to obtain material for me; others granted long interviews; many suggested yet others who could help me. To all of them my thanks.

Among them were:

In Newfoundland: Mr. Chief Justice Robert Furlong; Mr. Ed Kavanagh, small plane pilot who flew me low over the coast to simulate the start of the 1919 trans-Atlantic flights; Mrs. Augustus Lester; Mr. Justice James Higgins; Mr. Ed Roberts, leader of the Opposition in the Newfoundland Legislature; Mr. W. J. Carew, secretary to many former premiers; Mr. Peter Dawson and Mr. John Maunder, both of the Newfoundland Museum; Mr. F. Burnham Gill and Mr. John Green, of the Newfoundland Provincial Archives; Mrs. Bride Sutton, of Trepassey; Mr. James J. Collins and Mrs. J. J. Collins, son and widow of the St. John's Marconi station operator in 1919; Mrs. Genevieve Drayton, second wife of William Drayton, former owner of the Cochrane Hotel; Mrs. Mary Laws, daughter of Mr. Drayton's first marriage; the staffs of the Arts and Culture Building library and the Gosling library; Mr. C. F. Rowe, meteorologist; Mr. Bill Parsons, of Harbour Grace; Mr. Albert Perlin, journalist; Mr. Ted Henley and Mr. Doug Wheeler, of the Newfoundland Department of Tourism; Mr. Martin Lee, of the Conception Bay Museum; Captain D. C. Fraser; Mr. E. R. Bearns; Mr. T. J. Dalton; Sir Leonard Outerbridge; Dr. David Parsons, son of Dr. Will Parsons.

Elsewhere in Canada: Inspector Ian Glendinning, RCMP (rtd), now of

Edmonton; Mr. John Grey, of Georgetown, Ontario; Mrs. Lillemar ten Hooven, for translations from Norwegian; Major J. C. Newlands, librarian of the Royal Canadian Military Institute, Toronto; Mrs. Helena Jacob, librarian of the National Museum of Science and Technology, Ottawa; Olaf Solli, Norwegian consul-general in Montreal; the staffs of the bibliographic centre, newspaper archives, and science and technology branches of the Metropolitan Toronto Central Library; Mr. O. Lipholdt-Petersen, Danish vice-consul in Toronto; Mr. Richard Bower, publisher, *The Daily Colonist,* Victoria, B.C.; the staff of the newspapers section, National Archives, Ottawa.

In Scandinavia: Mr. Tryggve Gran, only surviving flying member of the British crews attempting to fly the Atlantic in 1919; Henning Henningsen, director, Danish Maritime Museum, Helsingor, Denmark; Reide Lunde, chief editor, *Aftenposten,* Oslo; Mr. F. Holm-Petersen, director, Maritime Museum, Troense, Denmark; staff members of the Berlingske Tidenden newspaper in Copenhagen.

In Eire: Capt. Jack Kelly-Rogers, of the Irish Aviation Museum; Mr. Jack Millar, chief press officer for Aer Lingus.

In U.S.A.: Captain Robert Lavender USN (rtd), the only surviving member of the U.S. Navy's attempt to fly the Atlantic in 1919; Ms. Anna Urband, assistant head, media services branch, Department of the Navy, Washington; Ms. Catherine Scott, librarian of National Air Museum, Smithsonian Institute, Washington; Dr. Jerome Hunsacker, Boston; Ms. Janet Irwin, Museum of Science and Industry, Chicago.

In Britain: Captain E. S. J. Alcock, brother of Sir John Alcock; Sir Geoffrey Taylor, retired professor at Cambridge University; Mr. Norman Clark of Swansea; Mr. Frank White, Ministry of Defence Library, London; Miss Ruby Evans of Swansea; Mr. Tony Austin, features editor, *Western Mail,* Cardiff; Mrs. C. E. Underwood, sister of the late F. P. Raynham, of Long Buckley, Warwickshire; Charles Andrews and Alan Jeffcote of the Vintage Aircraft and Flying Assocation; Mr. Windsor, of the Science Museum library, South Kensington; Mr. John Blake, of the Royal Aero Club; Mrs. Dilys Jenkins, Ferryside, Carmarthenshire; Mrs. Edna Grey, of Swansea; Mr. J. S. Howell, former ship's radio operator, of Swansea; The staff of Manchester Central Library; Mr. D. C. Brech, archivist, Royal Air Force Museum, Hendon; the library staff of *The Guardian* newspaper, Manchester; Mr. A. W. Naylor, of the Royal Aeronautical Society, London; P. Short, University of Manchester Institute of Science and Technology.

BIBLIOGRAPHY

Alcock, Sir J., and Whitten-Brown, Sir Arthur. *Our Transatlantic Flight,* William Kimber, London: 1969 (includes Alcock's account written for the September 1919 issue of Badminton magazine).

Brackley, Freda. *Brackles: Memoirs of a Pioneer of Civil Aviation,* Putnam: 1952.

Boughton, Terence. *Story of British Light Aeroplanes,* John Murray: 1963.

Brett, R. Dallas. *The History of British Aviation,* 1939.

Brockett, Paul. *Bibliography of Aeronautics 1917-1919,* Smithsonian Institution.

Bryden, H. G. *Wings: An Anthology of Flight,* 1942.

Burbidge, William. *From Balloon to Bomber,* John Crother, London: 1948.

Chadwick, St. John. *Newfoundland: Island into Province,* Cambridge University Press: 1967.

Cherry-Gerrard, Apsley. *The Worst Journey in the World,* originally published 1922; published in Penguin Books: 1937.

Churchill, Randolph. *Winston Churchill,* Heinemann.

Clarke, Tom. *My Northcliffe Diary,* Gollancz: 1931.

Collinson, Clifford, and McDermott, Captain F. *Through Atlantic Clouds,* Hutchinson: 1934.

Croix, Robert de la. *They Flew the Atlantic,* Norton: 1958.

Dixon, Charles. *The Conquest of the Atlantic by Air,* J. B. Lippincott: 1931.

Ellis, F. H. and E. *Atlantic Air Conquest,* Ryerson: 1963.

Ferris, Paul. *The House of Northcliffe,* Wiedenfeld and Nicholson: 1971.

Fyfe, Henry Hamilton. *Northcliffe: An Intimate Biography,* Allen and Unwin: 1930.

Gibbs-Smith, C. H. *A History of Flying,* Battsford: 1953.

Greenwall, H. J. *Northcliffe, Napoleon of Fleet Street,* 1957.

Gwyn, Richard. *Smallwood: The Unlikely Revolutionary,* McClelland and Stewart Limited: 1968.

Hamlen, Joseph. *Flight Fever,* Doubleday: 1971.

Harrison, Michael. *Airborne at Kitty Hawk,* Cassell: 1953.

Hawker, H. G., and Mackenzie-Grieve, K. *Our Atlantic Attempt,* Methuen: 1919.

Hawker, Muriel. *H. G. Hawker, Airman,* Methuen: 1922.

Hewings, Ralph. *Gran,* W. H. Allen: 1974.

Hildreth, C. H., and Nalty, Bernard. *1001 Questions Answered About Aviation History,* Dodd Mead Co.

Horwood, Harold. *Newfoundland,* Macmillan: 1969.

Jablonski, Edward. *Atlantic Fever,* Macmillan: 1972 .

Kerr, Mark. *Land, Sea and Air,* Longman's Green: 1927.

Lanchberry, Edward. *A. V. Roe,* The Bodley Head: 1956.
Lewis, Peter. *British Racing and Record-Breaking Aircraft,* Putnam: 1970.
McDonough, Kenneth. *Atlantic Wings 1919-39,* Garden City Press: 1966.
Murchie, Guy. *Song of the Sky,* Houghton Mifflin: 1954.
Napoleao, Aluizio. *Santos-Dumont and the Conquest of the Air,* Ministry of State for Foreign Affairs for Brazil.
"Neon." *The Great Delusion: A Study of Aircraft in Peace and War,* Ernest Benn: 1927.
Pound, Reginald and Harmsworth, Geoffrey. *Northcliffe,* Cassell: 1959.
Raleigh, Sir Walter, and Jones, H. A. *The War in the Air,* 6 vols. Oxford Press: 1922.
Roseberry, C. R. *The Challenging Skies, 1919-39,* Doubleday: 1966.
——— *Glenn Curtiss: Pioneer of Flight,* Doubleday: 1972.
Russell, Franklin, (ed). *The Atlantic Coast.*
Santos-Dumont, Alberto. *Dans L'Air,* Century Co., New York: 1904.
Scammell, A. R. *My Newfoundland,* Harvest House: 1966.
Shepherd, Edwin Colston, *Great Flights,* Block: 1939.
Smallwood, J. E. (ed.). *The Book of Newfoundland,* 4 vols. Newfoundland Publishing Company.
Smallwood, J. R. *The New Newfoundland,* 1931.
Smith, Richard K. *First Across: The U.S. Navy's Transatlantic Flight of 1919,* Naval Institute Press, Annapolis: 1973.
Sprigg, C. St. John. *Great Flights,* Nelson: 1935.
Stierman, Hy, and Kittler, Glenn D. *Triumph,* Harper and Brothers: 1961.
Thomas, Lowell, and Thomas, Lowell Jr. *Famous First Flights that Changed History,* Doubleday: 1968.
Turnball, Archibald D., and Lord, Clifford. *History of U.S. Naval Aviation,* Yale University Press: 1949.
Turner, P. St. John. *The Vickers Vimy,* Patrick Stephens: 1969.
Wallace, Graham. *The Flight of Alcock and Brown,* Putnam:1955.
Whitten-Brown, Arthur. *Flying the Atlantic in 16 Hours,* Stokes: 1920.
Wrench, Evelyn. *Uphill,* Nicholson and Watson: 1934.
Wykeham, Peter. *Santos-Dumont: A Study in Obsession,* Putnam: 1962.
Wykes, Alan. *Air Atlantic: A History of Trans-Atlantic Flying,* Hamish Hamilton: 1967.
I also referred to the files of the following newspapers for 1919 extensively: The London Times, Daily Mail, Manchester Guardian, in Britain; New York Times, New York World, in the U.S.; Toronto Telegram, Toronto Star, Globe and Mail, Halifax Chronicle, Halifax Herald, in Canada; and the St. John's Evening Telegram, St. John's Evening Herald, St. John's Star, and St. John's News, in Newfoundland.

Extensive reference was also made to the following; Flight, The Aeroplane, Flying, L'Aerophile, Aero Digest, and National Aviation News.

224